PRAI

GODDESS
pages

"In this engaging, inspiring, empowering guide, Rev. Laurie Sue Brockway shows women how to find the goddess who dwells within. Filled with exercises, rituals, and ideas for drawing upon the power of the goddesses, this wonderful guide combines the practical with the spiritual, the daily with the divine. Open these pages and find the gifts of the Goddess with which to create a rich, free, and authentic life!"

—Phyllis Curott,
author of *Book of Shadows, Witch Crafting*, and *Wicca Made Easy*

"Laurie Sue Brockway gives voice to goddesses of many pantheons and traditions, allowing us, as mere mortal women, to access their power, beauty, and brilliance in our own lives. Her insightful guidebook is a blessing to women everywhere."

—Arielle Ford,
author of *The Soulmate Secret, and Turn Your Mate Into Your Soulmate*

"Rev. Laurie Sue Brockway's wonderful book *The Goddess Pages* empowers women to find the goddess within and discover a more mystical side of themselves."

—Judith Orloff, MD,
author of *The Empath's Survival Guide, Positive Energy*, and *Second Sight*

"The Goddess is a girl's best friend . . . and so is Laurie Sue Brockway. Enter her world, and you will never be the same."

—Laura Day,
author of *Practical Intuition*, *The Circle*, and *Welcome to Your Crisis*

"Laurie Sue Brockway is a gifted writer who embodies the spirit of the Goddess. She inspires women to connect with their inner strength and express their feminine power. In her unique way, she combines wisdom and practical advice that inspires growth and love—as well as fun. Her book is a must-read!"

—Dr. Judy Kuriansky, radio personality and author of many books,
including *The Complete Idiot's Guide to Tantric Sex*

"This book is a must-have for every goddess in your life, starting with *you!* This book will serve to inspire millions and help level the spiritual playing field, balancing masculine and feminine for a more healthy and rewarding existence on Earth."

—Shelley Ackerman, may she be of blessed memory,
astrologer and founder of Karmic Relief

These reviews appeared in earlier editions of this book.

the
GODDESS
pages

the GODDESS *pages*

36 DIVINE FEMALES TO GUIDE YOU TO MORE LOVE, SUCCESS, AND HAPPINESS

LAURIE SUE BROCKWAY

GODDESS COMMUNICATIONS, LLC
NEW YORK CITY

The Goddess Pages: 36 Divine Females to Guide You to Love, Success, and Happiness

Publisher: Goddess Communications, LLC
Cover Design and Interior Formatting: Qamber Designs & Media
All Images used under license from: Shutterstock.com and DepositPhotos.com
Additional research provided by: Rev. Dr. Victor Fuhrman, D.Scd, MSC, RM

History of this Book:
A version of this book was originally published as *A Goddess Is a Girl's Best Friend: A Divine Guide to Finding Love, Success, and Happiness* by Berkeley Publishing Group, a division of Penguin Putnam, in 2002. This is a revised and expanded edition.

It was then updated, revised, and renamed *The Goddess Pages: A Divine Guide to Finding Love and Happiness and published by* Llewellyn Worldwide in 2008.

In 2020 it was introduced for the first time in digital edition and was accompanied by an updated paperback edition, with a new subtitle: *The Goddess Pages: 36 Divine Females to Guide You to Love, Success, and Happiness*. Both are published by Goddess Communications, LLC. Rights are retained by the author, Laurie Sue Brockway.

First Edition and Printing, *The Goddess Pages*, 2008
First Digital Edition, 2020
Second Edition and Printing, 2020

"There Are So Many Goddesses" © 2008 by Laurie Sue Brockway.

Paperback ISBN: 978-1-941630-20-4

I dedicate this book to my mother, Shirley Brockway.

She was a true goddess who ruled her universe and did things her way.

She was also
loving,
kind,
nurturing,
and wise.

Cover Design and Interior Formatting by Qamber Designs & Media
Images used under license from Shutterstock.com and DepositPhotos.com

Cover: Goddess of the Universe
BLACKDAY/Shutterstock.com

Part 1: Eva and the Red Apple
CaroDi/DepositPhotos.com

Part 2: Face of Quan Yin
Gow27/DepositPhotos.com

Part 3: Antique Marble Statue of Aphrodite
James Smirnoff/DepositPhotos.com

Part 4: Hawaii Goddess Pele Creating Lava
Ja Ja Kang/Shutterstock.com

Part 5: Lakshmi, Goddess of Blessing and Abundance
MiSt21/Shutterstock.com

Part 6: Amaterasu Holding a Cat
Designspace/Shutterstock.com

Page Dividers and Affirmation Crowns
Olia Fedorovski/DepositPhotos.com

THERE ARE SO MANY GODDESSES

There are mild goddesses
and there are wild goddesses.
We need them all.
They show us how to
embody all that we are.

There are light goddesses
and there are dark goddesses.
We need them all.
They show us deeper levels of the self,
and they help us know our truth.

There are famous goddesses
and lesser-known goddesses.
We need them all.
They teach us about the mysteries
and help us reach our dreams.

There are maiden and mother goddesses,
queen and wise woman goddesses.
We need them all.
They guide us on the path we're meant to travel;
they help us become more skillful and wise.

There are goddesses who will stand by us
and guide us as we remember
how to rebirth ourselves at any stage and stand again in our own
full power as we claim what is rightfully ours.
We need them all.

—LAURIE SUE BROCKWAY

CONTENTS

Acknowledgements   *xiii*

Test Your Goddess IQ   *1*

Inroduction   *7*

PART ONE: RECLAIMING EVE

| EVE | Rediscovering Feminine Wisdom and Self-Esteem | 1 |

PART TWO: GODDESSES OF SELF-EMPOWERMENT AND STRENGTH

HATHOR	See How Beautiful You Truly Are	13
LILITH	Discover Your Dark And Wild Side	20
OYA	Welcome The Winds Of Change	27
NIKE	Claim Your Victories In Life	35
MARY	Connect To Your Healing Power	43
SOPHIA	Learn To Trust Your Inner Wisdom	51
KUAN YIN	Be Compassionate With Yourself And Others	59
GREEN TARA	Feel Safe And Protected	67
WHITE BUFFALO CALF WOMAN	Create Peace In Your World	74

PART THREE: GODDESSES OF LOVE AND ROMANCE

VENUS	Be The Ultimate Self-Love Goddess	85
OSHUN	Bring Out Your Sensuality	92
FREYA	Be A Man Magnet	98
PERSEPHONE	Liberate Yourself From Bad Relationships	105
GAURI	Get Ready For Marriage	113
RADHA	Discover Soulful Love	120
ISIS	Rescue Your Relationship	127

PART FOUR: GODDESSES OF FAMILY LIFE AND FRIENDSHIP

THE GREAT GODDESS	Transform Your Relationship to Your Mom	137
PELE	Channel Anger And Heal Hostility	145
KALI	Dance With The Hungry Ghosts of Your Past	154
SAINT LUCY (LUCINA)	Bring Light And Vision To Your Family	163
THE MUSES	Celebrate With Sisters And Friends	170
MARY MAGDALENE	Survive The Loss Of A Loved One and Other Endings	177
VESTA	Create A Place You Can Call Home	184

PART FIVE: GODDESSES OF WORK AND FINANCES

AURORA	Discover Your True Path	193
ARTEMIS	Pursue Your Career Goals	200
BRIGID	Find Your Inspiration	207
LAKSHMI	Increase Your Income	214
NEMESIS	Embrace Your Inner Saboteur	221
DURGA	Draw Your Boundaries	228
SAINT TÉRÈSE	Get The Job Done	235

PART SIX: GODDESSES OF PLAY AND LIGHTHEARTEDNESS

BAST	Be Playful As A Pussycat	243
UZUME	Burst Out In Laughter And Sunshine	250
IRIS	Catch A Ride On A Rainbow	256
BUTTERFLY MAIDEN	Come Out Of Your Cocoon And Fly	262
FAIRY GODMOTHER	Believe In Magic	269

Closing Thoughts	*277*
Chapter Notes	*278*
Goddess Resource Guide	*292*
Bibliography	*296*
About the Author	*298*

ACKNOWLEGMENTS

This book is very special. It has been blessed by the goddesses of publishing three times! It was first published by Perigee Books in 2002. It came alive again in its second, updated, and revised incarnation from Llewellyn Worldwide. And now, it is reborn, for the first time as an e-book and in a new paperback edition, from Goddess Communications.

A lot of love went into this book. I am so grateful to all those who helped this book come alive and stay alive.

It would not exist without the support and original efforts of Arielle Ford, Brian Hilliard, Jennifer Repo, Christel Winkler, Michelle Howry, Heather Connor, and my beloved hubby, Rev. Victor Fuhrman.

I am so grateful to Llewellyn publisher Bill Krause for making the second edition possible. I thank my wonderful editor, Mindy Keskinen, for gently editing this book to make it even better; and I thank literary agent Julie Hill for her expertise and guidance on that edition.

And I thank my sister, Nikki Fiske, for proofing this new edition, as she did the first time, and helping me update it for its new venture out into the world.

My gratitude soars out into the universe to all the teachers, deans, mentors, friends, and counselors who have been part of my path to the Goddess. A special hug to Ammachi, known as Amma, who gave me my first experience of the Mother Divine in human form. Loving gratitude to Rabbi Joseph Gelberman, founder of The New Seminary, who taught me to embrace the Divine by all names and of all faiths, with the understanding that we are all one. May his memory be a blessing. And a heartfelt thank you to the original NYC Media Goddess group that helped me grow and cheered me on.

I thank all the goddesses and spiritual heroines of so many traditions for allowing me the opportunity to be a scribe of higher wisdom that will hopefully help women have richer and happier lives.

TEST YOUR GODDESS IQ

Goddesses are in our consciousness even more than we realize. They are casually referred to, and spoken of, constantly in our contemporary culture; their images and stories have sunk into our awareness. Before you meet the awesome archetypes of The Goddess Pages, test your own Goddess IQ.

1. Cleopatra was the most famous Egyptian pharaoh, legendary for her love affairs with Julius Caesar and Marc Anthony—and her attempts to rule the world in partnership with each. In ancient Egypt, all rulers identified themselves as gods and goddesses in human form. Which goddess was Cleopatra's guiding light?

   A. Nut
   B. Hathor
   C. Isis
   D. Maat

2. Who is the Greek goddess of war and wisdom, born out of her father's head?

   A. Artemis
   B. Hera
   C. Athena
   D. Hestia

3. Which of these divine females was born as a fully formed woman from the womb of the sea?

   A. Lakshmi, Hindu goddess of fortune and beauty
   B. Venus, Roman goddess of love and beauty
   C. Aphrodite, Greek goddess of love and beauty
   D. All of the above

4. Name the mother goddess who searches the earth for her beloved daughter Persephone, who has been captured by the ultimate bad boy, Hades.

   A. Gaia
   B. Demeter
   C. Astarte
   D. Tamuz

5. Which goddess is friend to the Dalai Lama, Richard Gere, and many other famous Buddhists who evoke her in Tibetan chants? She shares a name with a famous place in a classic movie.

   A. Tara
   B. Eve
   C. Joy Luck
   D. Crouching Dragon

6. Although the Jewish religion does not personify God, the tradition of mystical Judaism has long identified the feminine nature of God as an "indwelling presence." What is her name?

   A. Sarah
   B. Sophia
   C. Shekinah
   D. Rebecca

7. According to Jewish mysticism, Adam had a first wife, before Eve, who huffed out of the Garden of Eden one day and was later demonized as a wicked *femme fatale*. Today, some admire her as a powerful bitch goddess who owns her own life and takes charge! Female rockers named a huge music festival after her. Who is she?

   A. Sarah
   B. Beth Sheba
   C. Ruth
   D. Lilith

8. In many ancient cultures, temple priestesses were considered "sacred prostitutes." It was their role to initiate men to the goddess through lovemaking; this was a fully accepted rite of passage. Who was the Sumerian goddess the sacred prostitutes prayed to?

    A. Inanna
    B. Aphrodite
    C. Venus
    D. All of the above

9. One of the earliest and most famous images of the Goddess depicts her as a rotund and curvy female. Her pendulous breasts represent the hills and mountains; her big belly is the rich and fecund earth. What is the name of this statue that dates back about twenty to thirty thousand years?

    A. Venus on a Half Shell
    B. Mother Earth
    C. Gaia
    D. Venus of Willendorf

10. Who is the most famous Hawaiian goddess? Her legend comes to life on Hawaii's Big Island, where she is said to live in an active volcano.

    A. Haumea
    B. Laka
    C. Maui
    D. Pele

11. The first goddess of the Hindu pantheon was birthed by the collective energy of the male gods to fight a mighty buffalo demon that the guy gods could not destroy alone. She is pictured with eight arms, wielding weapons and one lotus flower, and she usually rides a tiger. What is her name?

A. Lakshmi
B. Saraswati
C. Parvati
D. Durga

12. Using tiny boats launched from the shores, Brazilian women make offerings of food and flowers to a beloved Yoruban ocean goddess whom they credit with helping them heal their lives. By what name is she known?

A. Oshun
B. Seala
C. Oya
D. Yemaya

13. When searching for inspiration, the ancient Celts prayed to this red-haired triple goddess of poetry, blacksmithing, and brides. She was later transformed into a Catholic saint. She is:

A. Dana
B. Cerridwen
C. Guinevere
D. Brigid

14. What is the Greek name for the goddess whose image we might see on a courthouse façade or a lawyer's business card? She is often depicted delicately balancing the scales of justice.

A. Grace

B. Fortuna

C. Themis

D. Blind Justice

15. Goddesses show up on lunch boxes, T-shirts, skirts, and other clothing. Which victory goddess has a successful line of sports shoes and apparel named after her?

A. Puma

B. Adidas

C. Nike

D. Keds

THE ANSWERS
1. C. Isis
2. C. Athena
3. D. All of the above
4. B. Demeter
5. A. Tara
6. C. Shekinah
7. D. Lilith
8. A. Inanna
9. D. Venus of Willendorf
10. D. Pele
11. D. Durga
12. D. Yemaya
13. D. Brigid (a.k.a. Saint Brigit)
14. C. Themis, goddess of justice
15. C. Nike

SCORING
- 15 correct answers: You may already be an expert, but you're about to meet some new goddesses in this book.
- 7 to 14 correct answers: You have great "goddess awareness." Now expand it!
- 0 to 6 correct answers: You don't know what you've been missing! Read on to discover more.

*I*NTRODUCTION

It's only natural that the Goddess should have special significance
for women, who long to know, too, that they are made in divine image.
—JALAJA BONHEIM, *GODDESS: A CELEBRATION IN ART AND LITERATURE*

*Y*EARS AGO I WAS GIVEN a special book and deck
of divination cards: *The Goddess Oracle* by Amy Sophia
Marashinksy, with awesome illustrations by Hrana Janto. This gift
came into my hands just as I was making a huge career transition—
from magazine editor to minister. My father had just died, my love
life was a mess, and I was raising a little boy as a single mother.
I was grieving, confused, worried, stressed, and overwhelmed as I
began the process of leaving a longtime career and taking a leap into
the unknown. I yearned for a wise and all-knowing helping hand to
guide me on the spiritual path. After receiving this gift, I used the
oracle deck often, laying the goddess cards out in "spreads" in search
of insight. I loved the idea of being guided by the goddesses, but at
the time I saw them as mythological figures and archetypes. I didn't
quite understand how to create a truly sacred relationship with the
Goddess—the Divine Feminine. But I sure was happy to begin to
get to know her!

It wasn't until I was deep in my studies of comparative religions
in seminary school that I began to truly see and get acquainted with
the many feminine faces of God, known collectively as the Goddess,
as she exists in so many of the world's religions and traditions. My
path included many bumps, questions, and doubts along the way.

Having been raised in a fairly traditional religious culture, I found it hard to believe—and perhaps even sacrilegious to consider—that the male God of the Bible is but one of many interpretations of Divine presence that exist in the world's religions.

Fortunately, I was trained by a seminary that encouraged free thinking and exploration. Its motto is "Never *instead of,* always *in addition to.*" In order to embrace all faiths, we were taught that God is one source, but a source that manifests in many ways, through many paths, religions, and spiritual practices. And that God is represented by a wide range of deities with different names. To my delight, I discovered that so many of them are female and even pictured with curves, real hips, and a touch of lipstick!

The first goddess who found me—and adopted me—was Lakshmi, Hindu goddess of fortune. One day as I was praying to her for money to take care of my son, I panicked when a thought occurred to me. *As I continue my seminary program,* I wondered, *what if the male God—the one my parents told me about—gets mad at me and cuts me off?*

I was rattled by the fear that I was praying "inappropriately" or asking the "wrong deity" for help. That fear moved me to find out more about Lakshmi and how she is honored and perceived in her faith of origin. I began to study Hinduism in earnest and hang around Hindu temples and worship services. Often I simply sat in front of the Lakshmi icon and watched how naturally the priests honored her with chanting, *puja* devotional rituals, and offerings. I saw how commonplace it was for Hindus to pray to Lakshmi—and all the goddesses—in their daily worship. Eventually, I began to know in my heart that I was just as entitled and welcomed to pray to this goddess. That is what she is there for—to be honored, to be worshipped, to bring us good things, and to help make dreams come true.

If that was the case with Lakshmi, I surmised, then every goddess must have a relevance beyond her own tradition of origin. Every goddess must be a universal goddess, available to all. How cool is that? We really can connect with any goddess we feel called to.

By the time I graduated from seminary, I had a burning hunger to know the Goddess and meet her in her many forms. I wanted to learn about every divine female I could find! I scoured every book and embarked on countless spiritual adventures in search of Isis, Hathor, Kuan Yin, Tara, Pele, Freya, Brigid, Durga, Kali, and so many more.

I was still raising a small child, so I couldn't really travel around the world. I had to find other ways to connect with these goddesses and bring them into everyday life. I couldn't get to Egypt, but I could go to the Egyptian exhibition at the Brooklyn Museum and see the antiquities up close. I wasn't able to travel to Tibet, but I could take a taxi to New York's Tibet House and sit in the temple there to feel the energy. I wasn't going to Lourdes in France, but I could walk into any Catholic church and commune with Mary and the saints. Eventually, I filled my home with goddess icons and created my own temple.

That is how I now know that we can connect with the goddesses anywhere, anytime, as long as our hearts are pure and our intentions are sincere.

As a writer, interfaith minister, supporter of women's dreams, and true fan of the Goddess, I decided to follow my natural response to my search for the Divine Feminine: I would write a book that would help other women do the same. Having covered women's issues as a journalist for many years, I have found that one of the biggest challenges we face is low self-esteem. It seems to be at the root of so many other problems—dating the wrong men, being underpaid, letting people take advantage, not saying "no" enough, fear of pursuing our dreams, and feeling that we are not worthy or capable enough.

If women can connect with the many goddesses of the world, I wondered, won't that also help us recognize the Goddess within? So this book is designed to bring the goddesses into your life—to help with your everyday challenges and to keep you connected to your true aspirations. This book can help you connect to your own power and stand firmly for what you believe in as you passionately and happily pursue your dreams.

THE GODDESS IS A GREAT ROLE MODEL

Once you get to know her, you'll agree! She's got powers in the world, and she's connected to all that is. She's got attitude, she's got sass, and she's got presence. She does things her way. She is the source of her own power. When we tap into her energies, we tap into the vast creative force of the universe.

You'll find that there are thousands of goddesses from many cultures, known by various names and images and representing not only the feminine aspects of divinity, but also aspects of our humanity. They're wild and mild, powerful and soft, compassionate and passionate; they're virgins and queens, mothers and daughters. They're rulers of the universe who can transform the planet, nurse a baby, and love their consorts simultaneously. Their images, energy, and the very concept of female divinity can heal us, empower us, instruct us, and help us find our way on life's rocky path. They give us permission to be all we can be.

Goddess history dates back to the earliest civilizations. It's well documented that ancient societies worshipped feminine forms of God— typically as mother, Earth, nature, Holy Spirit, or as deities who personified feminine attributes. The earliest signs of such worship date back as far as forty thousand years. One of the most famous artifacts of the Divine Feminine is the stone statue known as the Venus of Willendorf, believed to have been carved twenty to thirty thousand years ago. And while she looks like a rotund female, pregnant and voluptuous, when a replica of the statue is placed flat on her back, she takes on the form of the earth—the hills and valleys, mountains and ravines, are all in her body. And that is how some of the ancients worshipped the Great Mother—Mother Earth and Mom Nature. The Great Goddess Mother was the planet: alive, growing, pulsing with life, but always incorporating death and regeneration, as witnessed in nature's cycles.

Our early ancestors saw the Divine Feminine as the source of All That Is, and they depended on her to sustain their very lives. Her power was expressed in the image and stories of literally thousands of goddesses. Many of the world's cultures continue to worship, honor, and pray to female deities. The Hindu, Buddhist, and Tibetan civilizations, and the indigenous cultures of the Americas and Africa, are among those that have always communed with the Divine Feminine.

Obviously, conventional monotheistic religious belief is dominated by references and images of a male Divine, but the feminine has whispered ever so softly between the lines. Catholicism, especially, has given us our most tangible mainstream connection. Mary, mother of Jesus, along with a handful of popular female saints, has been the most visible aspect of the feminine in traditional Christianity for about two thousand years. Because of that, she cuts across religious boundaries. She is, in many ways, the adopted spiritual mother of all women; people of many faiths embrace her.

WELCOME TO THE GODDESS PAGES!

This book brings you thirty-six goddesses and spiritual heroines— including Mary and some beloved Catholic saints—who can enhance your spirituality as they assist with various aspects of your life. It was hard to pick just three dozen! All are noted for the special place they hold in their traditions, yet this book also presents them in the context of our own lives: our specific situations and challenges to which each goddess can bring her special skills and loving guidance.

The Goddess Pages brims with insights, history, mythology, prayers, invocations, meditations, affirmations, exercises, rituals, and modern interpretations of ancient wisdom to help women connect with each goddess personally. Originally published as *A Goddess Is a Girl's Best Friend* in 2002, this was my first book about the divine feminine. It was updated, revised, and republished in 2008 as *The Goddess Pages*. It features five goddesses that were not in the first edition.

Even though times have changed, this book has not changed too much. I wrote the first edition after the attack on the World Trade Center and while I was working as a volunteer chaplain for The Red Cross during recovery in New York City. Under the influence of those devastating events, I added a number of protection goddesses into this book and addressed various aspects of upheaval and loss. I think all the sacred females herein still offer guidance that is relevant today.

Each chapter gives you directions and suggestions on how best to honor that particular goddess or spiritual heroine. Every story, every ritual and prayer is shared here to empower you, help you enhance your own life, and help you tap into your own power—the Goddess within.

MEET THE GODDESSES: A PREVIEW

Reclaiming Eve

Eve, considered the mother of us all in the Judeo-Christian world, is our first link to the Divine Feminine in human form. Reclaiming Eve is the first step toward getting to know the Goddess within.

Goddesses of Self-Empowerment and Strength

Hathor, Egyptian goddess of love, beauty, and pleasure, helps you to see your inner light and shows you how truly beautiful you are.

Lilith, the Hebrew goddess said to be Adam's first wife, was demonized historically but is an empowered woman in the Kabbalah and in contemporary feminine spirituality. She helps you discover your hidden and wild side.

Oya, Yoruban, goddess of wind, hurricanes, and wild weather, helps you welcome the winds of change.

Nike, Greek goddess of victory and herald of success, helps you claim your victories in life.

Mary, mother of Jesus, is not *considered* a goddess in the Catholic faith, yet has the powers of the Feminine Divine and has been its primary representation for two thousand years, making her the spiritual mother for us all. She helps you connect to your healing power.

Sophia, goddess of wisdom in Gnostic Christianity, is also referred to in Hebrew texts and the books of Solomon. She helps you tap into, and trust, your own intuition.

Kuan Yin, Chinese goddess of healing and compassion, helps you find compassion for yourself and others.

Green Tara, Tibetan Buddhist goddess of protection, helps you feel safe and shows you how to stay calm and centered in a crisis.

White Buffalo Calf Woman, Native American spirit woman, is the mystical feminine force who taught great sacraments to her people. She helps you connect with the true nature of the soul and create a more peaceful life . . . and world.

Goddesses of Love and Romance

Venus, quintessential Roman goddess of love and beauty, shows you that self-love and appreciation is the first step to embracing your own divinity and empowering your sense of self-worth.

Oshun, Macumban goddess of sensuality, beauty, and womanhood, helps you tap into your sensual side—and express it.

Freya, Norse goddess of sexual prowess and war, guides you to be a "man magnet" and enjoy every minute of your life's sizzling sexual energy.

Persephone, Greek goddess of springtime who was abducted by the god of the underworld, shows you how to liberate yourself from bad relationships and set forth a new path in your love life.

Gauri, Hindu goddess of love and marriage, shows you how to prepare for a serious relationship and gently encourage your true love toward the altar.

Radha, sacred consort of Hindu avatar Krishna, helps you discover your soulful, higher lover.

Isis, famous Egyptian mother goddess, is hailed for her healing, magic, and resurrection powers. She helps you rescue troubled relationships and get them back on track.

Goddesses of Family Life and Friendship

The Great Goddess is the divine female energy of All That Is. She represents life itself, as well as death and regeneration, and can help transform your relationship with your own mom by connecting you with the power of your female ancestry.

Pele, the fire goddess who dwells in the volcano on the Big Island of Hawaii, shows you how to channel and express anger and heal in a healthy, holistic way.

Kali, Hindu goddess of life, destruction, and regeneration, shows you how to own up to your dark side and dance with the hungry ghosts of your past.

Saint Lucy (Lucina) is the cherished Catholic saint who originated as the Roman goddess of a newborn's first light. She can help you open your spiritual eyes, see family in a new way, and bring light to the shadow side of family life.

The Muses, the nine Greek deities who joyfully presided over the arts, are among the most familiar mythical women and goddesses. They help you celebrate creativity and connections with sisters and friends.

Mary Magdalene, the spiritual heroine who is closely linked as soul companion to Jesus, helps you survive the loss of a loved one.

Vesta, Roman goddess of the hearth, assists you in creating a true home.

Goddesses of Work and Finance

Aurora, Roman goddess of the dawn, assists you on the path to your true calling and helps you open your spiritual eyes.

Artemis, Greek goddess of the hunt, helps you pursue your career goals with passion and focus.

Brigid, Celtic Irish goddess of inspiration, poetry, birth, and blacksmithing, helps you find your inspiration and let your creativity flow.

Lakshmi, Hindu goddess of fortune, gives you a hand—or four—to boost your income, your financial potential, and your ability to plan for your future.

Nemesis, Greek goddess of retribution, helps you handle office politics and troublemakers while showing you how you can avoid sabotaging yourself, too.

Durga, Hindu, mother goddess of protection and war, helps you draw your boundaries and protect yourself from negative energies.

Saint Térèse, the beloved Catholic saint known as the Little Flower, is a spiritual heroine for women of all faiths. She helps you complete even the most menial tasks by showing you the relevance, power, and sacredness in life's little chores.

Goddesses of Play and Lightheartedness

Bast, Egyptian goddess of play, felines, and females, shows you how to be playful as a pussycat.

Uzume, the Japanese shaman goddess responsible for inspiring laughter, shows you how to bring sunshine and levity into your life.

Iris, Roman goddess of the rainbow, helps you add color and zest to your life.

Butterfly Maiden, Native American spirit woman, takes you from cocoon to butterfly and helps you transform your life.

The Fairy Godmother, a goddess-like figure many girls grow up with, may be an icon of fairy tales and movies, but she is also an inspiration for activating magic in our lives at any age.

May you enjoy meeting the goddesses and working with them. We can all greatly benefit from an intimate connection with the Divine Feminine!

Many blessings,
Rev. Laurie Sue Brockway
New York City

Part I
RECLAIMING EVE

$\mathcal{E}$VE

REDISCOVERING FEMININE WISDOM AND SELF-ESTEEM

Eve was framed.
—POPULAR T-SHIRT SLOGAN

I'M NO BIBLICAL SCHOLAR, BUT I think Eve got a bum rap. Although she should be exalted and honored for her role as the first woman on Earth, the Mother of Us All, she has been vilified and held out as an example of all that women should not be.

The stern interpretation of Genesis that has been Eve's legacy tells us that women who are curious and disobey male authority and ideology bring bad karma to their families: they wreak havoc on marriage, turn out dysfunctional children and are, in general, seductresses who cannot be trusted around men! And as if messing up her own life weren't bad enough, Eve is credited with making the planet a living hell for the rest of us.

Oy vey. Is it any wonder that women in our culture have self-esteem issues? *If we came from her and she did all that, how could we possibly be any good?*

Eve is the first daughter and therefore our first link to the Divine Feminine in human form, and yet her tale is riddled with fear-based messages that have long made women cringe at their own curiosity, power, and self-expression. Could it be that the Mother of Us All was such a *bad girl*? Or has she just been victim of some of the worst negative spin doctoring in human history?

1

I vote for the latter.

The mystical Islamic school of Sufism and the Kabbalah of Judaism both take a view of Adam and Eve that is useful for us all: the story is really a metaphor for something we all must go through. It was time for the children to leave the father's house and go out into the real world. The human world had to expand, evolve, and grow. Eve initiated the beginning of history. Had she not dared to taste that apple, had she not prompted her man to share the discovery, none of *us* would be here.

What was Eve's sin, really? She tried to seize a little knowledge beyond what was handed down to her as law by her father and she "initiated" her husband. Bucking authority is part of evolution. We grow when we step out of the box that people try to contain us in. We find our power by pressing up against resistance and people who try to control us. For women, turning our men on to the new things we discover is part of being in a relationship. What Eve did was a natural part of human development.

But we have had that nasty notion of the "original sin" droned into our brains since childhood. That blame, shame, and underlying fear of retribution is, unfortunately, an insidious hallmark of the female experience, ingrained in us even if we rarely, if ever, give it a conscious thought. Whether we know it or not, women come into the world fulfilling an ancient, unconscious agreement that we are not as good as men, not as worthy, and certainly not as divine. It affects us all in some way, on some level.

As the "daughters" of Eve, we carry on her legacy. So many of us, consciously and unconsciously, suffer from the "Eve Problem." We have bought into the belief that our "foremother" was weak and unworthy—and thus, so are we. For generations, women in general have been plagued by a small voice, an imaginary serpent that hisses in our ear: "*Who are you to be powerful, strong, capable, prosperous, and successful?*" It is time to put that hiss in its proper perspective, make the serpent recoil, and transform its tune from negative self-talk to inspiration for success, spiritual development, and personal evolution.

It is time to redefine and reclaim Eve from a woman-friendly point of view. We now have the opportunity to reinterpret our personal history and feel more connected to our Divine Mother. We can help shape our destiny, rather than be dragged along by it.

"RECLAIMING EVE" MEDITATION

The story of Adam and Eve, in many ways, is a very romantic tale about soul mates. The idea of Eve being created from Adam's rib, being of one flesh with him, is the stuff of romantic fairy tales. She was given the chance every woman dreams of—to live in a heaven on earth with her honey. Instead of believing that she *blew it*, we can consider her a pioneer, a courageous woman who was strong enough to establish the human race. Tasting from the Tree of Knowledge was the fulfillment of her life purpose—opening the gates of wisdom to the rest of us for all time!

To fulfill our destinies as powerful women, we have to go back to the Garden of Eden to reclaim Eve. When we look at the pleasant and unpleasant sides of her story—both the dark and the light—and come to a more empowering interpretation, we give ourselves a fresh start. We also embrace, and perhaps say goodbye to, the little serpent who lives on our shoulder and hisses: "*You are not good enough, smart enough, powerful enough, and who are* you *to be doing* this, *anyway?*"

Journey to Eden

In this reflective exercise, you'll reinvent your relationship with Eve. Read it through first and set aside the time you'll need.

1. **Go back to the garden.** Make plans to visit a beautiful garden, a park, your backyard—any place that puts you in touch with nature

in an environment that at least evokes the sense of Eden. Do you live near an apple orchard? In a pick-your-own orchard, you can pay a few dollars during the autumn and take your own fruit home after enjoying the beauty of the groves. For this meditation, a fruit orchard is ideal—but any outdoor setting will do. If you can't get out into nature, simply stay inside and use your imagination to place yourself, energetically, in the Garden. Either way, you'll be beginning to contemplate Eve in a powerful way.

2. **Connect to the Tree of Knowledge.** Find a comfortable spot where you can spend an undisturbed fifteen or twenty minutes in quiet reflection and meditation. Sitting with your back against an apple tree, or any tree, would be ideal so that you can feel the energy of Mother Earth coming into you, connecting you with the energy of the Tree of Knowledge. Prepare yourself to enjoy a few moments with Eve. Set your intention to come away with a more positive image of Eve and to feel proud of her as your ancient foremother.

3. **Imagine the Garden of Eden.** You are observing one of the most powerful moments in time, the moment that is said to have altered human history, when Adam and Eve tasted of the Tree of Knowledge. See this Garden as you believe it must have looked, replete with splendor and beauty, plants and animals— the elements of the story that are familiar to you, and those images that come to you now. Even though this is *the* Garden of Eden, it is a garden of your own creation. Invent whatever you wish for it.

Follow your creative heart and your imagination to see Eve, along with Adam. Let them come alive in your mind's eye— happy, playful, fulfilled, in love, safe. Observe the moment when the serpent invites Eve to taste of the fruit, and see that she is not motivated by darkness or evil, nor is her behavior bad. She is innocent, exploring and tasting of a new fruit that is part of their life's evolution—and our evolution. Allow yourself to be there with her, watching, knowing, and seeing who she really is. Feel her fear at trying something new, and her fear of angering her father, but sense her moment of power as she responds to the call of her own soul.

Without judgment, observe the moment when Adam and Eve eat the apple and God discovers them. Tune in to the crisis—and how Adam and Eve handle it. Rather than seeing an angry God raining wrath down upon them, see him gently saying to his children: *"I tried to protect you from the darker side of this world that I have brought you into. But now it is your time to leave, explore, discover your life's mission, and find your way to your own personal wisdom."*

Then hear the voice of the Divine Mother speaking, too: *"The apple is sweet, and it is tart, as is life outside the garden walls. Now that your consciousness is open to All That Is, life will bring you a wide range of experience, dark and light, pain and joy. I cannot shield you from all, but I will come with you, out of this garden, so that you always carry a little part of it with you and you can find your way back home to the source of who you are."*

Now see if you receive an additional message from the Mother or the Father, or Eve and Adam. Just listen for any thoughts or ideas or small still voices that whisper in your ear. Keep your eyes closed. Stay still for a while until you feel your time in the garden is complete.

Now say goodbye to the garden and any messengers you met along the way. Thank Adam and Eve; God and Goddess; All That Is.

4. **Redefining Eve.** Combining the elements you love about the story of the Garden of Eden, the vision you had of Adam and Eve in your meditation, and any new thoughts about this ancient

tale that are beginning to emerge from you, redefine Eve. Write a brief statement about how you see her now—such as *Eve was bold and she never got credit for her chutzpah.* Write down whatever is a true belief for you now, personally. If you have not arrived at a new belief yet, write down the one you would most like to adopt.

When we redefine Eve, we inspire a new role model: a first woman who knows she has permission to evolve and express her power. Step into your power with the renewed energy of Eve—and the Goddess—as your guide. Take this opportunity for a fresh start at reinventing your own life and reclaiming your power.

A CELEBRATION OF EVE AND HER APPLE

Was the Tree of Knowledge actually an apple tree? There is still a debate on this subject. Some say the forbidden fruit could have been a fig, especially since Adam and Eve quickly ended up with fig leaves on their privates—remember, after they bit into the fruit of knowledge, they realized for the first time that they were naked!

But let us honor Eve and her apple, long a symbol of her downfall, so that we can reclaim the power of the feminine that lies within its sweet fruit.

The apple has been used as a symbol of evil—recall the wicked queen who fed Snow White the poison apple, for example—and has been linked with death and deceitfulness. But it is largely considered a fruit that is delicious, nutritious, and symbolically sacred.

The apple symbolizes fertility, love, joy, knowledge, and wisdom in many of the world's religions and mythologies. Offering an apple is often seen as a symbol of love. The Greek goddess of love, Aphrodite, and her Roman counterpart, Venus, were both known to woo with golden apples that evoked love and desire. Apple blossoms are associated with the bridal day and are Chinese symbols of peace and beauty. As a fruit found in the garden of Norse goddess Freya, the apple symbolized immortality. The apple tree has mythically been associated with health. In addition, scientific research from the University of California-Davis has showed that in fact, "An apple a day keeps the doctor away," because the fruit is loaded with healthy substances.

On Rosh Hashanah, the Jewish New Year, it is a special blessing to eat apples dipped in honey, meaning, "May you be inscribed for a good, sweet year." The apple is also a sacred symbol of the Divine Feminine. Cutting open an apple, we see at the core that it is shaped somewhat like a woman's vulva; we also see the natural design of the five-pointed star that is linked with earth religions that honor the Goddess. In addition to all this, they taste yummy and sweet. And even if you bite into an apple that has a bitter edge, it still gives a sweet taste—a symbol of life, in a way.

Apple Juice and Apple Ceremony

With this celebration, you'll join together with friends to reclaim Eve as sisters.

1. Invite a few girlfriends over for a celebration of "Eve Night."

2. Prepare a tray of juice and delicious apples. Slice one apple in half laterally and rest it on the tray as a centerpiece, with its star-shaped core turned up. Pick a facilitator for the evening, a friend who is good at leading group activities, or let everyone share the task.

3. Gather everyone in a circle. You can open with this prayer:

   Mother, Father, God, Goddess, All That Is . . . Please fill this place with your sacred presence . . . Please open us to your love, light, and wisdom . . . Please reunite us with our divine selves and prepare us to reunite with our first human mother,

Eve.

Empower us to heal her . . . that we may heal ourselves.
Amen. And so it is.

4. Speak the intention for the ceremony.

   We now celebrate and affirm our communion and positive
   connection to the Divine Feminine and to the human mother
   of us all, Eve, through the sharing of apple juice and apples.
   The apple represents the feminine, as it held the key that
   opened the door to knowledge and wisdom; wisdom, in most
   traditions, is referenced as feminine in nature.

5. Ask everyone to wave a hand over the food in the gesture of
   offering a blessing, and bless the apple together.

   We bless this apple juice, and these apples.
   We ask Goddess to instill them with her divine energies,
   We ask God to instill them with balancing qualities of the
   divine male.

6. Offer participants the tray and let them take a juice and an apple.

7. Offer this prayer as they partake of the sweet fruits:

   May this apple symbolize wisdom, courage and living our
   personal truth. And may it symbolize our permission to bite
   into life—with passion. Take a bite!
   May this apple juice symbolize the nectar of feminine power,
   and may it connect us more fully to the Goddess, and espe-
   cially, to the Goddess within. Take a sip!

8. Afterward, sit in quiet communion. Play a soft, stirring piece of
   instrumental music.

9. Then bring the sacred ceremony to a close with this blessing:

   May the light of God, Goddess, All That Is, please guide
   us to reconciliation with the story of Eve that has wounded

woman. **May our hearts replace untruth with truth. May our experiences and opportunities in life empower us to grow. May we all be the powerful and empowered women that Eve was.**

EVE AFFIRMATION

"May the light of God, Goddess, All That Is, sustain and empower us and lead us to personal truth and evolution. Amen. And so it is."

Part 2
GODDESSES OF
SELF-EMPOWERMENT
AND STRENGTH

$\mathcal{H}$ATHOR

SEE HOW BEAUTIFUL YOU TRULY ARE

I feel pretty . . . oh so pretty!
—MARIA, IN *WEST SIDE STORY*

THERE ARE A HANDFUL OF supermodels in this world—and then there are the rest of us. We grew up in a culture intent on making us believe that beauty is something external, a culture that pressures us from an early age to pursue images and ideals of beauty most of us will never achieve. That's why it is so important that we connect with our true inner beauty and light.

Glossy women's magazines, Madison Avenue, and Hollywood have been hypnotizing us for decades, trying to make us believe that being tall and rail thin, well dressed in designer clothing, and made up with pouty lips is what makes us beautiful and lovable. But beauty—however clichéd it may sound—comes from within. It is a sad fact that there is an epidemic of low self-esteem among women in American culture.

Our culture tends to assign goddess-like stature to women of astounding beauty and sexuality, yet women who do not fit the physical ideal of perfection are often left to feel unworthy. And we also end up working very hard to feel beautiful, instead of simply *accessing* the great reserves of beauty within. Despite anything you have been led to believe, now you must believe this: you are a beautiful woman!

Call upon Hathor when it comes to owning your inner beauty and inventing a personal style. She helps you see your truest beauty and also helps you use the realm of fashion and self-care to empower yourself. At the same time, she opens your spiritual eyes to the gorgeous soul that exists beyond physicality and fashion. She represents inner beauty and self-admiration.

WHO IS HATHOR?

The beauty of your face glitters when you rise, O come in peace.
One is drunk at your beautiful face, O Gold, Hathor.
—HYMN TO HATHOR INSCRIPTION FROM A TOMB IN THEBES

Hathor (*HATH-or*) is the Egyptian goddess of love, beauty, and pleasure, and a guardian of women. A multifaceted divine female, she manifested in many forms to the ancient Egyptians. She was a fiery solar deity and close consort to Ra-Horakhty, a lover who is a combination of the sun god Ra and the god Horus. She was a favorite among common folk and was also embraced by Hatshepsut, one of the few female pharaohs, whose rule encouraged the cult of Hathor. Her religion was considered joyful. Her main place of worship was in Dendera, a city that thrived on ongoing celebration.

As one of Egypt's most ancient goddesses, she's been blended with many popular deities. She is sometimes indistinguishable—in look and role—from Isis; she is also said to be the sister, or the milder aspect, of the lion goddess Sekhmet. Hathor's first form was as a cow goddess and a mother deity who empowers and feeds devotees with her rich milk. Hathor was believed to materialize during childbirth to help women through; she was a special guardian spirit of women and female animals. She was often depicted holding a mirror, and thus the mirror is a ritual reminder of the goddess's energy. The Greeks were especially fond of Hathor, equating her with their own goddess of beauty and love, Aphrodite. Hathor is usually seen as a trim

Egyptian woman with dark hair and dark eyes highlighted by kohl; she wears a wide, jeweled neckpiece and a headpiece created from a solar disk atop a pair of cows' horns.

HOW TO INVITE HER INTO YOUR LIFE

The women of Hathor's Egyptian culture were big on beauty treatments, cosmetics, essential oils, wigs, and personal adornment. Women rich and poor partook in rituals of beauty and self-care—to feel better, protect themselves from the elements, and enjoy their own expression of beauty. Hathor encourages the enjoyment of femininity—without stress. To look at Hathor's image is to see a woman who looks like *most* Egyptian women: an attractive figure, but not necessarily a ravishing beauty. Yet she decrees that all women are beautiful and can evoke their own special charm. Devotees were often said to be overwhelmed and intoxicated by Hathor's glittering appearance.

You, too, can evoke the beauty of the Goddess within when you begin to see yourself through new eyes and through a special looking glass—one that offers a more soul-inspired vision of your loveliness.

Look into Hathor's Mirror

Just as we contemporary women all own a mirror or two, almost every woman in ancient Egypt possessed one. The mirror of Hathor was the most popular style. The handle was sculpted in the image of the goddess, with the horns of her headpiece rising to hold the glass; the round mirror was her sun disk. Women were encouraged to admire themselves in Hathor's looking glass. Each morning, they sipped milk, the drink of the cow goddess, to replenish their *ka* (spirit), and gazed at themselves in the mirror. It was a way to start the day feeling connected to Hathor's power.

You can tap into Hathor's power by enjoying a few moments of self-admiration. At the very least, you can turn your morning experience of applying make-up into a self-love fest, connecting to Hathor as you put on lipstick and blush. Hathor's warmth is considered life itself, warmth that can help you see your true beauty. The way to access your inner beauty is to connect with and honor the Goddess within. Hathor's mirror can help you look deeply into your own eyes and love who you see.

1. **Identify your special mirror.** Select a mirror you look into often— such as your morning make-up mirror or the one you use when you dress. Or purchase a special mirror that you can keep on your vanity, in the bathroom, or any place you use frequently. Designate it your Mirror of Hathor.

2. **Find an image of Hathor.** Purchase, download, or copy a small picture of Hathor that really appeals to you. If you are not yet familiar with or connected to her image or energy yet, Hathor will understand if you prefer one of her more familiar Roman or Greek counterparts— Venus or Aphrodite. Select any image, artwork, or holy art that inspires you and connects you to what you deem to be the true beauty of the goddess.

3. **Attach the picture to the mirror.** Place it off to the side, so that Hathor's image is in the corner of your eye as you look at yourself in the mirror—whether it's a hand-held, full-length, or bathroom mirror. Make sure it's big enough for you to see clearly, but it doesn't block your view of yourself. You should catch sight of it easily with a slight eye movement or with your peripheral vision.

4. **Try a few eye exercises to meld with the goddess.** Keep your head still but let your eyes take you on a journey. Look at yourself in the mirror, and then look at the goddess. Look at yourself and, again, look at the goddess. Don't worry—you're not being narcissistic. This is a simple way to blend your beauties so that

you can come to see that there is no separation between you and the goddess. She truly lives inside you.

5. **Connect to your own beautiful essence.** As you look back and forth at yourself and then at the goddess, you may feel slightly dazed, but this is actually the goddess's beauty trance; you become more open to receiving her love. Think of it this way: Madison Avenue and the media have been hypnotizing you for years to believe in their version of beauty, and now you are hypnotizing yourself to see and know the beauty of your own soul. Allow yourself to feel her true beauty. This link to the Hathor/Venus within exists in us all. It cannot be bought in a bottle or worn on your body. It is a pure essence that comes from within. Don't be afraid to love that part of you. From that glorious dimension, your true beauty pours forth into the world and permeates all of your life.

6. **Try these modern mantras.** As you get used to the idea of truly seeing yourself as a goddess, you will know that you can access anything. It helps to support the visual exercise with language. Whether you feel this way or not, whether you feel it sometimes and struggle with it at other times, treat these statements as facts that are completely and absolutely true. When you are ready, look at the goddess and look at yourself and affirm:

> I *am* divine.
> I *am* beauty.
> I *am* love.
> I *am* a magnificent being.
> I *am* a goddess.

7. **Plant these messages into your heart and mind.** Say them as often as possible. Together, make them your own personal mantra if you like. Do this exercise as often as you can. You might even

want to put a sign near the picture of the goddess that reads, "*I am divine; I am beauty; I am love; I am a magnificent being; I am a goddess.*"

8. **Love being a girl.** Hathor showed the women of Egypt how to really love their beauty and personal adornment as an activity of self-pleasuring. Forget about trying to look exactly like the models we see in the magazines. That's so much work that it's painful! Somehow, the clothes, hair, and make-up are never as perfect when translated from the slick magazine pages to us. Trying to be the models we see instills in us a feeling of hopelessness that wounds us deep within. Don't go there. Instead, get some cute ideas and find things that are right for your personal look, and use those models for ideas—rather than ideals.

9. **Create your own style.** Hathor was known for wearing a *menat* neckpiece—a beautiful, wide beaded necklace of many strands that fit across her chest—and a form-fitting dress. She had a personal style, and you do too. You never have to be a slave to fashion. Select the kinds of clothes you love, feel comfortable in, and feel good in. Go for personal style over trends.

10. **Let the goddess guide you as you dress.** Make the act of adorning yourself in clothing and jewelry sacred, and always trust your first choice in outfits. We may spend hours trying on everything in the closet before heading out on a date or to a social occasion, yet we almost always end up wearing our first choice. Learn to trust the first instinct and go for it, as this is Hathor whispering in your ear. Trusting your clothing choices will lead to greater confidence in your appearance. It will also save a lot of frustration, not to mention time rehanging and refolding everything.

HOW TO KEEP HATHOR WITH YOU

Treat yourself well, regularly. Manicures, pedicures, and facials are empowering and beautifying because they relax you, give you some down time in which to connect with your own beauty, and help you feel good about yourself.

Enjoy a reflexology session. This ancient Egyptian healing practice of massage targets areas of the feet that affect the whole body. Reflexology relaxes, rejuvenates, and enhances feelings of well-being and inner beauty. It stimulates your natural tendency to feel good.

Install more mirrors in your home. Learn to love looking at yourself and connecting to your own eyes.

Carry a Hathor mirror in your purse. Purchase a beautiful compact mirror. Designate it and bless it as your mirror of self-appreciation.

Anytime you need a little extra encouragement, take out your mirror and speak your Hathor mantra.

HATHOR AFFIRMATION

"I see my beauty inside and out."

$\mathcal{L}$ILITH

DISCOVER YOUR DARK AND WILD SIDE

You're either a goddess . . . or a doormat.

—PABLO PICASSO

BEING NICE IS NOT ALWAYS a virtue. Playing the good girl and acting sweet does not always get us what we want in life. Women who are living their dreams do not necessarily get there by being dainty and darling. They get there by being wild, daring, provocative, hungry. They demand what they want into existence, and they do what it takes to make it happen. That could mean breaking a few rules . . . breaking a few hearts . . . and breaking a few habits along the way—especially the habit of constantly apologizing for who you are and what you think, say, or do in the world.

If, like so many women, you were trained to *mind your manners* and *act like a lady,* it may be painfully difficult for you to break out of the mold—or it may be painfully difficult not to! If you're suppressing yourself because you're afraid of your own dark side, you might as well recognize the wild woman bitch goddess within before she bites you on the butt in an attempt to get your attention.

Sometimes we've got to access our internal power through external connections and role models, until we manifest it into being. Just like children—who learn to *become* by pretending they *already are*—you may have to fake it until you make it. Think of all the fun you can have pretending to be a fierce female, tough chick, and force-to-be-reckoned-with, evoking those energies from within. Consider it an exercise in seizing personal power.

Call upon Lilith when you're ready to unleash the wild woman within and take the lid off your self-expression. She may seem nasty, but she is simply an exaggerated metaphor for rising above meekness and doing whatever the hell you want to do—regardless of what people think or say or how they react. She represents freeing the wild woman within, exerting personal power, and living without apology.

WHO IS LILITH?

He then created a woman for Adam, from the earth, as He had created Adam himself, and called her Lilith. Adam and Lilith began to fight. She said, "I will not lie below," and he said, "I will not lie beneath you, but only on top. For you are fit only to be in the bottom position, while I am to be in the superior one."
-THE ALPHABET OF BEN SIRACH
(DATED SEVENTH TO TENTH CENTURY A.D.)

Lilith (*LILL-ith*) is a Hebrew goddess known to possess great personal power and sexual appetite. In goddess spirituality and Jewish feminism, she is revered as fierce, potent, and wild. According to some tales from mystical Judaism and Jewish folklore, she is considered Adam's first wife, while Eve is seen as God's more malleable second try (although some believe Lilith represents an aspect of Eve's fuller power). Legend says Lilith was created in exactly the same way Adam was and at the same time, but Adam refused to treat her as an equal partner; he tried to push the male domination routine and insisted on male-on-top missionary-style sex. Lilith refused to be beneath him and bolted. The Garden was too restrictive to her; she wanted to become queen of her own domain. She opted for a romp by the Red Sea with a bevy of fallen angels considered demons. Lilith was not only branded a *femme fatale* and a bitch, she went down in history as an evil she-devil who birthed hundreds of mini-demons a day and populated the earth with negative beings. But she never looked back and she never apologized. Although she lives in demon mythology as a succubus who kills children and takes sexual possession of men while they sleep, Lilith has been reclaimed as a role model for female power. She's often depicted with female face and serpent body; sometimes seen slithering about, she's often thought of as the snake who tempted Eve to taste from the Tree of Knowledge.

HOW TO INVITE HER INTO YOUR LIFE

Few of us crave the kind of heartless powers that are attributed to Lilith, but just a "little bit of Lilith" can go a long way in teaching us to stand up for our rights. Getting what we want sometimes requires us to "come out of ourselves" and be a little wild. One of Lilith's most coveted attributes is her ability to seek fulfillment of her goals without concern about other people's beliefs and judgments about her. If you're *too nice, too meek, too wishy-washy* or *too much of a doormat,* just a whiff of her stance on life might help you find a path to expressing more personal power. Lilith can help reveal the wild woman within you—at your own pace and comfort level.

Lilith revels in the energy of living in her prowess. She eats life, devours egos, laughs at the idea of anyone being superior, and doesn't give a hoot what people think of her. She does what she wants to do. She may tend to be a dark goddess, yet she is willing to explore that part of herself. That's what makes her wild—she will go into the places others don't dare go. Lilith is all about freedom of choice. Good or bad, dark or light—she makes the rules. She owns her shadow self and all the dark desires that filter up from within. She does not oppress or distress herself over anything—ever. She may use the metaphor of sexual dominance to rule her universe, but it goes way beyond sex. She is an uppity chick who will not be told what to do or how to act—by anyone! She doesn't exist in this world to appease others. You shouldn't either!

Try these techniques for getting in touch with your inner Lilith.

1. **Watch movies that celebrate "Lilith energy."** She's a little nasty and she's got attitude! She knows what she wants—and gets it. She's the woman most people refer to as a bitch, because she knows how to "work it." There are many films that feature women characters who express their wild side. Classics include *Body Heat,* starring Kathleen Turner; *Fatal Attraction,* starring Glenn Close; and *The Last Seduction* with Linda Fiorentino as man killer Bridget Gregory. Fiorentino is the *darkest* side of Lilith, personified as the clever, scheming, and oh-so-hot *femme fatale* who is completely in control of her universe.

2. **Practice being fierce.** Lilith fosters a sense of anticipatory fear. There's something scary about her. Like a dominatrix or a "dangerous woman," she seems armed, but hers is an unseen power. Just as people don't argue with or mess with a woman perceived to be armed, they do not mess with a female who radiates an inner fierceness. You can opt for one of the most fun ways to evoke inner fierceness—clothing. Go shopping in a very cool store that has *femme fatale* clothing—maybe even a costume shop. Try on clothes and play around with "a look" that makes you feel fierce: maybe a wide-brimmed black hat with veil, a bustier, tight short skirt or leather pants, and long evening gloves—whatever helps bring out your wild side. You don't have to buy anything, or even wear it in public. But if it would be a breakthrough for you to don something devastating and wear it into your world, do it!

3. **Take charge by speaking clearly and giving directives.** Instead of molding yourself to the way things are, *mold your life to the way you are.* Essentially, there are those people who like to be

in control and people who like to give over control. Lilith likes to call the shots. Don't resist your own desire to take charge. People in your world are just waiting for you to tell them what to do. Communication with a bit of an edge is often just the thing to move people to get things done. Most people respond to a clear directive—do this, by such and such a time—that also has an embedded message about consequences. This is not being harsh; it is just a way to keep life flowing with a sense of certainty. Notice the kind of language and ways of speaking that get results and practice them in everyday life, out in the world.

4. **Develop an attitude that lets people know what you stand for.** Lilith takes a queen-like stance as if to say, "*Worship me.*" Anything less than utter reverence is unacceptable. Sometimes you have to train people around you through actions, words, and subtle threats—just as you'd train a puppy! But first it has to come from within. Look at yourself in the mirror and practice saying, over and over again: "*I am a goddess and you must worship me*" until you begin to get that you are worthy of reverence. Then look deeply into your own eyes and blow yourself a kiss. You may feel funny, stupid, out of your element, but see if you can get into the groove. It will enhance your sense of self-reverence and help you magnetize what you want. When you're willing to own your goddess nature, people will want to serve your needs.

5. **Stay firm in your choices, without apology.** If you give someone an ultimatum or tell them how it's going to be, stick with it or you will lose power. Don't second-guess yourself or wimp out of right decisions. When Lilith left the Garden, they tried to talk her back in. Whether she made a good choice or not, *she made a clear choice.* No one can argue with that. Practice making decisions that are in your best interest and impenetrable by others. If you chronically apologize every time you set forth a

decision others may not like, you'll negate yourself. Did Lilith say "sorry" to Adam for not wanting him on top of her? No. She said "ta-ta." For one day, take notes on how many times you say "I'm sorry." The next day, think twice about it and assess whether an apology is truly called for. By the third day, you should find that once you stop apologizing for nothing, you have more time to really express yourself!

6. **Don't blame others if you don't have what you want in life.** Lilith ditches whatever and whoever does not empower her. If a man will not honor her choices, or if an environment does not support who she is, she is outta there. *You, too, always have choices.* Choose what and who in your life is worth your continued effort and attention. Then take right action. If you are giving your power away, take it back! Try being just a little bit stern—especially if you are someone who is generally passed over, ignored, not taken seriously, or is always giving to others. There is no need to become dark and disturbing, but it is important for you to seize your personal power, make your own choices, and shape your own reality. Lilith encourages you to own your wilder side and express it when called for; it will help you claim the rights and privileges that are yours.

HOW TO KEEP LILITH WITH YOU

Allow for your dark desires. When it comes to expressing our power in the world, the rule of thumb is that it's got to be legal, moral, and cause no injury to self or others. You may not want to go down to the Red Sea and do what Lilith did, but certainly a dark thought or two may pass through your head. Allow the thoughts to surface and do not judge them. Then let them go.

Be queen of your world. Lilith left the Garden to conquer a new world. Keep a globe in your home or office to symbolize that you rule your personal universe. It's a metaphor for being in charge and on top of the world: you don't have to live at the mercy of anyone else's whims.

Get a T-shirt fit for a goddess. Lilith, obviously naked, was able to get her point across—but you can declare your attitude on your chest. Invent a slogan or find a T-shirt emblazoned with words like "I'm on top" or "Bitch Goddess."

LILITH AFFIRMATION

"Treat me like the goddess I am."

$\mathcal{O}$YA

WELCOME THE WINDS OF CHANGE

There is no holding on in this world.
—FROM THE MOVIE *I DREAMED OF AFRICA*

CHANGE ISN'T ALWAYS EASY TO accomplish or accept, even when it's "for the best." While common sense tells us that certain things in our lives must change if we are to grow, there's a part of us that resists like crazy. Even great, wonderful, blissful change can be a fright because, while we know our starting point, we have no idea where we will land. Even when we *desperately* need a change, still, a part of our personality wants to cling to that which is familiar and comfortable. For better or worse, it's what we know. Creating change requires risk, and risk often takes us out of our comfort zone—but it can also lead us to success in life!

Change can seem painful and scary, yet our fears about it are often more exhausting than the change itself. Some of us approach any kind of transition as a jail sentence, and we go kicking and screaming. But the thing that we refuse to change is what keeps us locked in a prison of our own making! Life will be much happier and more balanced when we learn to surrender more gracefully to the winds of change, working with them to create the life we choose. When an opportunity to grow or correct an imbalance through change comes along, grab it! Because the universe has a way of changing things for us when we can't find the wherewithal or courage to do it ourselves.

Call upon Oya when it comes to making changes in your life. She will not tolerate any clinging to the shreds of a dead relationship, job, or lifestyle. She presses you to do all the things you *said* you wanted to, and to fulfill as many dreams as you dare. She represents the surrender of the old and the radical rebirth of the new.

WHO IS OYA?

Great Oya, yes
Whirlwind Masquerader, awakening
courageously takes up her saber.
—JUDITH GLEASON, OYA: IN PRAISE OF THE GODDESS

Oya (*OY-yah*) is the goddess of change and mother of chaos, hailing from the Yoruban and Macumban traditions of Africa and Brazil. She's a warrior goddess whose domain is major shifts in weather, such as hurricanes, tornadoes, earthquakes, and storms of all kinds. As the *orisha* (spirit) responsible for whirlwinds, Oya rides the wild whirlwinds herself as they bring great change to the landscape— and sometimes, devastation that forces people to reevaluate and rebuild. Her name means "Tearer." Her consort/husband is Shango, the powerful thunder god; together they are *fierce*. She is sometimes called the "Mother of Nine" because nine is her sacred number. Oya's nine children were born out of a sacred rainbow cloth, a cloth sometimes called Grant-That-I-May-Live-Long. Closely associated with the cemetery, she is believed to be a special spirit link. Oya represents the ancestors and the greeting committee when you cross over; she lives between the worlds. She is also guardian of the marketplace and considered a shrewd businesswoman. Sometimes seen as an Amazon who rides the winds wielding a beaded horsetail and a saber, Oya is also thought of as a tall and stately African woman.

HOW TO INVITE HER INTO YOUR LIFE

Change or be changed—that's Oya's general theme. She is not the goddess relished by slowpokes and procrastinators: she is aggressive, wild, and unpredictable. Sometimes the best you can do is surrender to her powers and work with her as gracefully as possible. She is more than willing to let you catch a ride on the air she breathes, but she will blow you away if you disrespect the powerful forces she brings to bear.

Oya's saber is considered a sword of truth and wisdom, a weapon that helps cut away stagnation. If we work with Oya's energy to *create change*, we are better equipped to handle it and have more resilience when it comes. In order to grow, we must stretch beyond where we are, into the unknown. Each time we take responsibility to change our lives for the highest good, we gain confidence and trust in our ability to let go of whatever holds us back. We learn to let a part of us die or dissolve—we learn that that is okay and part of life—and then we allow ourselves to be reborn and transformed and new.

Oya has a way of correcting imbalances when we refuse. Resist, and she creates a whirlwind around you to bring your attention to the areas where you are due for a change. If you resist, she persists, urging you to take a second look at what you truly want in life. It works something like this: If you stay in a job, relationship, friendship, home, addiction, or habit longer than it takes to get the lesson or move on, Oya takes initiative and begins to *move you on*.

1. **Get a special "Time to Change" notebook.** Make it a loose-leaf that can be easily added to and changed. On the very first page, dedicate it to Oya: "*Mother Oya, my transformation and my awareness are my offerings to you. I surrender what no longer serves me and ask you to help me manage and master the winds of change.*"

WRITE WHAT IS GOOD. Jot down things you appreciate, like, and value in yourself. This can include physical attributes, abilities, talents, attitudes, spiritual awareness, the way you are with others, accomplishments.

WRITE WHAT IS NOT SO GOOD. Next, make a list of people, places, and things in your life that you know are holding you back or keeping you stuck. The idea is not to judge yourself, or them, but to clarify which aspects of your life need your attention. What's wreaking havoc; what's standing in the way of your growth? Is a particular job, friend, lover, family member, lifestyle, living arrangement, neighborhood, attitude, fear, or pattern of neglect in handling something? If so, jot it down. Be honest. Look at all the things that jam up the process of living and create stress, as well as things that are cluttering your life or draining your energy. Acknowledge the dark or dysfunctional aspects of your life; it's challenging but worth it.

PRIORITIZE AND AFFIRM. Review the list of things that keep you stuck and prioritize which need your attention first. Rewrite them as positive goals, phrased as if you've already achieved them. For example, "*I hate my weight*" becomes an affirming present tense statement: "*I am slimmer, healthier, and feel better about myself.*"

DELETE THE OLD. After you've rewritten all the affirming statements, get rid of the "not-so-good" list. As a symbolic gesture of the change you are willing to make, tear the list into tiny pieces and flush it down the toilet—or shred it, burn it in the fireplace or outdoor barbecue pit, bury it near a tree, or roll it into a tiny ball and feed it to the garbage truck.

GIVE YOURSELF A FRESH START. Now create a list for your new life. What and who will be in it? Create your new reality on paper so you have a place to head for as Oya helps you disengage from the places you've been stuck.

SAY A LITTLE PRAYER. Always ask Oya to make life's changes as gently as possible. *"Oya, guide me to make changes at an appropriate pace and in a way that harms no one—including me!"* Let her know that if she can do anything to soften the experience, you'd appreciate it. Tell her you want to make your life great and that you want to learn how to work with her gracefully.

MAKE AN OFFERING IN HER HONOR. Oya is sometimes worshipped with animal sacrifices. It may sound gross, but for millennia people have made such offerings to the gods to appease them and win favors. *Your offering can be something very personal; it will be just as pleasing.* Oya loves things in nines. Why not create an altar upon which you offer her nine each of some of her favorite things—such as nine grapes, red gemstones, or pennies. You can also offer her a sacrifice of one negative behavior that is causing you pain or keeping you stuck—whether it's an addiction to buying shoes or to smoking cigarettes. Every day for nine days, stand at the altar and offer her your gratitude for helping you find a way to gently release your challenge. This will let her know you mean business: you want to work with her, not against her, to change your life!

2. **Use cowrie shells for small changes.** Not ready for a major change? Work your way toward it with *small changes.* Take one issue at a time— such as finding a new doctor, updating your resume, doing your taxes— and handle it step by step until it's completed. Then take the next thing, then the next, until you get the momentum to rampage through your physical, emotional, and spiritual space, cleaning up your life and making room for the new.

Try this practice for the step-by-step approach. You'll use cowrie shells, sacred to Yoruban goddesses. Porcelain-like shells that were originally home to sea snails, they are considered the mouth of the orishas. Cowries are also called money shells, as they were used as currency in Africa. They are found in the Indo-Pacific region and can be easily and affordably purchased by the dozens from shell stores online.

A COWRIE A DAY KEEPS OYA'S STORMS AWAY. There's an ancient proverb: "The woman who removes a mountain does so one stone at a time." In this case, you move *one shell* at a time! Get eighty-one cowrie shells. This is Oya's sacred number times itself—nine times nine. (Or, to start smaller, choose another nine-based combination such as twenty-seven, which is three times nine). Put the shells in a big jar labeled "My Change." Get another big empty jar and label it "Completed."

SMALL CHANGES ADD UP. Identify each smaller subject—such as finding a new job—and identify every small step toward it. Move a cowrie shell to the other jar every time you complete a related task. For example, you unearthed your resume: that's one shell. Sitting down to review it: that's another. If you begin to revise it: that's another. Each small task equals a cowrie. The point of this exercise is to gain an understanding of how each small task adds toward a larger accomplishment. There may not be eighty-one steps to each major task, but if you count every small effort you make, you'll feel that you're making great progress! It's like a tick sheet or an abacus. As you watch the "My Change" jar empty and the "Completed" jar fill up, a sense of accomplishment and pride will come over you. Your subconscious mind, and Oya, will get the message you are someone who takes care of business.

START AGAIN. When you've named all the shells and transferred them to "Completed," soak them in sea salt to clean the energy, dry them overnight on a windowsill, and start again, filling the "My Change" jar. Now look ahead in your life again. What are your next small tasks that will add up to something big? Do the whole process again, and again, until you've developed a good sense of how to move energy and create change by acknowledging each step.

3. **Know what change teaches us.** Change is an ongoing process. Every day of our lives we shed a little of our old skin and regenerate new skin. Over the course of a lifetime we may undergo a million tiny deaths and passing phases. Everything

must eventually change. Work on accepting these statements:

CHANGE IN SMALL INCREMENTS IS BEST. Making small changes at a slower pace helps you to adjust to a new reality rather than feeling shocked by it. Weight loss is a good example. It's a change you crave, yet if it happens rapidly, you have no time to process the emotional changes; being thinner can make you feel vulnerable when you're used to that "padding." Slow weight loss is healthier and gives you time to adjust to the new you! Whenever you can, choose change at a slower and gentler pace.

YOU CAN COPE WITH A SUDDEN CHANGE. If a big sudden change comes your way, you will find the strength to handle it. When Oya blows into your life like a tornado or a hurricane, at first it's hard to accept that there's anything good about it. And you will need to grieve your loss. But in the darkest night of the soul we somehow come to understand that whatever the loss, there is a reason. From the depths of our pain, we can find a way to process the confusion and not just survive, but also thrive, and find our true power.

CRISIS CAN BE A PATH TO EVOLUTION. If you find yourself in the winds of sudden, scary change—a job loss, a health scare, an unexpected breakup—trust that it is all in divine order. A breakdown opens the way for something new. It reveals the lies we live and gives us an opportunity to change them.

YOU WILL RISE FROM THE ASHES. Oya shows us the true impermanence of life. She teaches us that, like the phoenix, we must let go and surrender to each moment, trusting our ability to release whatever holds us back. She teaches us we must allow a part of us to die or dissolve, and then allow ourselves to be born anew.

YOU ARE NOT A VICTIM. You may feel like one at times; you may have a "victim consciousness." But if you choose to be queen of your own destiny, you must begin to see that you sometimes unconsciously draw Oya's dramas and disasters to you to precipitate change.

IT'S HEALTHY TO KEEP TOSSING OUT THE OLD. Take a big black

garbage bag—or ten!—and dump things. Let go of anything that ties you inappropriately to the past. Allow Oya to move you through the process like a wild woman in heat, blood pumping as you surrender your unused, unneeded, and unhealthy stuff! Give anything you don't need anymore to the garbage goddess or to charity.

HOW TO KEEP OYA WITH YOU

Keep on keeping on. When you can't figure out your next step, when intellect does not apply, when you just don't know what to do—surrender it to Oya. Go with the flow. Release yourself into the hands of the divine and let her figure it out.

Calm yourself with shea butter. The goddess of change is calmed with shea butter, and you can be too. It's found in cosmetics, sold as a moisturizer, and used in chocolate and as cooking oil in West Africa. Dab a little on the wrists to calm your senses.

Listen to her drumbeat. The famed African drummer Babatunde Olatunji offers a passionate ode to her in "Oya" on his *Drums of Passion* CD.

Read for practical insight. Consider *A Year to Live* by Stephen Levine. He describes a process to engage more fully in life by operating on the assumption that you have only one year to live. The book explores many compelling questions, including this one: If you had so little time, would you waste it on resisting growth and change?

OYA AFFIRMATION

"I am willing to change my life for the better, now."

*N*IKE

CLAIM YOUR VICTORIES IN LIFE

Just do it.
—NIKE CORPORATE SLOGAN

ON YOUR MARK . . . Get set . . . Go!

Some of us are born with the desire to win. We're up and running right out of the cradle, ready to compete and always aiming for victory. Some of us crave the kind of success that will make us stars and bring public recognition. Others just want be able to *make things happen* and manifest everyday dreams into reality. Success, winning, victory . . . these all have different meanings for different women. Regardless of the ultimate goal, when you feel compelled to make your mark on the world, it's time to pick up the pace for making dreams come true.

Even if you don't see yourself as a go-getter, or fancy yourself as someone who is "out there," there comes a moment when you realize the time has come to pursue bigger, brighter, better dreams and goals; it's time to step to the fore so you can let your light shine for all to see. There's nothing wrong with *wanting it all!* The ultimate success in life is to achieve true balance and to have excellence in all areas. Like so many powerful women before you, when you are ready to uplift yourself in all ways and create the life you choose, it's time to put aside all childish ways and old hurts from the past, put

35

on your running shoes and just do it!

Call upon Nike when you need help focusing on and achieving success at the highest levels and attaining victories of all kinds. She brings a focused, edgy, active approach to tasks at work, at home, and in your personal life. Nike ensures success at the outset because she inspires you to find the wherewithal to reach the finish line. She represents success on all levels, personal greatness, and winning at the game of life.

WHO IS NIKE?

The statue of Athena is upright with a tunic reaching to her feet . . .
she holds a statue of Nike about four cubits high,
and in the other hand is a spear.
—PAUSANIAS

Nike (*NY-key*, although the Greeks pronounced it *NEE-kay*) is the Greek goddess of victory. The winged daughter of the giant Pallas and the river Styx, she is a fierce and focused river goddess, known for her ability to sprint to the finish and celebrate victory. She is famous for success in war and battle, but was said to deliver victory in all forms of competition and accomplishment. Considered the divine messenger who brings the coveted laurel wreath to victors, Nike is the goddess the ancients prayed to when they competed in any forum. In all sorts of human undertakings, such as culture and athletics, Nike came to be recognized as a mediator of success between gods and humans; she was an important deity at the Olympics. Although she was at one time indistinguishable from Pallas Athena, also a dispenser of victory who will not abide defeat, Nike became known as a separate entity who still served as cheerleader and support to the goddess of war.

Very little has been written about Nike, yet she abounds in ancient images. Both Zeus and Athena are often seen carrying small figures of Nike, indicating she is an important aspect of their success. Some believe she is Athena with wings, but when they are pictured together, Nike is wingless. When depicted alone, she is a winged, barefoot young goddess in a flowing tunic. She often carries a palm branch, wreath, or shield of victory, and sometimes a cup, jug, and incense burner. In the famous Nike of Samothrace in the Louvre, she is a headless presence, yet still fluid.

HOW TO INVITE HER INTO YOUR LIFE

As a divine harbinger of success, Nike can inspire your winning spirit by motivating you with enthusiasm and desire for victory. The ancient Greeks connected to Nike with a prayer before any major endeavor, asking her to bring success. Nike travels the path alongside you from start to finish on your adventures. She is a cosmic mover and shaker who sees to it that you stay on track to fulfill your destiny and dreams. Petition Nike with very specific requests. This is the key to gaining her attention and assistance. She thrives on your clarity.

Try these ideas to honor Nike.

1. **Build a victory altar.** Because of her close association with war goddess Athena, Nike is especially fierce and powerful when it comes to getting things done, but she also operates with a cool head and calm demeanor. There is a small temple on the Acropolis of Athens dedicated to Athena Nike, honoring Athena as goddess of victory in military encounters and political intrigues—and Nike as the wind beneath her wings. Athena brings deeper insight, a calm bearing, and extraordinary powers of strategy to the mix. The two together bring a double whammy of winning.

   FIND IMAGES OF NIKE AND ATHENA TOGETHER. Figures of the two are easy to find in statuette form. Athena is dressed in armor, looking kind of macho. Nike is more feminine, always in a flowing gown with wings. They are the balance of masculine and feminine energies. In some images of them together, Nike is in Athena's hand. You can also find classic pieces of art of each to frame and place on an altar. While Nike is the primary deity to call upon for victories, Athena offers a steady hand to the process.

KEEP A DREAM BOX ON YOUR ALTAR. It will be the keeper of all your desires, filled with requests you leave at the feet of the goddesses. Consider it a temple for your dreams. Buy a beautiful Greek-style box, or a metallic or wood box; or, if you are creative, fashion your own out of a shoebox, covering it with images of famous sites in Greece and emblems and images of Athena and Nike.

KEEP A BOWL OF LAUREL (BAY) LEAVES. You can find them in your kitchen or local supermarket. They symbolize protection and manifestation of Nike's gifts of victory. In ancient Greece, a laurel wreath was always placed upon the head of Olympic winners, and it was also used to crown poets and scholars (that's where the phrase *poet laureate* comes from, and *baccalaureate* too). It was the crowning glory of Nike's domain.

2. **Do a victory ritual.** Use your laurel leaves to further your own goals.

CELEBRATE SUCCESS. The way to create more success is to celebrate all that you've already achieved. Appreciate life's little victories; they are the precursor to bigger dreams. Never judge your station in life; just seek to change it when you are ready for bigger things. Before taking on any new endeavor, make sure to list, or at least mentally review, all your recent achievements. Thank Nike for all her help getting you where you already are.

CLARIFY GOALS. Take a few moments to think of what's next for you. Do you have any truly pressing or urgent goals? Are you focusing on several general life-enhancement goals? Do you need to revise your goals because you've attained the last batch? Have a felt tip pen handy so you can write some of your dreams down.

WRITE ON LAUREL LEAVES. Use Nike's symbol of victory to create more victories for yourself. Sort through your bowl of bay leaves and find the smoothest, best-formed leaves in the bunch. The very act of selecting them is a symbolic gesture: you now choose the best. Leaning on a hard surface—pressing the pen lightly so it won't rip the leaf— begin to write your goals, one on each leaf. For example: Annual salary of $100,000, beautiful new home, great relationship, the respect of my peers, fame, delirious joy, travel to exotic locales, great adventure, or whatever you seek. Just make them short enough to fit on the leaves.

PRAY AND ASK FOR DIVINE ASSISTANCE. Place the bay leaves with your goals in your dream box. Hold the box in your hands and pray to Nike to please come to you and help you manifest these dreams.

Then pray to Nike and Athena to please bring the power of wisdom and strategy. Try these words, or your own.

> **Dearest Goddess Nike: With fleet foot and wings, please bring your grace to the manifestation of these goals. Bring me strength, stamina, and passionate desire to make it to the finish line and claim my prize.**

> **Dearest Goddess Athena: With the power of knowing all that is, please connect me to the inner wisdom so I know what I must do to make my dreams come true, and bless me with the gift of strategy so that I can follow right action and good timing to bring my goals to victory.**

> **To Nike and Athena, thank you both. And so it is.**

GIVE YOUR DREAMS OVER TO THE VICTORY ALTAR. With your intentions placed into the leaves by your own hand, and your goals now empowered with prayers and petitions for divine help, place the dream box back on the altar. Promise to make your success an offering to the goddesses.

MAKE OFFERINGS. Legend has it that Nike spends her mornings studying the victories of men and women and considering which ones she will help. As she does so, she takes her meal of ambrosia and nectar, the gods' drink of immortality. It was said that if an altar was prepared featuring her bright flame, Nike would fly down and pour a libation on the altar as a sign of victory to come. Sometimes she carried incense to the site of victory so the winner could be cleansed. Reach out to her by burning incense for your own purification, lighting a candle in honor of her victorious spirit, and placing a small glass of nectar (perhaps mango or pear juice) nearby for her pleasure. For Athena, leave a small owl statue or image to honor her wisdom and powers of strategy.

COMMUNE DAILY. The trick to winning is to *assume* victory. Go forward with the notion that you will win and you will make dreams come true. Nurture this notion by communing with the goddesses daily. Just sit by the altar and talk to them. Tell them what you've accomplished so far and where you are in your journey. Ask for help along the way. Do not be afraid to speak up; trust that you will be heard.

3. **Take responsibility for your life.** Decide what you want in life at every stage, on all levels, and go for it. Support your goals spiritually as you pursue the practical and active aspects. Take inspiration from the action-oriented approach of successful sports stars, music stars, film and television stars, and writers who inspire you.

4. **Be impeccable in all you do.** Be elegant, not arrogant. Be appreciative, not abrasive. Be a diva but not a brat. Create what you want in life by calling upon the grace and refined skills of Nike. Pursue your goals with strong intentions, but don't let them consume you. Be someone who is a pleasure to work with, to know, to love.

5. **Include financial power in your plan.** Part of success is the financial ability to pursue dreams, and the promise of greater

things to come. Don't shy away from taking responsibility for finances, including making money, managing it, saving and spending, paying bills, taking care of debts, signing contracts, making major purchases and commitments, making investments, and using finances wisely.

6. **Face challenges head on.** Success in life does not always equal comfort. Nike knows that the last few yards before the finish line are the toughest, the place where many women give up and discount their dreams. It can be a lot of work to launch an extraordinary life, but if you take it on and face life's challenges along the way, you are halfway there. Nike always helps the devoted to the other side of the finish line.

7. **Tune out naysayers.** The mark of all great athletes and stars of every field is their willingness to follow their own hearts and surround themselves with people who empower their *perceptions* of what success is. Everyone will have opinions, but it is not your job to internalize them. Try this polite, noncommittal answer to anyone with advice on how to run your life. Smile and say, "Thank you for sharing."

8. **Choose battles wisely.** On the track to success, there will be bumps, and others may try to block you so they can get to the finish line first. Focus only on the things that will move your goals forward. If you encounter little skirmishes or jealousies along the way, avoid engaging in petty battles. They can be draining and overwhelming. Save your energy for the important stuff.

9. **Take charge of your own destiny.** Believe in your dreams. Live your life fully, every moment, and seize all the good moments to empower your spirit; use the difficult times to build character and fortitude. Set forth a vision for your future and follow it like a religion. Never, never give up. If you fall down, pick yourself up

and get back in the game. See the laurel wreath that waits at the other end of every goal in progress. Know that Nike will help you draw closer to victory, as she draws victory closer to you.

HOW TO KEEP NIKE WITH YOU

Wear her on your body. Since this goddess is especially famous as the inspiration for the Nike corporation, maker of athletic shoes and clothing, purchase a pair of Nike sneakers.

Run and work out. Access your power through physical exertion and expression.

Watch birds in flight. As a winged goddess, Nike is associated with victory just as the flight of the soul is associated with victory over death. Watching birds in flight offers the sense of freedom and possibility that is part of Nike's gift to us. See how the birds scale the heights so naturally and elegantly—and then translate that into smoothness and grace in your everyday life.

NIKE AFFIRMATION

"I am victorious in all things."

$\mathcal{M}$ARY

CONNECT TO YOUR HEALING POWER

In joy and woe—in good and ill—
Mother of God, be with me still!
—EDGAR ALLAN POE

NO MATTER HOW OLD WE are, whenever we feel sick, exhausted, or bullied by life, it's nice to be able to run home to Mommy. The warmth and comfort of a mother's touch has long seemed the antidote to many ills. Even if we don't have a great relationship with our own mom, or if we've lost a beloved mother, most of us need motherly love at some time in our lives—or the kind of unconditional and soothing comfort associated with it. Some of us can even find that in elders, sisters, friends, and by reaching out for professional counseling and support.

But what about life's most pressing challenges? The kind that not even Mom can help resolve? Sometimes life events seem to stretch us beyond our coping skills; some challenges seem far greater than our own capacity to heal. In those times when illness, injury, or deep emotional distress comes our way, it's nice to know that we need not be alone with our burdens. It is in those times that we can seek healing of the highest order and use every health and wellness challenge that comes our way as an exercise in calling forth our own healing abilities and powers.

Call upon Mary when it comes to healing. She is the mother whose arms await you when you need a shoulder to cry on. She's the witness to your sadness and the warm heart to let you know everything will be okay. With love and understanding, she makes you feel better as she shows you how to be your own healer. She represents the all-encompassing energy of the healing mother, and the power to heal that lives within.

WHO IS MARY?

I salute you glorious virgin, star more brilliant than the sun, redder than the freshest rose, whiter than any lily, higher in heaven than any of the saints. The whole earth reveres you, accept my praise and come to my aid.
—ANCIENT PRAYER OF PROTECTION,
TRANSLATED BY ANDREW HARVEY

Mary of Nazareth is an icon of the Catholic Church, and yet she is spiritual mother to all women. She is the virgin called upon by Archangel Gabriel to carry God's only begotten son . . . the Jewish mother to the rabbi prophet whose birth, death, and resurrection are the foundation of Christianity . . . the Holy Spirit who balances out the triad of the Father and the Son. She holds a sacred place in the heart of Catholics as the mother of Christ and conduit between the earthly plane and heaven. While her church has not titled her a goddess, she clearly possesses the clout, divine connections, and magical healing powers of a goddess and is afforded the worship, reverence, and prayer of a divine female. It is through her high profile in the Catholic Church that the feminine principle has been represented most prominently in Christianity for over two thousand years. Yet she represents even more. She is the virgin maiden. She is the great mother. She is the queen of heaven. And she is the wise woman. She is all of it! She continues to be honored around the world as Mother Mary, the Blessed Virgin, Our Lady of Immaculate Conception, Our Lady of Lourdes, Our Lady of Guadalupe, Stella

Maris, Star of the Sea, and many other names. In many parts of the world, such as Mexico, her adoration equals that of her son's. Countless images of Mary worldwide make her one of the most widely portrayed women in the history of art.

HOW TO INVITE HER INTO YOUR LIFE

Mary has long been a widely adored, accepted, and accessible Spiritual Mother. Because of her extraordinary popularity and iconic presence, Mary cuts across religious boundaries. She is respected for raising her son as a strong, loving, true believer in the power of a kind heart and social equality. Like all moms, she's got influence! In the Catholic tradition she is a major intercessor between her son and those who seek his healing, she is one to whom devotees run with all manner of broken parts and hearts—and she is a healing hand and wholesome energy unto herself. While those raised in the Catholic faith have the chance to relate with her from the start of their spiritual lives, she is also an adopted spiritual mother for all women. People of many faiths embrace her as a Universal Mother.

She is there for all of us, always, at any time, and it is very easy to connect with her—in ways like these.

1. **Go into any church, any time, to commune with her.** She is so prevalent and visible in our culture, and so easy to be with. (More Catholic churches are named for her than for her son!) When you are hurting, suffering, dealing with your own illness or coping with a loved one's illness and trying to help them heal, you can find her almost anywhere in the world. No matter what your religion, you can always sit in the quietude and sanctity of a church and be in the presence of her grace. Many Catholic churches offer a way to kneel before an icon of Mother Mary, light a candle, and petition for her help. As a thank you, you can leave a financial offering to the church.

2. **Perform healing rituals in your own home.** You can ask Mary
    into your life, into your home, into your very being. Many people
    who swear to have sighted or experienced her tell of miraculous
    spontaneous healings and ongoing heavenly help.

    FIND AN IMAGE OR ICON OF MARY THAT YOU LOVE. You can find
    her image everywhere and anywhere. She is depicted holding baby
    Jesus, standing with arms outstretched in a protective blessing, or
    revealing her sacred heart. Find the image that connects you to her
    healing grace. Keep it in a sacred place in your home and visit her
    whenever you are hurting. Ask her to take your pain away.

    MEDITATE WITH MARY. Close your eyes. Imagine she is in you.
    Not outside, not above, not separate. If you are sitting in a chair, see
    her in the same chair, sitting in the same position. In your mind's
    eye, with your spiritual sight, know that you and she occupy the
    same space at the same time—and you can call upon her healing
    powers as if they are your own.

    IDENTIFY AND NAME YOUR PAIN. Tune in to the part of you
    that is hurting. If you are ill or in pain, try to identify or pinpoint
    the source of your suffering. If you are emotionally distressed, give
    your distress a name (for example, sadness over a loss, fear about
    medical tests, devastation over drastic life changes, deep despair
    over a financial or work situation). Allow yourself to feel Mary's
    presence with you. She holds your head gently in her hands, calming
    your emotional upsets with the soothing light of heaven. She places
    her hand on whatever hurts and fills that place with love. And she
    helps you illuminate your aching heart, opening it to goodness and
    protecting it with her own sacred heart. Feel her healing energies
    within you as if they are your own.

    CARRY HER INSIDE YOU. Many Catholic mystics acknowledge
    that Mary is the Holy Spirit, the aspect of Christ that enters us, heals
    us, and makes us whole. Few devotees will dispute her magnificence
    and her healing ways. The amazing woman who assumed the light of

God to give birth to her sacred son has, for more than two millennia, offered her healing to us. While many believe that she is *the cure*, she might argue that she delivers healing light at the exact moment you are ready to receive it, and hence, your own inner healing is awakened. Pray that she fills you with her healing spirit. Catholics have always evoked her gracefully by saying the Rosary and repeating this invocation:

> Hail Mary, full of grace,
> The Lord is with you.
> Blessed are you among women,
> And blessed is the fruit of thy womb.
> Holy Mary, Mother of God,
> Pray for us (sinners),
> Now and at the hour of our death.
> Amen.

3. **Call upon her with healing waters.** Millions of people have made the pilgrimage to see her shrine at Lourdes in France. They follow in the footsteps of young Bernadette, who saw Our Lady of Lourdes at the opening of the grotto and received a message about the miracles of the body and soul that would be performed at Lourdes. Mary appeared with rosary in hand and yellow roses at her feet. Over time, Bernadette received a series of messages, falling into ecstatic trances of communion. Through Mary, Bernadette's healing powers opened. One day she scraped away some soil from the side of the grotto and a spring suddenly appeared. Water trickled out, and then poured out. To this day, the spring provides twenty-seven thousand gallons of fresh water that replenishes itself daily.

ANOINT YOURSELF AND LOVED ONES. The healing water is available in small bottles that can be ordered from the Lourdes Center in Boston. While the water is not considered "holy water" or "magic" it is believed to have healing qualities and many people say the Blessed Mother has granted healing favors in conjunction with its use.

APPLY THE WATER TO WHERE IT HURTS. While it is always best to seek your physician's approval for use of anything not prescribed, many people use Lourdes water as an adjunct to medical care; they often drink it or apply it to affected areas of the body. People at Lourdes bathe in it without ill effect. When you apply it, imagine with all your might that the hand of the Mother is touching you and making you whole as she activates the healing powers of your own touch. You can also anoint loved ones, with their permission.

PRAY TO HER. Holding the intention for healing is powerful, but it is always nice to commune with her in prayer. This prayer from the *Novena to Our Lady of Lourdes* is perfect. You can adapt it if you are praying on behalf of a loved one.

> **Mother of Mercy, Healer of the Sick, Comforter of the Afflicted,**
> **You already know my sufferings and my needs; look on me with mercy.**
> **At Lourdes you have given us a sign of your compassion and your love.**
> **Many sufferers have already found healing through your intercession.**
> **I come before you with confidence in your motherly care.**
> **I ask that you listen to my requests and grant my petitions.**
> **In gratitude, I will try to imitate your life so that**
> **I may have some share in the glory of the kingdom.**
> **O Mary, conceived without sin,**
> **Pray for us who have recourse to you. Amen.**

4. **Remember that a health or wellness crisis can be a gift.** Illness may be our body's way of telling us to slow down, take time out, and nurture ourselves. Many spiritual schools of thought believe that we should enhance medical treatment with a complementary approach that supports the body, mind, and soul. When we are pressed to find ways to get better and search for solutions, we often discover a fuller power emerging in our lives as we participate in self-healing. Great healers, such as

medicine women and shamans, come into their own being by healing themselves of grave illnesses. Each breakdown of the physical, emotional, mental, or spiritual system is an opportunity for discovering a way to rebuild, renew, reemerge, and grow.

5. **Help loved ones.** Mary shows us how the power to heal can surge through us. From the dawn of time, women have been healers—the unlicensed doctors, the counselors, the family ministers of health. Women of the ancient worlds offered health care to their family and villages, using herbs, homemade medicines, and the power of their touch. They were so connected to the cycles and rhythms of nature and the body's innate healing capacity that they simply did what came naturally. Mary brought her baby into the world by Immaculate Conception and birthed him in a manger to a wonderful welcome—but she couldn't save him from his death, and she wasn't meant to. The hardest work of a healer is to know when we can help and when it is simply out of our hands; no one's ultimate health or fate is ours to decide. Sometimes the best healing we can bring is love. Love is like medicine from heaven.

HOW TO KEEP MARY WITH YOU

Choose a rosary. No matter what religion you practice, the rosary brings Mary to you, along with her blessed son. She resides in each bead; you can hold it in your hand and call to her.

Wear a Mary medallion. Buy a small Mary medal to keep her with you, by your heart, wherever you go. They can be purchased for less than a dollar in any Catholic shop or church store.

Seek her out in a pilgrimage. Mary appears in visions to mystics and civilians alike and has reportedly been sighted in visitations around the world. It's said that many of Mary's shrines, cathedrals, sacred springs, and "appearances" are at ancient goddess sites.

MARY AFFIRMATION

"I feel the healing power in me."

OPHIA

LEARN TO TRUST YOUR INNER WISDOM

From ancient times, intuition has been equated with the feminine.
—JUDITH ORLOFF, MD

I N THE HUSTLE AND BUSTLE of our overly busy lives, we sometimes forget that we possess something that can be even handier than a cell phone, and more constructive than a board meeting—a sixth sense that has often been referred to as "women's intuition." But when we're about to make a big decision, many of us check in with all our best friends, business associates, assorted experts, and a psychic here or there, before we even think of trusting our own gut. Ultimately, we end up more confused than when we started, with too much input and opinion from others.

Women's intuition is our pipeline to divine messages and wisdom, and we all have the ability to receive inner guidance. Our challenge is, first, to *hear* all the great advice that is channeled through us, and then to *trust it*. We must learn to have faith in the quiet times, to live inside the silences without getting so antsy. Through those silences come great messages of wisdom that can guide us in everyday life, and even help people we care about.

It's easier than you may think to learn to trust your own inner knowing and access it at any time. Intuition is demonstrated in small ways every day of our lives: You think of someone, and "out of the blue" they call. You have a "feeling" you should attend a certain event and you meet someone there who leads you to the next great job or boyfriend. Intuition also manifests in signs and sensations that tell you something isn't quite right, such as nausea, headache, dizziness, or a sense of dread. It's that "bad vibe" you get about something that tells you to steer clear. The trick is to go with your intuition even when you don't have "evidence" that it is "right."

Call on Sophia when it comes to hearing the still small voice within, the voice that whispers the wisdom of the feminine. She is the essence of female intuition, in that she *knows*. Source of infinite wisdom and a divine counselor, Sophia represents inner knowing, self-trust, and truth of the highest order.

WHO IS SOPHIA?

I was sent forth from the power, and I have come to those who reflect upon me, and I have been found among those who seek after me. Look upon me, you who reflect upon me, and you hearers, hear me. You, who are waiting for me, take me to yourselves.
—*SOPHIA SPEAKS, IN THE THUNDER, PERFECT MIND*

Sophia (*so-FEE-ah*) is the goddess of wisdom, personified in the Gnostic Christian tradition and referred to in the Judaic holy writings. In the Gnostic Gospels she is called the Mother of the Universe, Mother of the Creator God (Yahweh), and Bride of God. In the Hebrew texts Proverbs, Sirach, and the Wisdom of Solomon, "Wisdom" is a woman who has relationships both human and divine. Sophia is her Greek name; her full name in that language, Hagia Sophia, means "holy female wisdom." She is known as *Hokhman* in Hebrew and *Sapienta* in Latin. Many feminist theologians also call her the Holy Spirit. She was embraced as God's equal partner in the early Judeo-Christian tradition, when her wisdom balanced his force. One of the first references to Wisdom as a feminine entity unto herself was in the Old Testament's Book of Proverbs, which depicts her as a loving partner or consort, a co-creator. She also plays a prominent role in the Apocrypha (the body of work that came after the Old Testament and preceded the birth of Jesus by two centuries). Although they contained elements that were eliminated from the "official" Jewish and Protestant Bible, the books of the Apocrypha survive to this day as an appendix to the Old Testament in the Catholic Bible. *The Book of ben Sirach* contains sonnets and poems to, and attributed to, Sophia; the *Wisdom of Solomon* is like a love poem to her.

In the Gnostic Gospels, Sophia is also referred to as the "Wisdom of Christ" and the consort of the divine male who created the universe. It is said that she was hidden, stashed in those texts since the fourth century BC, as part of the Christian movement to remove anything that did not completely espouse Christianity from the popular Roman perspective. (The Gnostic Gospels are part of the Nag Hammadi scrolls unearthed by an Egyptian farmer in 1945.) Sophia is depicted in Eastern Orthodox icons with stars around her head and her feet standing on the moon. In Michelangelo's "Creation of Adam" on the ceiling of the Sistine Chapel in the Vatican, God is pictured reaching out and touching Adam's finger with a finger from his extended right hand. In the same fresco, his left arm is wrapped around a wide-eyed woman whom many say is Sophia, God's consort and partner in creation.

HOW TO INVITE HER INTO YOUR LIFE

Although we all love to get really great advice or insight from others, there is nothing like being able to trust your own wisdom and hear your own truth without an intermediary. When communing with Sophia, you are communing with your soul, the highest aspect of yourself. Her divine thoughts become your thoughts. Her divine wisdom becomes your wisdom. If you've ever wrestled with a problem, then suddenly had the answer come to you in a moment of silence—you might already know Sophia's handiwork! Now you can learn to seek her out. It's been said that in prayer, you speak to the divine; in meditation, the divine speaks to you.

Spending time alone to seek out and listen to that sacred voice within will teach you how to become a natural receptor of divine wisdom. Meditation, or a meditative state of relaxation, is the most powerful way to connect with Sophia. It reduces stress, puts you in a relaxed state, and helps you open your "channels of communication" to the divine.

MEDITATE. It will give you the ultimate sacred connection to Sophia. Read these steps all the way through and prepare before you begin.

PREPARE. Find a comfortable, quiet place where you'll be undisturbed for twenty minutes. Draw the shades, light a candle if you like; you might play a suitable piece of relaxing music. Sit comfortably with your legs uncrossed and your feet gently but firmly touching the ground. Keep your back as straight as possible without too much effort, and allow your hands to rest gently on your lap with your palms turned up. If you possibly can, record the meditation that follows so you can replay it and use it as a guide.

OPEN WITH A READING. Begin by evoking Sophia with an ancient reading on wisdom. There are many, but start with these words of Solomon, considered the wisest Hebrew king, who many believe took his lead from the Bride of God.

> **Wisdom is bright and unfading,**
> **And she is easily seen by those who love her,**
> **And found by those who search for her.**
> **The person who rises early to seek her**
> **Will not have to toil,**
> **For this person will find her sitting at the gate.**

To think of her is the highest understanding,
And the person who is vigilant for her sake
Will soon be free from care.
She goes about in search of those worthy of her,
And she graciously appears to them on their paths,
And meets them in every thought.

IDENTIFY THE ISSUE YOU NEED HELP WITH. Name it, formulate a question, and hold it in your mind as something you will address to Sophia. If you have a short memory, write it down before going into meditation. Keep pen and paper handy to write down any insights Sophia offers. Before the end of the meditation, you will have a chance to be a scribe and channel the answers you need.

BECOME THE DAUGHTER OF WISDOM. In the Hebrew tradition, a female is described by her given name, and as daughter of her mother. "Daughter of" is conveyed with the word *beth*, for example, "I am Gabriela Shoshanna *beth* Sura Ruchel." Now, as you begin your meditation, bring your complete awareness to the experience by saying your own name (it need not be Hebrew), the name of your mother, and the name of Wisdom. For example, "I am Gabriela Shoshanna *beth* Sura Ruchel *beth* Sophia."

PRACTICE THE MEDITATION. Now close your eyes, take a deep breath, and hold it for three counts . . . one . . . two . . . three . . . then exhale slowly all the way out with a big sigh. Again, inhale deeply and hold it for one, two, three and exhale slowly. One more time, inhale and hold for one, two, three and exhale slowly and completely. Allow your breath to return to its normal pace and start focusing on it. Get into the experience of breathing and revel in how good it feels to breathe. Each cycle of inhalation and exhalation renews you, relaxes you, and makes you feel so good. As you relax, begin to let go of any tension you are holding about whatever challenge you are dealing with. Give yourself the gift of being in this perfect moment . . . your moment to unwind, release, and enjoy the simple pleasure of just breathing . . . inhaling and exhaling . . . relaxing and healing . . . letting go. If an occasional thought crosses your mind and takes you away for the moment, don't fight it. Think of it as a cloud passing by in a beautiful blue sky. Acknowledge it, see it pass, and let it go.

Continue to be aware of your breath. Now imagine that you are in a beautiful place that is spiritual and joyous. You could be in a temple, or on a ranch in Montana gazing up at a sky full of stars, or floating on a cloud in a place that feels like heaven. In this place, you feel totally at ease and connected to All That Is. Although you can see distinct forms and images that are outside of you, let yourself feel that they are actually part of you. Keep breathing and allow your comfort to increase. Know you are in total security, balance, and comfort. See yourself there, enjoying the essence of this perfect place, whatever it is to you. Feel the winds of heaven blow gently against your soul. Sense a presence that is larger than yours, yet the same as you; an energy that is dynamic to you here on earth, yet natural and part of you in this heavenly place. Hang out there and keep breathing . . . becoming more a part of All That Is with every breath.

Continue to breathe comfortably, staying in touch with the sensations of this glorious place and its nuances—a breeze that caresses your skin, a sight, or a scent. As soon as Sophia gives you the go-ahead, ask your question. Dwell in the question for a few moments, and then open your eyes and start writing her answers. (*When recording this passage, pause here for a moment*). If you hear her voice, enjoy the intonation and communication, but keep writing down what she says. Don't edit or analyze, or even read it. Just write whatever comes. When you are done—when you feel all that must be written has come through— return to the meditative state.

Pay attention again to your breathing and renew your sense of your surroundings. This is your special place, where Sophia and the wisdom of the feminine dwell. She is a part of your soul, and you are a part of her. Know that this special place is yours to return to whenever you choose and whenever you seek wisdom and guidance. Ask for a sign, a special emblem or sensation, so you can always connect with Sophia through your special signal (it could be a flying dove, a breeze, a floating cloud, a sound, a sense somewhere in your body). Then gently bid it farewell, feeling gratitude for the time of quiet and guidance. Slowly journey back to the present place and time ... slowly coming back as you deepen your breathing and ever so gently begin to move your fingers and toes ... your hands and arms, your neck gently from side to side ... Now, keeping your eyes closed, take three more deep cleansing breaths ... one for the body ... *(pause)* ... one for the mind ... *(pause)* ... and one for the spirit *(pause)*. Allow your breath to return to normal and when you are ready, open your eyes. May the spirit of wisdom always be with you!

CLOSURE. You can close your meditation with this short prayer:

**May the spirit of wisdom
Shine her light in my consciousness
And connect me to my truth
And my highest mind,
Now and always.**
Thank Sophia and ask her to stay close.

KEEPING SOPHIA WITH YOU

Meditate regularly. Just ten minutes of meditation daily can help you develop your intuition, awareness, and wisdom. These regular quiet times let you "check in" with Sophia for her impressions and insights, and also help you establish an ongoing channel of communication that you can easily tune into anytime.

Keep the sign of the dove. The dove is a symbol of peace and an emblem of Sophia. Keep a picture, image, or small statue of a dove to remind you of her.

Stay connected to her ancient presence. Any time you doubt the wisdom of the feminine, study references to her found in holy texts, such as the Gnostic Gospels and Song of Solomon.

SOPHIA AFFIRMATION

"I am guided by feminine wisdom."

KUAN YIN

BE COMPASSIONATE WITH YOURSELF AND OTHERS

You've got to be your own merciful mother.
—BARBARA AZZARA, PSYCHOTHERAPIST AND TEACHER

SOME OF US ARE HAUNTED by an internal battle that places us in direct opposition to ourselves. We fret, regret, and feel remorse over the tiniest things, continuously beating ourselves up. We can't forgive ourselves for our indiscretions of the past, or for something dumb we said a minute ago. If someone else were beating up on us the way we do on ourselves, we'd have to fight back in self-defense.

Some of us have a hard time giving ourselves the love and compassion we deserve. We judge, hold grudges, and never let ourselves off the hook. We are unforgiving of ourselves. Sometimes we take the blame for things inflicted on us by others—the mean teacher or boss, the emotionally abusive parent or partner—and turn it against ourselves. Our depression may be anger that is really meant for another, but that we turn inward on ourselves because we're afraid to express what we really feel. Sensitive women tend to be like sponges, soaking up other people's "stuff."

By the same token, when we cannot give to ourselves all that we deserve, it is impossible to fully give it to others. We can "pretend to care" and "act nice" toward others. We can be very accommodating, maybe even bordering on codependent, but when we do not love and give to ourselves, we cannot authentically offer love to others. If we lock ourselves into an unforgiving attitude, it acts as a chain on our hearts.

Healing the pain within that robs us of self-love takes time and patience. But the only way to start to dissolve the ill will we have toward ourselves is with compassion—a compassion born of understanding and fully accepting our true feelings without judgment. When we give this to ourselves, we can make it available to others and offer a helping hand to those in need.

Call upon Kuan Yin when it comes to forgiving yourself and finding the deep well of compassion that lives within you. As the embodiment of loving kindness, she brings a wonderful presence to any difficult moment and offers a cosmic shoulder to cry on. She also enables you to reach a hand out to help others. Kuan Yin represents compassion, mercy, and unconditional love.

WHO IS KUAN YIN?

Many women coming from Asia to live in the United States bring with them stories of Kwan Yin. They learned to revere her as little children, taught by their mothers or grandmothers at the family altar, encouraged to offer flowers and fruit and incense to this powerful goddess.
—SANDY BOUCHER,
DISCOVERING KWAN YIN, BUDDHIST GODDESS OF COMPASSION

Kuan Yin (*KWAN YIN*) is the Chinese Buddhist goddess of compassion, mercy, and healing. She is the "compassionate savioress" worshipped for centuries throughout China, Japan, Korea, and Southeast Asia. Known also as Quan Yin, Guanyin, and Guan Shih Yin, she is the patron and protector of women, children, sailors, artisans, and those who are imprisoned. She is as popular as the Virgin Mary is in Western culture. She's frequently called upon by women having difficulty conceiving and is seen as a great source of fertility and feminine vitality. Statues of her divine form bless every Buddhist temple in Asia, and today almost every Chinese home is adorned with art depicting Kuan Yin. Her name is translated as the being *"who hears the cries of the world."* She is a *bodhisattva*, which in Buddhism is a human being who has completed all karma and reached enlightenment. Although her bodhisattva status entitled her to enter the paradise of nirvana, Kuan Yin decided to remain on earth until all suffering was ended.

Various cultures have different tales of Kuan Yin's beginnings. In one, she began life as a male. Another legend tells us that she once walked the earth as the princess Miao Shan, whose father ordered her execution because she disobeyed him and refused to marry; some versions say she was spared from death and lived her days in a nunnery. Kuan Yin is often depicted as a classic Chinese beauty wearing a flowing white gown with her hair pulled up in a headdress. She's seen seated on a lotus or majestically riding a dragon. Sometimes she's pictured as the Thousand-Armed Kuan Yin. She's seen carrying many special emblems, such as a willow branch that she uses to dispense flower essences and ambrosia; a porcelain vase that carries these pure, healing unguents; scrolls or books of Buddhist prayers and wisdom; or a crystal rosary used for meditation.

HOW TO INVITE HER INTO YOUR LIFE

It is said she never turns away anyone in pain. Kuan Yin can be your bodhisattva, your personal savioress. If you are too tough on yourself and others, or if you are struggling to open your heart to compassion, she will be right there with you, helping you cast out self-criticism and negative judgment. When she hears the cries of humanity she manifests in any form needed—perhaps as a helpful passerby, an angel who can help in a crisis, or even as a friend who shows up just when you need her.

Get in touch with Kuan Yin in these ways.

1. **Chant to her anytime.** Her powers and gifts can be invoked by calling her name or chanting the famous mantra known as "mani":

Om mani pad me hum
(Oh-m mah-nee pahd-may hoom)

This mantra celebrates and honors her altruism and selflessness and acknowledges her as the "jewel in the lotus." Kuan Yin's custom often suggests that we do things in threes or nines, as those are auspicious numbers. So always chant at least three times or preferably nine, especially when you need to connect deeply with her.

2. **Perform a healing ritual.** Give your sorrows to Kuan Yin: she has compassion enough to embrace all the tears of the world. You can pour your tears into hers, release your pain, and open to her compassion. (Note: This is a simple ritual, but it is powerful. Strong feelings may arise, and you might need some help processing them afterward. If you don't have that kin d of emotional support right now, you might want to save this ritual for another time. If you are in therapy, check with your therapist before doing this work, or schedule an appointment for soon afterward.) Make sure you have an undisturbed hour or so, and gather the ingredients before beginning this ritual.

Get a dozen white carnations (you will use nine and hold on to three). Have two small vases or glasses with water for the flowers handy, but don't put the flowers in there yet.

Fill a big bowl with water and add a half of a cup of sea salt. Place the bowl on the floor or a table (where it will be comfortable for you to sit for a while) with a big towel beneath it to catch any splashes.

Find some *nag champa* incense, or your own personal favorite, and some matches.

Have a CD player and preselected instrumental music nearby. To begin the ritual, choose some soulful, sad music that stirs your heart and helps you maintain a reflective state. To close the ritual, choose music that is uplifting.

Set up a small altar with incense, the vases, an image of Kuan Yin if you like, and a picture of yourself.

BEGIN WITH THE MANI, INCENSE, AND MUSIC. Call to Kuan Yin by chanting the "mani" invocation nine times. Light a stick of incense to honor her, and send healing prayers up to the heavens on the smoke. Play the soulful, sad music.

FEEL THE SADNESS WITHIN. Take three deep breaths and center yourself. Bow your head in reverence to Kuan Yin and also in acknowledgement of your pain. Go into a state of sorrow and reflection, and look within at all the unhealed parts of you that need *your* love—the places where you lack self-compassion, where you are mean and unforgiving with yourself, where you feel guilty or like a bad person. Tune in to those places where you hold yourself accountable for other people's problems or hold the blame for things others have done. Allow yourself to know and feel the depth of the pain in your heart. It hurts, and it has been getting in the way of your happiness, and your life. Let all the painful feelings surface so you can shine Kuan Yin's light of love upon them. You are giving your pain over to Kuan Yin, for she can handle all of it and more. She shows you how to deepen your own ability for self-compassion and healing, and how to forgive yourself.

PUT YOUR PAIN INTO THE FLOWERS AND THE FLOWERS INTO THE WATER. The carnations symbolize the white lotus the goddess sits upon. They are pure and untouched, as she is; and willing to take on your pain, as she is. Hold nine carnations on your lap or rest them on the table near your hands (save three for later). Having evoked the sadness within, begin to name it. Name everything that gets in the way of your compassion for yourself and ultimately, others. For each pain you name, using one flower at a time, pull off a petal and drop it into the bowl of salty water. As each feeling comes up, let it go into the flower, then let the flower petal go into Kuan Yin's healing waters. Surrender your sorrow to her. She will bear witness to it and take it from you. Cry, express yourself, scream—verbally release whatever is there. Drop as many flower parts into the water as you feel moved to and, as you wrap up this part of the ritual, make sure all nine flowers—stems and all—end up in the water.

BRING YOUR SORROW TO A CLOSE. Having released your pain, sit and reflect. Relax and begin to feel the sense of relief come upon you. With the act of tossing flowers into the water, you have made a physical statement of release. You might even feel as if a weight has been lifted.

When that feels complete, change the music to the more uplifting instrumental. Take the remaining three intact carnations and hold them close to your heart. Ask Kuan Yin to fill you with the compassion and self-love you need to live a loving life. Meditate on that for a moment as you feel your heart opening, no longer shut down by pain.

OFFER THE THREE WHOLE CARNATIONS TO KUAN YIN AND YOU. Place one in a vase next to the image of the goddess, one next to the picture of you, and one on your pillow to inspire loving compassion as you sleep. Let the flowers symbolize a healing that helps you feel loved and loving.

OFFER UP YOUR FINAL RELEASE OF PAIN. Before the end of the day, release the water and pulled-apart flowers into another body of water, ideally saltwater, if you live near the ocean. Returning it to the source— the salty waters of the mother—is a strong gesture, but a river or stream is fine too. You can transport it in a bucket or leak-proof plastic bag. Or if you can't visit a natural body of water, don't despair. Just flush the water and flowers, a bit at a time, down the toilet and say your goodbyes.

BEFORE YOU GO TO SLEEP, GIVE THANKS. Look at the flower near the image of Kuan Yin and thank her. Look at the flower near your picture and thank yourself. When you lay down your head, let the carnation rest nearby. May it bring the sweet smell of healing and loving compassion to your sleep and your waking the next day. A new possibility has begun.

3. **Practice connecting to others.** It is a longtime Buddhist and Hindu tradition to greet fellow and sister travelers with the Sanskrit salutation "namaste." The spoken term (pronounced *nom-a-STAY*) is accompanied by a hand gesture or *mudra* that looks like praying—two hands together, in the prayer position, right in front of your chest—simultaneously with a slight bow of the head. It is a gracious and cool way to acknowledge others. It means *"The divine in me honors the divine in you."* When we take the time to greet people with a spiritual salute, it gives us a chance to transcend the pettiness of life and rise above our egos; from that perspective we have more patience and compassion for the suffering of others.

4. **Volunteer to help others.** The ultimate offering to Kuan Yin is to help her with her work in the world. Once we have healed our own hearts with self-compassion, we are fuller beings with more to offer others. Find a cause you can get behind, a group doing something you believe in, a charity helping people in way you support, and volunteer. Give of yourself and your time, and watch your capacity for compassion begin to expand.

HOW TO KEEP KUAN YIN WITH YOU

Savor her energy in tea. Conjure Kuan Yin in lotus tea, which is said to promote inner radiance and the essence of the lotus flower. It is soothing, calming, and helps you feel like a goddess. It smells sweet and pure the way you imagine a goddess would.

Wear pearls. Kuan Yin is often pictured with pearls (or a rosary) around her neck, and her purity is said to live in these precious white spheres. She wears a necklace of pearls; you can too, allowing it to hang right over your heart. You might accessorize with earrings and a ring. Pearls also connect you to the energy of the moon, which also symbolizes compassion, love, and an open heart.

Bow to her. Prostration, also known as deep bowing, is an ancient Asian and Buddhist custom. It is believed to purify and humble us as well as offer homage—to the divine and to one another. Practice bowing deeply to Kuan Yin—an image or to her perceived energy— and you will connect more deeply to your compassionate self.

KUAN YIN AFFIRMATION

"I forgive myself for any ways in which I have disappointed myself or others. And I forgive others for disappointing me."

GREEN TARA

FEEL SAFE AND PROTECTED

Adversity is the diamond dust heaven polishes its jewels with.
—ROBERT LEIGHTON

FEW OF US LEAVE THE house in the morning in search of bad news or trauma. But most of us eventually find ourselves faced with one of life's terrifying moments or crossing paths with a crisis we can't control.

Even if you believe that things "happen for a reason," bad news can hit with stunning force. It hurts to hear you've been laid off, that the person you love is leaving you, or that someone you care for is seriously ill or injured. If the bad news is that you are in the middle of a traumatic event—an accident, fire, or crime—no one would blame you for freaking out. When your world is in the process of being rocked by a crisis, it may not be easy to "be spiritual" about it. That's why it's so important to strengthen ourselves spiritually on a daily basis, and not just when emergencies occur.

Building spiritual stamina can help us remain calm and centered in the face of fear and extreme stress. The first response any of us has when we are faced with very difficult news or a traumatic event is shock and denial—*No, this can't be happening.* Hopefully, down the line, we will find ourselves on the path of reckoning with reality and healing from the shock and trauma. Perhaps there will even come a time when we can search for and find a deeper meaning, or hidden lesson, in the pain that was endured.

But when it is happening, it is terrifying and confusing. Our greatest power is the willingness to stay present in the moment of truth and pain and lean into the forces of the universe that are there to love and protect us in our darkest hours. Our greatest test is to trust that, no matter what is happening to us or in our lives, we are enfolded by divine arms.

Call upon Green Tara when it comes to handling bad news and very high stress situations that may involve perceived danger or threat to your physical or emotional well-being. Tara is the all-embracing, all-knowing mother savior who takes us in her arms at our hour of greatest need and feeds our souls with manna from heaven to help us cope. She helps us get through the physical and emotional reality of a crisis. In Tara we find the ultimate protection and grace of the cosmic mother into whose spiritual arms we can run—and rest.

WHO IS TARA?

The worship of goddess Tara is one of the most widespread of Tibetan cults, undifferentiated by sect, education, class, or position; from the highest to the lowest, the Tibetans find with this goddess a personal and enduring relationship unmatched by any other single deity.
—STEPHEN BEYER, THE CULT OF TARA

Tara *(TA-rah)* is the beloved Tibetan Buddhist mother goddess. Monks and devotees around the world chant and evoke her energies daily, calling upon her for everything from world peace to inner peace and protection. Considered a female Buddha, she represents All That Is; her energy can permeate all things. Tara is worshipped in both mild and wild forms, and exists in a rainbow of colors reflecting her various attributes. The Green Tara and White Tara of the Tibetan Tantric tradition are the most popular forms, with

Green Tara seen as her fiercer, most dynamic form. As such she is a goddess of action, strength, and special protective powers, who wards off evil and shields you from spiritual harm. According to mythic tale, she was born from the tears shed by Avalokiteshvara, the Buddha of compassion, as a gift to end the suffering of all creation. The tears trickling down the left side of the Buddha's face formed the motherly and mature White Tara and the salty drops on the right birthed the fearless and youthful Green Tara. Her legend is somewhat similar to Kuan Yin's; some believe that she was a human princess who lived a life of the highest compassion and spiritual aspiration, dedicated to serving the Buddhist monks. Because of her path, she earned the right to be reborn in male form and teach the ways of the Buddha. She told the monks that since the concepts of male and female were only illusory; she would remain in female form until all of humanity was liberated from illusion and reached enlightenment. She is depicted as a slender Asian woman with jade green skin and adornments, sitting on a lotus with one leg folded in front of her in the traditional meditation pose and the other leg extended and ready to leap into protective action.

HOW TO INVITE HER INTO YOUR LIFE

Tara is a protector who offers us her body and wisdom to shield us from danger. The ancient texts say she protected those who called upon her from the "eight calamities," which are described as Lions and Pride, Wild Elephants and Delusions, Fires and Hatred, Snakes and Envy, Robbers and Zealots, Prisons and Greed, Floods and Lust, and Demons and Doubts. It is said she is often the deity evoked by Tibetan nuns and monks who have miraculously survived arrest and torture in their native land. People in trouble pray to her for deliverance. Because she represents compassion in action, she becomes the bridge from fear and suffering to happiness and good tidings. Devotees trust that with Tara in their corner, even in the worst of situations they will somehow be okay.

Daily Rituals

1. **Chant her mantra.** The root of Tara's name is the sound *tri*, meaning "to cross." When we call upon Tara she immediately comes to our defense and helps us cross from danger to safety. Tara's protection and favors are granted instantly when we simply call her name or chant her mantra:

   Om Tare tu Tare ture soha

   (Om Ta-ray too Ta-ray too-ray so-hah)

   It essentially translates to: *"Hail Tara . . . Her enlightenment and compassion protect me and liberate me from external fears and internal delusion . . . May I honor this in myself!"*

2. **Meditate with Tara.** To develop resilience and spiritual preparedness for life as it occurs—with all its twists, turns, and surprises—connect with Tara every day. Meditating or quietly connecting with her in your own way can help you overcome chronic fears, phobias, and self-doubt, and can also bring clarity and strength that builds your everyday confidence.

   PREPARE AN ALTAR. For meditation, Buddhist practitioners often set up a small altar and comfortable pillow so they have a special place prepared for Tara in their home. You can set up a very simple altar with these items:
   - two green candles
   - a bowl of water for purification
   - incense (Green Tara incense is available)
   - a small icon or postcard-sized image of Tara
   - Tibetan *tingsha*: two brass cymbals that are chimed three

times to begin and to end a meditation. The distinct sound clears the negative energy of the room at the start, and restores you to normal consciousness at the end.

- bell and *dorje*: at some point, if you like, you can add these sacred symbols of Tibetan worship. They represent both the feminine (bell) and masculine (dorje) principles.

LIGHT UP. The candles represent healing and compassion. The incense is an offering to the goddess.

SIT BEFORE THE ALTAR IN A COMFORTABLE POSITION. Hold the tingsha in hand. Begin by taking a few deep, cleansing breaths. Close your eyes. Breathe deeply and release. (Chime the tingsha.) Feel your heart open. Breathe deeply, again, and release. (Chime.) Feel your mind open to new possibilities. Take another breath and release it with a sigh. (Chime.) Feel your spirit open to your own highest knowing.

CHANT. The traditional mantra for calling in Tara's presence is all you need:

Om Tare tu Tare ture soha
(Om Ta-ray too Ta-ray too-ray so-hah)

Repeat this chant at least three times; if it's comfortable for you, thirty-three times. (Metaphysical experts suggest chanting in repetitions of eleven, with eleven times three being especially powerful. If you need some inspiration and company, hear His Holiness the Dalai Lama lead a seven minute meditation with ongoing chanting of the "Green Tara Mantra." Check Amazon.com for other recordings of "Praise to Tara.")

LET TARA COME TO YOU. Inhale as deeply and comfortably as you can and exhale as you chant. With each repetition, the energy of Tara will come through stronger and stronger. When finished with the mantra, let your breath return to a normal rhythm.

Visualize Tara sitting behind the altar across from you in her traditional pose. Admire her beauty and strength. Look at her third eye and imagine a beam of pure white light connecting her third eye to yours. Sense this light as a conduit of her wisdom, courage, and enlightenment, and become one with her in this energy. Realize that all of these gifts have always been with you and that Tara has come as a mentor to assist you in self-realization. Dwell in this energy and release any doubts or negativity into the bowl of water to be cleansed and purified and returned to the universe.

CLOSE WITH A CHIME AND A VOW. When you're ready to end the meditation, open your heart to Tara and thank her for her sistership and love. Make a promise to nurture an internal image of her and hold her in the inner temple of your heart. Vow to call her when you need her help and to be open to her power when she comes. Begin to slow your breathing to help you feel grounded. When you are ready, open your eyes and end the ritual by chanting *"Om Tara . . . Om Tara . . . Om Tara . . . Om."* Chime the tingsha each time you say her name.

For Emergency Protection

SHOUT OUT TO TARA. This quick meditation and prayer can be used anytime or anywhere you feel or perceive danger, anxiety, or stress. Bring the energy of Green Tara around you to center you and help you feel more secure.

CALL TARA'S NAME. Either aloud or to yourself, call her name nine times.

VISUALIZE HER IMMEDIATELY APPEARING IN FRONT OF YOU. She is youthful, strong, beautiful, and fiercely determined to protect and defend. Tell her the source of your upset and ask for protection from those things in the material world. Tell her that you also desire clarity and understanding of whatever is welling up inside of you.

ASK HER FOR INSTRUCTIONS. Trust whatever insight comes to you immediately—the first thing—and combine it with your inner wisdom and instincts.

- Action may be key. If so, Tara will enable you to act quickly and wisely. Keep in mind that action may be something simple, such as "leave the room" or it may be more intense, such as "call the police." Honor whatever comes through to you and put aside any feeling that you may be overreacting; lay aside any fear you have about offending or embarrassing anyone else.

- She may even guide to you to stand fast, remain calm, and center yourself as the best defense, especially in stressful but nonthreatening situations. As always, thank her for her assistance.

HOW TO KEEP TARA WITH YOU

Carry a bottle of "Rescue Remedy." This is one of the mainstays of the Bach flower remedies, botanical essences used for healing and growth. Rescue Remedy is calming for humans and animals alike. If you feel nervous, just a few squirts under the tongue or on the skin will help. It's a natural flower remedy that is like Tara in a bottle. (Please check with a medical professional before using).

Wear green. Let her colors embrace you, hug your skin, protect your heart.

Serve the goddess. Tara's love is best served when we live in service to others, with nonattachment to the way things are, and an ongoing quest for enlightenment. As budding bodhisattvas, we can develop strength enough to help others so that if a crisis or bad news comes, our focus is larger than our own fear.

TARA AFFIRMATION

"I am safe and sound in the arms of the Mother."

$\mathcal{W}$HITE BUFFALO CALF WOMAN

CREATE PEACE IN YOUR WORLD

In the Native American culture, it is woman who is held in high
regard. Women are considered the peace seekers
in time of great disasters.

—DON EVANS, OJIBWA DESCENDANT

NOW MORE THAN ANY TIME in history, we need the
energy of the sacred feminine to balance our lives and balance
our world. We must be spiritual warriors, and this means harnessing
the most powerful aspects of feminine wisdom and directing them
toward peace within—and without. It means using the energies of
the Goddess and all mythical women to help direct the course of
history. It is the absence of feminine energy that kicks off a cycle of
destruction. It is the restoration of the feminine that will help heal
this imbalance. We *can* all partake in creating a more peaceful world.

Call upon White Buffalo Calf Woman when it comes to
activating your ability to build peaceful community and spread
peace. She helps you see the distinction between the masculine and
feminine approach, and she honors that both exist, side by side:
while men have historically been the fighters and defenders, females
seek to draw peaceful resolve to any situation. The important thing
is to have both, and a chance for balance—in women *and* men! She
represents the balance, and the peace, we all crave.

WHO IS WHITE BUFFALO CALF WOMAN?

It was told next time there is chaos and disparity, she would return
again. She said she would return as a White Buffalo Calf.
Some believe she already has.
—LAKOTA CHIEF ARVOL LOOKING HORSE,
MODERN-DAY KEEPER OF THE SACRED PIPE

White Buffalo Calf Woman is a Native American spirit woman considered a messiah, a holy woman-savior who came here to give instructions to "the People" for living the sacred life. In Native American culture, she's on the A-list of awesome women, a role model for teaching men how it should be and inspiring women to take their rightful place as leaders and facilitators. She is credited with helping the Lakota Sioux establish rituals and a sacred social life that would bring them closer to Great Spirit, the Great Mother, and one another; she also taught them how to perpetuate peace and honesty in their world.

As legend has it, many moons ago, amidst a great famine, two Lakota scouts went out in search of buffalo and instead came across a haze of smoke through which a beautiful woman suddenly appeared. She was, to their eyes, quite alluring and magical. One of the scouts was overly lustful and tried to make a play for the maiden; the other was respectful. The woman invited the lustier of the two to approach her; then both scouts disappeared in a puff of smoke. When the smoke cleared, the respectful scout stood there, and the lusty one was reduced to a pile of bones. The scout who honored the woman was given the task of taking her word to his nation. She told him to tell his people to "build a teepee" and prepare for her arrival. Soon she arrived and taught them the sacred pipe ceremony, along with the seven sacraments. She is often pictured as a beautiful young woman standing near a white buffalo, but sometimes she has a more mature appearance. She always has long flowing hair and a sacred pipe in hand.

HOW TO INVITE HER INTO YOUR LIFE

Many of the Native American traditions handed down by White Buffalo Calf Woman are still practiced today at certain special events, re-enactments, and ceremonies that are held in urban areas and on Native American reservations. Although they are not as accessible as Sunday mass, there are many places in the United States where you can attend and sometimes participate in authentic Native American traditions and learn more about the culture.

1. **Observe a sacred pipe ceremony.** Smoking the sacred pipe is a traditional Native American way to get in touch with the healing energy and peaceful ways of White Buffalo Calf Woman. Over time, it has been referred to as smoking the "peace pipe." The ceremony is conducted in a circle with others of like mind who hold the same intention for the ceremony. Ojibwa descendant Don Evans explains that in a state of prayer, the pipe is smoked and passed around. It contains strong ceremonial tobacco or the bark of a red willow tree. No one inhales—each person just takes a toke and releases, and as the smoke releases, so do the person's prayers. The prayers are said to travel to Great Spirit on plumes of smoke. The ceremony represents the truth being spoken. The pipe is considered a religious artifact—the bowl represents the feminine and the stem represents the masculine—and is used in a sacred manner.

2. **Host your own sacred ceremony.** As an alternative to a pipe ceremony, you can gather some friends of like mind and create a sacred healing circle dedicated to personal and planetary peace. Instead of passing around a pipe, pass a sacred object as a "talking piece"—a branch found outdoors, a store-bought crystal, or other meaningful object. Each person who holds it will have a chance to speak his or her truth while the others in

the circle bear witness.

SET AN INTENTION FOR THE SACRED CIRCLE BEFOREHAND. Make sure everyone knows they are attending a sacred ceremony and why they are there. Tell them, "We are gathering in the name of peace." Set a theme: sharing how we feel about peace in our world today, sharing individual ideas for creating a more peaceful life, and praying together for peace, for example. (Add whatever else you choose.)

SPIRITUALLY CLEANSE THE CEREMONY ROOM AND PARTICIPANTS. All Native American ceremonies include a spiritual cleansing of participants and the creation of a sacred space. First, white sage is lit to smoulder in an abalone shell; burning sage is believed to absorb and clear negative energies. Holding the shell and a feather, one person brings the smoking sage around the circle and gently fans it with the feather onto each participant, ritually clearing any negative energies. It's called "smudging." The person doing the smudging can also walk around the circle clockwise three times, creating a circle of sage smoke and ensuring a purified area for the ceremony.

OPEN WITH A SPECIAL INVOCATION. Native American traditions adhere to the belief that ancestors, spirit guides, and divine beings guide us. They exist in all dimensions and from all directions. The first invocation calls in the four directions (North, East, South, and West); then the directions Above (Father Sky), Below (Mother Earth), and Within (Great Spirit) are evoked. You can let several people participate by giving them each a direction to "call in."

> Caller 1: We call to the spirits of the East. We honor wind and ask that new opportunities for peace fill the air and that the white dove of peace flies freely in all nations.
>
> Caller 2: We call to the spirits of the South. We honor fire and ask that we be infused with warmth, enthusiasm, and passion for the mission of creating peace on earth.

Caller 3: We call to the spirits of the West. We honor water and ask that it cleanse the hearts and souls of all women and men and soothe our angers and wounds so that we may never again thirst for war.

Caller 4: We call to the spirits of the North. We honor the earth and her abundance. May we stand steady on her ground. May this dear planet and all her children grow stronger every day.

Caller 5: We call to the spirits of above, below, and within; we ask to be united with Father Sky, Mother Earth, and with God, Goddess, and Great Spirit of All That Is. With all the forces of the universe, we pray for harmony in our world.

LIGHT A CANDLE. The fire symbolically represents the sacred smoke of the pipe and brings the warmth and glow of White Buffalo Calf Woman into the circle. You can say, "We light a candle to White Buffalo Calf Woman and ask her to teach us and to guide us in this circle of peace."

SHARE THE CEREMONY. The "talking piece"—which has been selected beforehand—is passed around the circle and held by each person in turn.

- Each takes a moment to reflect and speak his or her truth.
- Since many people have personal concerns about peace, you might suggest that everyone pick one issue to share, and one solution. For example, issues may be "I feel fear in my heart and it is stressful" or "I am afraid of what is happening in our world today." Spiritual solutions may include "I promise I will pray every morning for peace" or "I will do volunteer work toward healing our planet."
- Request that people keep their issues and solutions brief.
- Each person who holds the talking stick should be given full attention and respect while speaking.
- There should be no commentary or discussion while someone is speaking. Reverent silence and bearing witness

to people's issues and their solutions is what this is about. However, after everyone has spoken, it is tradition for all in the circle to proclaim "*Aho.*" This is a sign of completion and agreement—something like a prayer that says, "And so it is."

CLOSING THE CIRCLE. Now all stand and hold hands for a final prayer, offering thanks to all energies and beings that attended and guided the sacred circle. (In general, it should always be initiated and summarized with a prayer related to personal and planetary healing and peace.) To close, we might say: "Thank you to the directions— East, South, West, and North; Above, Below, and Within—for guiding us in your ways. Thank you, White Buffalo Calf Woman, for your healing and compassion. Thank you, God, Goddess, Great Spirit of All That Is, for filling our gathering with your presence and grace. May anything expressed that needs healing be healed; may all dreams and declarations be made real. May we all leave here with peace in our hearts. Aho!"

HOW TO KEEP WHITE BUFFALO CALF WOMAN WITH YOU

Focus on peace, every day. Go to sleep with peaceful thoughts and you will wake with the same. Consider trading in the eleven o'clock news for a peace meditation or even a few moments of silence, a peaceful book or warm relaxing bath, or a loving experience with your mate, roommate, or child. Skip the TV: going to sleep after absorbing visual and verbal stimulus about the day's tragedies brings those elements into your dreamtime. Let bedtime be peacetime.

Take time out. During the course of your day, if you feel symptoms of stress overload, fear, or panic, take time out. In the spirit of the sacred pipe and the sacred circle, tell yourself the truth of the moment—*I am stressed, I am scared, I feel panicked*—and seek to right the imbalance by allowing feelings of peace to flood through you. Even if you have to walk out of a business meeting and sit in a ladies' room stall for five minutes to do it. Don't give unpeaceful feelings a chance to take hold. Peace within is always the first step to peace in the external world.

Try a Native American peace prayer. Take a "peace break" in lieu of a coffee break, and softly or silently chant: *Peace to my right. Peace to my left. Peace in front of me. Peace in back of me. Peace above me. Peace below me. Peace within me. Peace all about. Peace abounds. Peace is mine.*

WHITE BUFFALO CALF WOMAN
AFFIRMATION

"I radiate peace everywhere I go."

Part 3
GODDESSES OF
LOVE AND ROMANCE

$\mathcal{V}$ENUS

BE THE ULTIMATE SELF-LOVE GODDESS

To fall in love with yourself is the first secret to happiness.
—ROBERT MORELY

MOST OF US WANT LOVE, passion, and delicious romance in our lives. We want to feel the tingly excitement of going out on a hot date . . . the sheer joy of knowing someone really cares . . . the security of having a relationship we can depend on . . . the dream come true of marrying *the One*. Nothing in the world beats the feeling of falling in love with someone *so* fabulous that it makes your heart sing with joy!

We often put so much focus on finding love "out there" that we never get a chance to truly develop it within ourselves. If we seek love from another in order to feel happy and complete, we end up placing too many expectations and burdens on the other person. The healthiest way for two people to come together is for mutual sharing and support—not to fill a hole that exists within. We constantly draw to us people who mirror our internal feelings. If we don't give love to ourselves 100 percent, the person who stands before us isn't likely to, either.

It's so important to learn to love ourselves before trying to build a relationship with another. It's not narcissistic or stuck-up to care about oneself as much as—or even more than—you would care for another. It is, in fact, a prerequisite to mature and lasting love. Once we have nurtured ourselves along, we have a greater ability to make our relationships successful. Without self-love, we are like bottomless baskets: there's no foundation to uphold or contain love. Someone can love you with more heart than you ever imagined—but where will it go if you have no internal mechanism for recognizing pure love?

You deserve to have an amazing love . . . the perfect mate . . . the ideal spouse . . . the soulful partner . . . whomever your heart longs for. But your first love has to be *you.* If you are willing to give to yourself all that you wish to be given by a partner, you are making yourself ready for his love. It is a universal principle: Like attracts like. Give to yourself, and others will want to give to you. Believe in your own worth, and it will cast an alluring aura all around you, radiating wonderful vibes that say: "*I am lovable. I am hot. I am a female love force to be reckoned with. I am a love goddess.*"

Call upon Venus when it comes to self-love and self-appreciation. She is all that's divinely feminine, the essence of loving to be a girl. She loves her life, her men, her universe, and having it her way. She relishes gazing at her own reflection, admiring how stunning she is. Venus helps us open our hearts to ourselves and our eyes to our own value. She represents self-love, self-esteem, and a woman's divine worth.

WHO IS VENUS?

*With her, beauty comes. The winds flee before her
and the storm clouds; sweet flowers embroider the earth;
the waves of the sea laugh; she moves in radiant light.
Without her there is no joy or loveliness anywhere.*
—EDITH HAMILTON, MYTHOLOGY

Venus (*VEE-nus*), the Roman goddess of love, beauty, and sexuality, is one of the most famous goddesses on the planet. She even has her own planet—Venus, planet of poetry, music, pleasure, and love.

Her name is synonymous with all that is feminine, and with love and passion. She is reputed for her sizzling sexuality, her thorough enjoyment of her own exploits, and her complete and utter appreciation of self. Well aware of her own stunning beauty and status, she cherishes her power and, when expressing her dark side, will squash all annoying competition.

She has her generous side, helping mortals make manifest their own great love stories. Born as a fully formed female who arose from the sea on a shell, she represents the divinely independent female. Her love affairs with the hottest men of mythology are legendary. Volatile Mars and gorgeous Adonis are among her great paramours, but you won't see her waiting by the phone for her hunky god to call. She is more likely to go out and find a replacement to suit her current whim, or simply be happy left to her own devices. Venus possesses a magic girdle—crafted with love by her husband, Vulcan—and when she wears it, anyone around her will fall under her spell. She is often pictured naked, rising from the sea on her shell, covered only by her hands and hair.

HOW TO INVITE HER INTO YOUR LIFE

Venus does not feel she must fawn all over men or find her nourishment from them alone—nor should you! You honor her just by making sure you take care of your own needs. When you feel nourished, you have fewer expectations of others to meet your needs, and fewer disappointments and worries if a particular person doesn't give you what you're searching for. If you learn to feed your own soul and become your own best partner, you *lift yourself up*. You bring yourself to the level of quality that you seek in another.

Venus was born of water, and it is to the water she returns for purification and rejuvenation. In ancient Rome on every April first, women lowered the statue of Venus and ritually bathed her in honor of female sexuality and sensuality. It was a day for all women to celebrate the powers of the goddess. Later, they gathered for rituals in the temples. Some bathed in the famous Roman baths in honor of Venus, and it was said she would take their blemishes away. At the baths, attendants scrubbed them, removed unwanted hair, and rubbed them down with scented oil. You can bring elements of this ancient ritual home by creating your own special self-love bath.

Venus Self-Love Bath

Practice self-love by being a goddess for a day. This very act will bring you closer to receiving such pampering from another. It gives the subconscious mind the impression that you are someone who *deserves* divine treatment, who is *willing* to be nurtured like a goddess. It creates an energy "signature" in your being that *this is what a loving relationship will include for you.* And at its most basic level, a nice warm bath with candles gives you a chance to meditate and gain new perspective.

1. **Pick an auspicious day.** Friday is typically the day of celebrating Venus and doing love rituals in her name. Astrologically speaking, Friday is governed by her planet, and is said to help us access more of the feelings of love and joy that can raise self-esteem. But any day that feels right should be your day! Just make sure you have enough time to really relax into the experience.

2. **Let everything come up roses.** The rose is known as the flower of Venus. The scent generates her essence because it is associated with love and self-love. Get as many roses as you desire— and can reasonably afford—because you'll be using them in vases as well as for their petals. Red roses represent love and passion, the goddess herself. White are for purity. Pink are for appreciation (of self). Yellow are for joy. These are all qualities you want to evoke, so include as many colors as possible. Get a little basket for the rose

petals, and make sure you have rose water (if you prefer a lighter scent) or essential rose oil (for a heavier scent) and a small hand-held mirror. Venus loves looking at her own reflection; you can too.

3. **Turn the bathroom into Venus's Roman bath.** Replace the light in the room with a few candles to give off a nice glow. Set roses around the bathroom in a vase or two. Take the petals off the remaining roses and fill your small basket. Draw a delicious warm bath and place a half-cup of rose petals in the tub so you can enjoy the scented luxury of bathing like a goddess. (Save a few petals; you'll need them right before you get in). Add a little rosewater or a dab of rose oil to the tub for a stronger scent.

4. **Change into a flowing goddess.** Once the room is ready, prepare yourself by taking off your "civilian" clothes and putting on a pretty robe or flowing nightgown, white if possible; or wrap yourself in white sheet, like a toga.

5. **Play music that opens your heart.** Select romantic instrumental music or a recording of the sounds of the ocean, to take you back to the source of Venus. With the help of the music, put yourself in the mindset that you are about to love and be loved as you never have been before.

6. **Walk down the aisle to your altar of self-love:** In a wedding ceremony, the flower girl usually goes right before the bride, sprinkling flowers in her path to signify purity and a new life. Whether your walk to the bathroom is long or short, take your basket and be your own flower girl, sprinkling a trail of rose petals, as if you're a bride on your wedding day. Sprinkle any remaining petals into the tub. Step in and speak out loud as if making an offering to the goddess. *"Venus, goddess of love, I come to you pure of heart, mind, and spirit. Let me bask in your loving embrace and know what it is to evoke the great love from the goddess who dwells within."*

7. **Sit back, sink in, and relax.** Daydream and relish the feeling of the warm water on your skin. Let the goddess wash over you with scents, sounds, and feelings, and let her spirit move you. Contemplate what it would really mean in your life to treat yourself as a goddess, and be treated as one. What would you need in order to heal whatever is in the way of self-loving? What could you agree to do for yourself to make sure that your needs are always met?

8. **Take a vow of self-love.** Begin with a prayer: *"Dear Venus, hear me, please. I offer my vows to you for safekeeping and for assistance in setting them forth and honoring them always."* Take the hand-held mirror, and as you look at yourself, know you are looking at someone divine and deserving. Let your thoughts flow freely and try to express them as vows, for example: *"I promise to treat myself well and offer the same kindness, love, and compassion to myself as I do others; I will live my life in a manner that allows me to always nurture and love myself; I will embrace my sexuality and express my passion. I will always honor and cherish myself."* Whatever comes to mind, say it out loud as if you are speaking to Venus directly.

9. **Walk the recessional of the roses.** When you step out of your bath and walk back out through the rose petals, imagine that the goddess is walking with you toward a fresh start, a new beginning where you appreciate yourself, nurture yourself, and come to love yourself more and more each day.

SELF-NURTURE ON A REGULAR BASIS. A date with yourself is a powerful metaphor for self-nourishment. A "bath date" is just one way to take a sacred moment of self-honoring. You could also light a candle and incense and take fifteen minutes to relax in a favorite chair. Or take yourself to a movie, out to dinner, or to a museum exhibit you've been meaning to see. Many of us take time out for ourselves only occasionally; we neglect to create the foundation for ongoing revitalization. Carve out time and put things in order so that you can access these experiences regularly. This may mean keeping your favorite bath oil and candles on hand at all times or ensuring that you have several hours a week alone to yourself. Think of it this way: if you were dating, wouldn't you go out of your way to make time to see the person you are going out with and focus attention on the relationship? Do it for yourself, first! This lays the groundwork for someone to love you well someday—as well as you are loving yourself.

HOW TO KEEP VENUS WITH YOU

Write a love letter to yourself. Put pen to paper and say all the things you would want to hear from a beloved. Go for it—be mushy, romantic, loving, generous with praise, comforting, adoring, wild, and passionate. Comment in detail about your own beauty and grace; evoke the energy of the love you want to experience in your life. Mail the letter to yourself and when you read it, allow your heart to open even more to yourself.

    Reread the letter. Any time you feel a little beat up by the world, or just don't seem to feel connected to the love within you, read it and smile.

    Get your own personal "girdle of Venus." Venus wore a beautiful belt that was magical because she felt magical in it. Find a garment that makes you feel like a goddess and wear it to evoke the energies of Venus in your own heart and to feel good inside your own skin.

VENUS AFFIRMATION

"I am worthy of love."

$\mathcal{O}$SHUN

BRING OUT YOUR SENSUALITY

Sensual self-expression is a woman's birthright.
—CHARLOTTE ROSE

MANY OF US WISH WE could be completely comfortable in our own skin and feel liberated in our own bodies. We want to allow ourselves to express that raw, unedited female passion. Perhaps we dream of dancing on tabletops, skinny-dipping in the moonlight at the drop of a hat, or doing a slow, sensual striptease for an excited audience of one. Maybe our dreams serve our own sense of personal freedom and adventure, or maybe they enhance our confidence and pleasure. Whatever the personal motivation, sensual self-expression is healthy and good for the soul.

Some women are natural sensualists, completely at ease with their bodies. But many of us long to feel freer about expressing our sensual sides, yet feel we will never pull it off. It is important to recognize that sensuality is an inner glow and fire, an energy that we can nurture along and bring to life.

When we stifle our sensuality or limit ourselves from expressing it fully, it is as if a part of us is being hidden and denied. We have to reach into ourselves to bring out its essence. The effects can be wonderful—and fun—because they'll enhance your self-esteem, make you feel more beautiful, and help heat up your love life!

Call upon Oshun when you're ready to take the lid off your sensual self-expression and be completely natural with yourself, your lovers, or your mate. The ultimate wild woman, Oshun helps you bring out your raw and primal sensuality. She represents self-appreciation and giving oneself permission to have sensual pleasure.

WHO IS OSHUN?

Oshun loves bathing in cool waters, pampering herself with fragrant soaps and oils and wearing and changing her elegant clothing several times a day. —DIEDRE BADEJO, OSHUN, THE ELEGANT DEITY OF WEALTH, POWER AND FEMININITY

Oshun (*OH-shun*) is the Yoruban goddess of rivers and an *orisha*, or spirit, that sustains life. She is seen as the proprietress of sweet, flowing waters. Her worship is widespread, including in the United States, Cuba, Africa, Haiti, and beyond. Primary deity of the African Oshogbo religion, she is also revered in the religions of Santeria and Brazilian Macumba. Believers say that she honors them, in certain ceremonies, by coming into their bodies. She is the youngest orisha to be hailed as "Iyalode," meaning Great Queen; she's also called Lady of Secrets, Lady of Love, and Lady of Gold. She's a major love goddess who is prayed to for real and lasting love, good marriages, peaceful home life, and healthy babies; she governs diplomacy and brings support to the community as well. She also rules beauty and flirtation and evokes the essence of in-your-face sensuality. She is said to protect the abdominal area and teach pleasure and happiness to her devotees. She is often depicted as a sensual, brown-skinned woman, with full hips, wearing jewels and holding a mirror and a fan.

HOW TO INVITE HER INTO YOUR LIFE

The pathway to sensual liberation is feeling comfortable in your own skin. Comfortable enough to express and access power through your physical form and comfortable enough with your own nakedness. Oshun revels in the feel of her body. She is fluid, like the water; she loves to swim, to dance, to bathe, to writhe naked. She's fond of finer things and nice jewelry, and loves the feeling of jewelry jangling on her body.

She gets turned on by her own image and loves to gaze at herself in the mirror. It is said she wears a mirror on her belt so she can admire herself!

Oshun Beauty Ritual for One

If you're daring enough to explore your own body intending to love and appreciate it, try this sensual ritual with Oshun as your guide.

1. **Dance, dance, dance.** Pick a time when you know you will not be disturbed, put on some fabulous music and dance. Whether you think you can dance or not, start moving your body to the beat of music that turns you on and makes you feel excited. Dance the way you used to dance when you were a little girl— without inhibitions. Leap around, jump on beds, wave your arms all about, go wild—get lost in the music. This will raise your energy as it helps you rise above shyness and hesitation. In Nigeria, Oshun is honored with the Oshun festival, where dramatic ceremonies mark the day with numerous blessings and offerings. In one event, the women dance in honor of the goddess, hoping to be her favorite. It's said that when the goddess enters a woman, the woman dances wildly yet fluidly, as if she's swimming; she jangles her bracelets and jewelry and experiences a strong desire to look at herself in the mirror.

2. **Create a safe, sensual environment.** After you've had some fun dancing, turn down the music or pick a slow, sensual tune (or maybe beating drums: try some hot congas). Create an

environment in which you continue to feel loose and at ease. Dim all the lights and light a candle. Have a sip of wine if it will help you relax a bit.

3. **Look at your body without judgment**. Stand in front of a full-length mirror and strip off all your clothes. *All of 'em!* Notice your curves, your coloring, your breasts, your behind, and all the areas you don't normally look at: armpits, knees, toes, and fingertips. If your eyes begin to focus on parts of you that make you flinch, find another place to focus. The more you can begin to focus on seeing your most beautiful self, the more beautiful you will become, right before your very own eyes. Beauty, as they say, is in the eye of the beholder. If you are someone who has been critical of your own looks, it's time you recognize that as a distorted image of yourself based on old beliefs about what is beautiful and sensual, and what is not.

4. **Look into your eyes.** After you've surveyed the skin you are in, let your eyes catch those of the woman in the mirror. See the sparkle in those eyes, and then look beyond it. Try to connect to the sensual goddess within you. She is beyond your body, beyond the sparkle, and way beyond the critical beliefs you may have about your looks—and yet she is right there. She comes from a place where there's no such thing as unattractive, too fat, or too skinny. She is pure and untouched by a world that's tried to make her believe she isn't pretty or sexy or shapely enough. Look into your own eyes and see if you can find her there. Greet her with a loving smile.

5. **Give yourself a new name.** A new nickname that represents your newfound sensual identity—or who you hope to become—can be very inspiring. For example, if you feel connected to Oshun, you can borrow one of her own monikers or invent one of your

own, such as Queen of Sensuality, Princess of Passion, Mistress of Self-Expression, or Sexy-and-Loving-It-Woman. Use your imagination!

6. **Practice makes perfect.** Do this sensual beauty ritual as often as you like. Do it at home, or try it in other private settings if you can, such as in a hotel room when you are traveling. The more you move your body and get to know and appreciate your own physical form, the more comfort you will have in your own being. It will become easier to unleash your sensuality in your life—on a hot date, in your steady relationship, or just for the heck of it. As you go deeper into the process of unfolding sensuality, you can let your new name evolve, too. For example, you might begin as "Woman Who Loves Her Body" and as you grow more adept at expressing your true nature you might adopt a name like "Beautiful and Sensual." Maybe you'll graduate to "Hot, Hot, Hot Woman."

HOW TO KEEP OSHUN WITH YOU

Experience her in all of life's waters. When you bathe, shower, swim, wash your face, or even do laundry or dishes, think of Oshun and her sweet waters. Let her expressions of self-love flow into you with each drop of H2O.

Have a sensual breakthrough in the rain. Run into a rainstorm naked at least once in your life. Don't do it in the middle of rush hour, or during a dangerous thunderstorm, but when the moment comes when you're somewhere private and the rain beckons you to let it kiss your skin . . . say yes.

Wear her emblem on your body. Women honor Oshun by wearing a brass bracelet. It is said that Oshun herself owns five. On occasions when you especially long to have her with you, wear five brass bracelets that jangle a sensual tune with every movement of your arm.

OSHUN AFFIRMATION

"I am a beautiful, sensual goddess."

FREYA

BE A MAN MAGNET

Remember, there are only two things without limits—femininity,
and the means to explore it.

—FROM THE MOVIE LA FEMME NIKITA

SOME OF US FANTASIZE ABOUT being a sexual enchantress
. . . the kind of woman for whom it is second nature to allure,
seduce, and charm any man. And even if we're content with who we
are, and we're already in a relationship, we may just wish to be a little
more bold and expressive.

The art of magnetizing men is not just a sex thing. It's a matter
of communication, brainpower, and raising your sexual energy so
that it invites someone to get closer. It goes without saying that a
woman's sexual energy is a precious gift, not to be used to manipulate
or "hook" anyone. But you sure can learn to enjoy the natural sizzle
between men and women and have fun with it!

Instead of viewing sexuality as something located in the vicinity
of your underwear, experience it as a life force that flows through
you, something that feels like good energy pulsating through your
body. When a woman transmits that kind of energy to a man it is
extremely stimulating and sexy for both of you. Exploring sexuality
responsibly and consciously can be a turn-on as you awaken your
prowess and become a more skillful sex goddess in your own right.

Call upon Freya when it comes to owning your sexual energies and erotic impulses. She helps you express your sexual power in the world in a responsible way, and she also encourages you to draw the man—or men—of your choice, because she is the mistress of pure sexual essence and she is the power that inspires women to own their sexuality. She represents sexual self-expression and gives you permission to have pleasure and fun.

WHO IS FREYA?

Utterly promiscuous, she took all the gods as lovers.
—*PATRICIA MONAGHAN,*
THE NEW BOOK OF GODDESSES & HEROINES

Freya (*FRAY-ah*) is the Norse goddess of love and fertility, hailing from the family of deities known as Vanir. As the leader of the Valkyries, she chooses which warriors die in battle and then escorts them to the other side. Considered one of the most beautiful, fortunate, and powerful female deities in the Norse pantheon, she is a divine female of raw sensuality and vigorous passions—a vixen who is not shy about expressing herself. She is identified strongly with sexual freedom. Her residence is a beautiful palace called Folkvang ("field of folk"), a place where love songs are always in the air. Her passions include music, spring, flowers, and fairy folk. She is also host of her enormous Hall, known as Sessrumnir, which is large enough to receive half of those who die in battle. Rooted in a culture that accepted infidelity as a standard operating mode, rather than a deception, Freya is affiliated with numerous partners and yet also loved her consort husband. Although he was not her exclusive lover, when her husband Od (also known as Odr) went missing it's said the goddess cried tears of gold. When Freya wears her precious magical necklace that is a prized and magical possession, her allure intensifies and people fall under her spell. Some say she also wears a rainbow around her neck. Freya also possesses a cloak or skin of bird feathers, which allows its wearer to change into a falcon. She is often pictured riding naked—or clothed in a sensual pose—in a chariot pulled by two cats or by her "battle boar," who some say is her human lover in disguise.

HOW TO INVITE HER INTO YOUR LIFE

Freya shows us that when it comes to expressing female power, sexuality is a metaphor for life. Given that we're hormonally driven creatures, given to sexual urges and needs, it's healthy to desire pleasure, a decent selection of men to choose from, exposure to activities that enhance our sexual self-esteem, and even a little nookie if the right person comes along. When you feel sexually empowered, you're more likely to take risks in other parts of your life. It can be invigorating and confidence-boosting. Try these ideas to bring out your inner Freya.

1. **Create sex goddess runes.** As an oracle, ancient Viking, Germanic, and Anglo-Saxon peoples used "runes": stones inscribed with symbols based on the Viking alphabet. Reading the runes shed light on situations related to the present moment and lessons for the future, and people still consult them today. The ancient Norse people treated the runes and other natural markings on rocks as sacred inscriptions from the gods, and they had specific ways of deciphering them. You can create your own set of "sex goddess runes" on stone so that Freya can speak to you through them daily and lead you, day by day, to greater liberation.

   COLLECT NATURAL STONES. Go to a lake, a beach, a pebble-strewn park, or any place with a nice supply of smooth, round stones—preferably all of a similar color. Always ask the goddess for permission to remove stones from a public place or natural area first. Make the process of collecting them a passionate pursuit as you search for the most beautiful stones, appreciating their texture, running a finger over their tops to make sure they are smooth. Collect at least thirty-one, plus a few extra. Wash them at home and let them dry for twenty-four hours by a window that is exposed to sunlight and moonlight to bless them with the power of the sun and moon, masculine and feminine.

BUY THIN FELT TIP MARKERS TO WRITE ON THE STONES. Seek out the perfect pen, one that writes legibly but won't "bleed" on the rock. You may have to take a rock to the store to test a few.

GET INTO THE MOOD. Set up a table or "craft area" with your washed and blessed stones. Take out your new pen and get into man magnet mode. If you need inspiration, play sexy music, the kind that makes your hormones sizzle. You want to raise your energy and imbue the stones with your good vibes.

CREATE YOUR SEX GODDESS QUALITIES. Choose at least thirty-one qualities related to sexual expressiveness—qualities you would love to own. Be as daring as you are willing, and include some practical aspects, too. You might want to make a preliminary list. You can include some of the following, or make up your own: *hot, sexy, alluring, passionate, enticing, sensual, alive, queenly, goddess-like, attractive, tempting, bewitching, beguiling, beautiful, fulfilled, charming, enticing, mesmerizing, desirable, wild, popular, sought-after, beloved, confident, joyous, liberated, powerful, appreciated, ecstatic, skilled with pleasure, energetic, honored, satisfied, pure, open-hearted, tingling, erotic, poetic, romantic.*

WRITE THEM DOWN AND SPEAK THEM OUT. Write a quality on each rock, one for each day of the month. As you do, call it out: *I am desirable . . . I am appreciated . . . I am tingling . . .* and so on.

GIVE THEM A HOME. Find a pretty container or velvet sack in which to keep your sex goddess stones. Keep them in a sacred location—on an altar or by your bed, for example.

PICK ONE EACH DAY. Use them as a divining tool, your

communication with the goddess. For at least one month, choose a stone each day. Take a moment to visualize yourself surrounded by brilliant white light. Close your eyes, dig a hand into the container, and choose one stone. See what it says—that is your quality for the day! Take a moment to hold the stone in your hand and tune into the quality written on it. Think about what the quality means to you and let it begin to permeate your being. If the stone says "mesmerizing," then begin to feel like a woman who mesmerizes. Whichever stone you pick is Freya's advice to you for the day. You may carry the stone with you, or leave it on your altar. It's okay if you draw the same stone twice, or even many times— that just means the goddess wants you to practice!

GO ABOUT YOUR BUSINESS. The message on the sex goddess stone gives you a chance each day to practice *being in a state* of raised sexual energy and attention. On high alert, you might say. Let the quality of the day percolate within you as you go about your business *as if* you are sexy, alluring, popular, or whatever message you chose that day. By keeping it in mind, you may find that things occur that validate that you are indeed sending out specific vibes. The goal is that, eventually, all thirty-one qualities become a part of who you are.

Imagine it this way: Just as a radio tower broadcasts a signal and you hear music that makes you want to dance, you can broadcast "an invitation" across a room that can inspire a man to want to get to know you. Working with these runes can help you develop subtle energetic communication skills that will help you take charge of your own romantic destiny.

2. **Evoke the sex goddess within.** Freya lives in some of the classic tools of verbal and nonverbal communication. Once you've begun to boost your sexual expression using the runes, here are some ways to practice being aware, alluring, and authentic in interactions with men.

SHOW THAT YOU'RE OPEN AND INTERESTED. You have to let a guy know you want to meet him. Even if you feel a little nervous or unsure, don't shut down and then pretend you're not really interested. What draws a man is a woman who sends clear signals and is open to his approach. Be real. Let your body language show that you're relaxed and open. Smile.

BE REAL. Posturing and putting on airs defeats the purpose and sets up a dynamic you may not be able to live up to. When getting to know a man, you never want to give the whole enchilada in one sitting. Feed him slowly and keep him excited to know more. But be authentic. If you are smart, savvy, successful, funny, enthusiastic, fun, passionate about life—let him know that there's more to you than your sexuality.

GIVE HIM THAT LOOK. Your soul, your desires, and your intentions all come through your eyes. If you like a man, look him directly in the eyes and engage him with your look. Try not to turn your eyes away even if you get nervous. Stay present; stay with him. The longer you can keep his gaze, the more intense the connection.

Repel unwanted attention: Learn to fine-tune your "man antennae." That is, put out the right vibes for the right men, as opposed to drawing every male in the vicinity. Sometimes being a man magnet is expressed as a great, authentic feeling of confidence that glows from within and generates more of the same. But this can also lead to unwanted attention. If you find yourself getting hit on by people you want nothing to do with, imagine your sexual energy is like electricity that powers the lights. Flip the switch to "off" until you can get out of the situation.

HOW TO KEEP FREYA WITH YOU

Adopt a signature fragrance. A favorite perfume can help cast a spell on a man. It has to be a fabulous scent that makes *you* feel like a powerful goddess. At home, spray it in the air and walk through the mist so that it goes everywhere. Make sure it's strong enough to leave a *slight* scent trail as you walk. A man never forgets the scent of a goddess.

Try pheromones. Life is a pheromone fest. Like animals, we sniff the subtle scent of sex on each other and want to get closer. If you want to up the ante on the Freya experience, try some of nature's little helpers. Athena Pheromone 10:13 from the Athena Institute, mixed with your favorite perfume, enhances your natural charms and signals. It generates good feelings within, promoting a sense of attraction to your own energy, which energetically translates to others. Studies have shown that it has a direct effect on people in your immediate vicinity.

FREYA AFFIRMATION

"I magnetize men through the natural
expression of my feminine energy."

PERSEPHONE

LIBERATE YOURSELF FROM BAD RELATIONSHIPS

> A woman has got to love a bad man once or twice in her life, to be thankful for a good one.
>
> —MARJORIE KINNAN RAWLINGS, *THE YEARLING*

FEW OF US WILL ESCAPE the universal experience that initiates us all into the sacred sorority of being a woman: the bad relationship.

Let's hope you never find yourself in the grips of an abusive partner. But short of that, many of us still stumble into a union with someone who steals our heart only to abduct us into a "relationship underworld." Once there, we may find we're on a journey through Relationship Hell as we recognize that the man we believed to be Mr. Right is the lover we must leave.

His infractions may be relatively minor—he's cheap, unappreciative, unconscious, or just so unmotivated that it's impossible to build a relationship. Worse, he could be a cheater, liar, con artist, big-time emotional withholder, or someone who continually acts in a manner that is demeaning, mean, or makes you cry a lot. It might seem like a no-brainer that it's time to flee, but some of us stay—and stay—and become casualties of love. There is some invisible glue that holds us, or perhaps a forbidden fruit that tempts us.

A relationship that prompts you to feel bad about yourself, or that brings about symptoms of depression, despair, or rage (because you are not getting what you need) requires introspection and, eventually, action. Mr. Wrong may just be a blip on the screen for a brief moment in time, or you may find that you are living with him—or married to him. You may be toying with the idea of separating, or you could be crawling out of your skin, itching to get away, afraid if you stay another moment you will be forever lost. If you find you are exhausted and depressed from a relationship that takes so much work, ultimately, it may be time to learn your lessons, count your blessings, and move on.

Call upon Persephone when it comes to freeing yourself from bad relationships. She gives us great insight on what it feels like to be trapped and out of control in a relationship, and on how to extricate ourselves from unhealthy unions. She helps us evoke sunshine, springtime, and liberation. She represents balancing the light and dark aspects of a relationship, recognizing dysfunction, breaking free, and returning home to ourselves.

WHO IS PERSEPHONE?

He caught her up reluctant on his golden car and bore her away lamenting. Then she cried out shrilly with her voice, calling upon her father, who is most high and excellent. But no one, either of the deathless gods or of mortal men, heard her voice . . .
—HOMER, THE ILIAD

Persephone (*per-SEF-oh-nee*), Greek goddess of spring, was seen as the rich fertile earth, the seed that was planted in the earth so it could bloom. A virginal maiden who becomes a queen of darkness, she came to represent both the loss of innocence and a woman's occasional journey to the dark side with a man.

As the story goes, she was at play in a field, gathering flowers, when she came across the beautiful narcissus blossom. As she bent to pick it, without warning, the earth suddenly opened and out came Hades, god of the shadowy underworld and ruler of the dead, in a chariot. It turned out to be her surprise wedding limo. Frightened, kicking and screaming, she was carried off to his home in hell. Her mother, Demeter, freaked and confronted Persephone's dad, Zeus. It turned out that he had given Hades *permission* to take Persephone's hand—and more. Demeter roamed the earth in search of Persephone and could not find her. Finally she refused to let her grains and fruits grow until her daughter was returned and a deadly winter fell upon the earth. Eventually, Zeus gave in and ordered Hades to let Persephone go. But before Hades relinquished her, he persuaded her to eat from the pomegranate. Now, because she had tasted the food of the dead, Hades retained a claim on her. Persephone had eaten six seeds, so a deal was struck: she would spend six months of every year with Hades, and six with her mom. The cycle continues today: in spring, Persephone emerges from the underworld and nature blooms; in the fall she returns to Hades and her mother mourns.

HOW TO INVITE HER INTO YOUR LIFE

There is a jewel tucked into every relationship—even the bad ones— that can give us valuable insight into our own behavior (and help us move forward to a relationship that is more suitable). But once we find that jewel and polish it, we must decide whether we are meant to remain in a relationship with someone whom we know in our heart is not really right for us. As Persephone knew all too well, there is also a sweet fruit that can tempt us to keep coming back for more. But if a relationship is dragging you down into the underworld, holding you back from your power, bringing insanity to your life, there may come a time when you need to gather your strength and start again. The first task is to assess your situation honestly.

1. **Recognize denial.** When someone fulfills a particular need in us, we may tend to overlook even major flaws, wondering "Maybe my bad boy isn't *so* bad" or "Is my emotionally dysfunctional lover

really *that* dysfunctional?" Hades snatched Persephone, the very breath of spring-time, and took her to hell. He insisted she come to his world because he could never raise himself up to hers. After spending so much time there, she began to forget who she was. Some say she co-conspired to eat the forbidden fruit so they could be together—yet this was something Persephone would never admit.

2. **Review these healthy relationship checklists.** Love does not involve taking anyone hostage! The recovery movement has put forth a classic definition of a healthy partnership and healthy partners. Brenda Schaeffer outlines some of these qualities in her book *Signs of Healthy Love*. See how many you can check off on these two lists.

A healthy relationship:
- allows for individuality
- tolerates both oneness and separateness
- brings out the best qualities in both partners
- accommodates change and exploration
- encourages growth for both partners
- establishes true intimacy
- has built-in freedom and allows both partners to ask for what they want
- encourages each partner to experience giving *and* receiving

And a healthy individual, capable of a healthy union:
- endures endings well
- is self-sufficient
- has the ability to accept the limitations of self and partner
- is up to handling commitment
- has high self-esteem
- enjoys some alone time

- expresses feelings spontaneously
- welcomes closeness and is willing to take some risks
- treats self and partner as equal
- would never think of trying to change or control the other

3. **Inventory your past relationships.** Sometimes, even though we know a man is killing off our potential, we keep going back because of the *one thing* we think we can get only from him. The more willingly and skillfully we can identify the patterns we keep replaying in our relationships, the more consciously we can head toward healthier, happier relationships. Be gentle with yourself as you engage in this process of self-discovery. Make a list of all your boyfriends and significant partners and write down:

   - the significant problems and chronic issues
   - why you broke up, who initiated it, and how it ended
   - any message you might have told yourself about men after the breakup (*They always leave; They never love me enough; They can't be trusted,* for example). See if you can identify a "belief" you may have that keeps manifesting in your life.
   - any similar issues, fears, or feelings in your current relationship, if you have one
   - any insights about your standard M.O. for choosing men. Think about your relationship patterns. Do you have an antenna for bad boys? Do you seek out the wrong kind of men because they excite you? Do you accept less than love or let men make you feel small because you feel needy for love?

4. **Look honestly at your relationship with your father.** Everything begins with Daddy. Recognizing the root of some of your relationship issues is the first step to healing them. Persephone was betrayed by her father. Many women have been betrayed by their fathers in some way, or perhaps perceive that they have. Even if that is not the case, you can be sure there is some issue

related to Dad that begs to be explored. Whether he was mean, cold, or simply a well-meaning man with flaws, to a little girl, he was a god. Focus on gently discovering how your relationship with Dad may have affected or even interfered with your adult relationships with men. In quiet, alone time, explore these points.

ACKNOWLEDGE YOUR FATHER'S INFLUENCE. He is your first male influence, your model for how men are in the world. We tend to draw men who are like our dads, for better or for worse. Look through some old photos of your dad and remember what it was like growing up with him. Think about things he taught you about men, through his words and his way of being. Then ask yourself how you may attract men who replicate some of Dad's least desirable traits, and whether you sometimes "cast" your boyfriends as your father—a man to take care of you and be responsible for you.

HEAL THE DADDY WOUND. This can be a lifetime project, but with every relationship we get better at understanding how we've been hurt and disappointed. Write a letter to your father, whether he is alive or has passed on. This is *not* a letter you will send. Its only purpose is to help you clarify some of your pain and begin to liberate yourself from its grip. When you have some quiet time, go someplace healing—perhaps outdoors in nature, or at a beach—and take pen to paper. Hold the intention that you can be honest and strong enough to write anything you need to say to Dad and recognize anything you need to know about your relationship with him. Cry, laugh, feel whatever feelings come up. When you sense you've written all you need to share, fold the letter and put it somewhere special—maybe in a sacred book or favorite keepsake box. Choose to heal anything that stands in the way of a relationship with a man who is mature, balanced, loving, and appropriately attentive. Seek professional support for the tough parts.

5. **Use this pomegranate ritual to reclaim the right to a wonderful relationship.** Persephone's legendary descent to the underworld for six months each year brings us winter, and her ascent returns the spring and summer; the earth is reborn anew. You can rise up, liberate yourself, and come back to a new life—a life into which you only invite men who are truly worthy of your love. Perform the following rituals as symbolic gestures that you are ready to reach for your highest relationship potential.

SAY GOODBYE TO BAD RELATIONSHIPS BY PLANTING NEW SEEDS WITHIN YOU. Rather than letting the "sweet fruit" serve as a lure to hold us captive in a relationship underworld, get ready to reclaim the pomegranate and use it to empower yourself to liberation.

BUY A POMEGRANATE AND LET IT RIPEN. The inside of this fruit has dozens of tiny sacs of pulpy pink-red tissue, each holding a tiny seed. The seeds usually taste juicy and sweet, sometimes with a slightly sour aftertaste. The pomegranate is the only fruit from which we eat only the seeds. Selecting each seed, feeling its texture in your fingers, raising it to your mouth, and taking it onto your tongue makes eating a pomegranate very sensual and freeing. Pray for the lover who will someday feed the seeds to you with love and patience, but meanwhile, plan to partake of this pleasure by feeding them to yourself. You can declare your liberation from a bad relationship by asserting your dreams, hopes, and aspirations for love.

EAT THE SEEDS AND CHANT AS A SACRED ACT. You can do this exercise alone or with a nonromantic friend. Pick someone with similar relationship values. Cut the pomegranate into two even pieces. Play some fun, inspiring instrumental music to get you in the mood. Take turns eating the seeds one by one, and as you do, declare out loud a positive relationship trait that you seek in a man. Speak out: *He's sensitive . . . He adores me . . . He worships me in a healthy way . . . He's generous . . . He's spiritual . . . He's a nice person . . . My friends love him . . .* and so on. Calling out what you want creates a thought form that moves toward making it real in your world. As you swallow each seed after declaring a trait, you are embodying those qualities you seek in a man. It is a first step to creating a new reality. You may find that the man in your life becomes more of who you want— or you may see clearly that he is nowhere near the ideal partner you deserve. Then you can make a choice to move on. Either way, you have put forth a new relationship model and used the pomegranate as a tool for ascending from the relationship underground.

HOW TO KEEP PERSEPHONE WITH YOU

Wash that man right out of your hair. Anytime you feel the pain of loss or a broken heart welling up within, wash your hair and declare that sadness is moving out of your body and down the drain. Say a prayer to Persephone to bring back springtime in your life.

Let the sun shine. When you don't know what to do with yourself and you feel antsy from pent-up emotions, step out into the sunlight— like Persephone retuning to bring forth the spring—and let the sunshine warm your heart.

Explore spirituality. Go deeper into who you are and what you are about. You may have a tendency to focus on "him," what he did, and what he may be going through. Try some pursuits that take you out of your head—and out of his head! It might be a religious ritual or tradition, or it might be attending a lecture or class that's good for the body and spirit. Once you've been to the relationship underworld, the first glimmer of recovery is like the first sign of spring. Let Persephone help you come home and see the light.

PERSEPHONE AFFIRMATION

"I raise myself up."

GAURI

GET READY FOR MARRIAGE

You have become mine forever. Yes, we have become partners. Hereafter, I cannot live without you. Do not live without me. Let us share the joys. —FROM "THE SEVEN STEPS," TRADITIONAL HINDU WEDDING CEREMONY

THERE COMES A TIME WHEN we've sowed the oats of our wild-woman days, we've had our fill of solo journeys, and we're ready for a committed love relationship. Not just a boyfriend or a main squeeze, but a stable partnership with someone who is good "lifetime mate material." A husband, perhaps?

Once we yearn to feel the power of *that kind of love* in our lives, the search to find the right person to experience it with begins in earnest. Inviting true love into your life means making a relationship a priority and organizing your life to make room for the person who will love you like no other. This is a good time to pray as you have never prayed before for the kind of love you choose—and then to activate your "shout-out" to the universe for the love of your life.

Call upon Gauri when it comes to magnetizing the right mate, especially one who is solid and reliable. Gauri is the Divine Mother you can trust to guide you to a mate who is *really* right for you! She inspires you to make wise, wholesome choices and to develop the maturity needed for marriage. She represents working with your higher self to pave the way for true love and that walk down the aisle.

WHO IS GAURI?

After years of prayer to Gauri to bring her a "groom like Shiva," on her
wedding day the bride takes the groom to Gauri's abode in her family
shrine to thank the goddess for answering her prayer . . . and to show the
goddess the groom, the husband she is responsible for bringing.
—*DEPARTMENT OF ANTHROPOLOGY,*
CALIFORNIA STATE UNIVERSITY

Gauri (*GOW-ree*) is a Hindu love goddess who is worshipped as the bestower of "virtuous husbands." She is the goddess Parvati in her young unmarried state, the "Golden One" who ultimately lands the great god Shiva as her beloved. She is considered the bride of Shiva—just before the honeymoon. While most marriages are "arranged," according to ancient customs of India, many women consult Gauri, local protector of relationships and cosmic matchmaker. They believe she will help magnetize the best mate possible, because she was in fact able to do that for herself. She's the ultimate role model for success, having won the heart of Shiva! It is also said that some of the most notable heroines in Hindu history prayed to Gauri for good men.

Gauri is celebrated in the Gangur Festival in India, an event attended by married women who beseech the goddess to bless their husbands and families, and singles who pray for a suitable life partner. The festival is a females-only event featuring the goddess Parvati. On the final day, a bedecked and bejeweled icon of Gauri is wheeled through the streets. The women, balancing brass pitchers of water on their heads and wearing their finest, escort the icon to the temple of Gauri where the goddess is ritually bathed, her name chanted in many forms. The close of the festival includes the arrival of an icon or other depiction of Shiva, ready to escort his bride home, along with horses and elephants. A divine wedding, to say the least! Pictured as a beautiful young sari-clad Indian woman, sometimes sitting on a throne and displaying four arms, Gauri personifies purity and serious marital intent.

HOW TO INVITE HER INTO YOUR LIFE

It is Gauri's pleasure to bring good partners together and help create circumstances in which honorable people can marry. She brings a quality to a union that many of us find elusive—a sense of security born out of a deep and lasting commitment. Just before partaking in the marriage *samskara* (sacred rite), Hindu brides and their womenfolk often pray to Gauri for a blessed union. But they've already prayed to her long before the wedding, *for a wedding* to someone wonderful!

1. **Partake in Gauri's** customs. The Gangur Festival, which celebrates Gauri each spring and honors her marriage, gives women hope that they, too, will meet their own perfect mate. As well as enacting the coming together of mates, the festival also honors the evolution of the young goddess from girl to woman. As Gauri goes off with Shiva, she transforms into the sensual, worldlier Parvati, who becomes a consort supreme who through her energy (*shakti*) helps shape her husband's destiny. Women-created rituals to honor Gauri vary from village to village in India. While some celebrate with fancy, fabricated icons, other villages use cow dung (considered sacred) and mud. You can honor her in your own way in the privacy of your own home.

2. **Create a marriage altar.** If you want to keep a symbol of Gauri, select an object that represents her, such as a beautiful sari or a miniature throne. Or be creative, as many Hindu devotees are, and create an icon from a coconut, with the mask of a female face on it. To keep it simple, you can just light a pink candle or use a traditional oil lamp (you can buy a ghee or coconut oil

lamp with a small string wick online or at a store that carries Indian goods). To begin to imagine your own wedding, cut out a photo of a bride in a wedding gown you love with a dashing groom on her arm, and place it in a frame on the altar. Let your altar be the focal point for your prayers to the goddess that you will have the opportunity to marry a wonderful man.

3. **Divine a wedding date or a meeting date.** It is the Hindu tradition to find out the most auspicious day for a wedding by consulting a Vedic astrologer. If you are in a relationship—even if you have not heard a proposal or proposed yet yourself— you can consult an astrologer about what is the *most favorable time* for a marriage. If you are still single, you can ask for most potentially favorable time for meeting your true love. Called *Jyotish*, this kind of Hindu predictive astrology differs a bit from the astrology we know in the United States, but it is considered highly accurate. Don't get attached to an exact date, but there's certainly nothing wrong with *anticipating* a time frame for true love! It can help you use the law of attraction to support the stars in bringing true love closer.

4. **State your intentions with marriage paint.** *Mehndi* has become very hip and everybody is doing it. But in the Hindu culture, mehndi has long been associated with romantic love and marriage. It's the Indian art of hand-painted design using henna. Dry leaves of the henna plant are crushed into powder and made into a paste, then applied to a woman's hands and feet in an elaborate, intricate design. It's almost always a sign that a wedding is about to take place! Relatives usually do the bride's *mehndi* and then they do it for each other. Prefabricated mehndi kits are readily available; you can also go into an Indian beauty parlor. If you treat the experience as a sacred adventure befitting a bride-to-be, you may find that it is a nice symbolic gesture that

you too intend to marry—someday soon! The painted designs last about six weeks before wearing off.

5. **Do a "Get closer to marriage" ritual with Gauri.** To prepare, petition and pray to her with specific requests. Use some uplifting sacred music to help create a sacred space. This simple nondenominational ceremony will give you a chance to articulate your heart's desire and petition the goddess for true love.

MAKE AN OFFERING. Bring an offering of fruits and sweets. If you have set up an altar, place them there, or just leave them in a bowl as a gift you offer to the goddess before asking for her help.

BRING IN LIGHT. Light the pink candle or oil lamp to symbolize the love that already exists in your heart, and the heart of your beloved—wherever that person may be.

PRAY. Use the following prayer to call out to your divine matchmaker, goddess Gauri, and ask her to bring your perfect mate. (Feel free to revise it as you wish, or to write your own.)

First part of the prayer:

Dear Divine Matchmaker of All That Is,
in the name and spirit of the goddess Gauri, please fill this place with
your sacred presence. I ask for your guidance and your help
in finding my soul mate, my most perfect partner.
I seek a partner whose very being enhances me
who brings more love, joy, peace, and prosperity to my life . . .
who I can love fully and who can fully receive my love . . .
who loves, honors, and cherishes me completely, and always.

NOW, CONTEMPLATE THAT PARTNER AND THE RELATIONSHIP YOU DESIRE.

CALL OUT THE QUALITIES YOU SEEK IN A LOVE RELATIONSHIP. Describe that soul-to-soul relationship as if you are already in it. What do you love about it? If you choose, softly whisper those thoughts to Gauri, or write them down if you prefer. (Note: *Never* ask for the love of a specific person or make requests that may impinge on the will of others. You're describing the qualities of the relationship itself.) You might choose from these thoughts, and add your own:

- I am loved and able to love without conditions.
- We enjoy communicating and cuddling.
- Our spiritual life is the center of our universe.
- We listen to each other and we grow together.
- We are deeply connected by heart and soul.

CLOSE WITH THIS BENEDICTION:

I have spoken truly from my heart.
Please grant my desires for love—of self and with my true love.
I trust you will bring this to me lovingly and gently, at the exact right moment in time,
in a way that is completely right for my love and me.
I give thanks for your presence, your guidance, and your love.
Amen. And so it is.

TAKE IN SWEETNESS. In a typical Hindu *puja* ritual, the fruit and sweets that are offered to the deities before worship are shared with devotees after worship. It is called *prasad,* and taking it in allows you to take in the energy of Gauri. Eat a piece of fruit that has been blessed by your prayer.

TAKE GAURI'S DIVINE ADVICE. If you tell Gauri what you want, she'll align that with what she knows is in your highest interest, and she'll lead you to the right mate. She is the goddess who may, like a wise mother, tell you not to search for a lover you are frantically passionate about but to let yourself draw in a mate *who loves you dearly and would devote his life to you,* one who *is most committed to common goals.*

HOW TO KEEP GAURI WITH YOU

Keep praying and honoring the goddess. Praying regularly keeps you connected and keeps your goals alive in your consciousness and activated in the world. Try this Hindu prayer to Mother Gauri: *"Adorations to the goddess who is the auspiciousness of all that is auspicious, who is the consort of Lord Shiva, who is the bestower of every desire of one's heart. Adorations to you, O Devi, I have taken refuge in you."*

Read epic love poetry. Read poetry that stimulates your mind and your emotions and keeps the flame of your desire for love alive. Gauri lives in the epic poetry of India as Parvati, with her consort Shiva, and their relationship is hot and heavenly. Any poetry that enhances your yearning for love will help.

Daydream about your wedding. Think about what your marriage ceremony and celebration would be like: who you'd invite, what dress you'd choose, where it would take place, and at what time of year. What kind of ceremony would you have? What kind of vows would you speak? Allow your mind to run away with this fantasy and see yourself at the altar, speaking your vows to your soon-to-be-known beloved.

GAURI AFFIRMATION

"My true partner in life is here, now."

ADHA

DISCOVER SOULFUL LOVE

Whatever our souls are made of, his and mine are the same.
—EMILY BRONTË, WUTHERING HEIGHTS

SOME OF US ARE DESTINED to do love in a really big way. We don't just want a prince or a knight or a mere mortal love. We seek the love divine. For some of us, loving another is a religious experience and a sacred marriage.

When you get to this stage of the game, you have already come to know yourself as whole and complete unto yourself. And yet, it's as if you're searching for your other half, the one soul on the planet who can complete you: the one who, in many ways, is so much a part of you that there is no "I" or "you"—just "us." It's as if you already know one another . . . even if you have yet to meet. You can feel, taste, and sense that person drawing ever closer.

Many Eastern philosophies tell us that the sexual communion that comes from such intense and magical connecting has many transformative powers. Sex is the coming together, figuratively and literally, of the physical and the divine. It represents the merging of lower nature (human personality) and the higher self (God). When experienced in such a soulful manner, and treated as a sacred act, it elevates us to a soul-expanding awareness that allows us, as they say, to "feel at one with the universe."

Love divine can change our lives, and our status in life.

Call Upon Radha when it comes to soulful love and ecstatic sexual union, something that goes way beyond the realm of "good sex" into "transcendent sex." She helps us take sexuality to a sacred place and make it a high expression of love that helps shape who we are and who we are becoming. She represents devotion, sacred union, and completion in a relationship.

WHO IS RADHA?

And led by Radha's spirit, the feet of Krishna found the road aright.
Wherefore, in bliss, which all hearts inherit, together taste they
Love's divine delight.
—*FROM THE GITA GOVINDA*

In the Hindu tradition, Radha (*RAH-dah*) is the *gopi*, or cowherdess, who is said to be the most devoted and adored lover of the great avatar Krishna. It is widely believed that she was an incarnation of the goddess Lakshmi, and thus she is considered a goddess come to earth in human form. Lord Krishna—the flute-playing divine cowherd—was like the rock star of the gopi set, intensely popular and sought-after. And Radha was his favorite gopi gal.

Radha left her home and her family to fulfill her destiny with Krishna. They spent their time together in the groves, or by the lotus pond, often surrounded by other gopis; at night they'd meet at a special temple to make love. Radha was the divine temple into which Krishna could offer his Love Divine. He was lifted by her sweet *shakti* (female energy) and she was empowered by his male energies. As human female and divine male, together they personify God's love for humanity, and humanity's desire to be one with God. To many devotees, their union is seen as strictly spiritual. But some followers believe that they also embody the Tantric principle; that they are two aspects of the divine, male and female, that together form one unit. Some see their relationship as devotional love taken to the utmost spiritual heights. Some imagine it as erotic love. Pictured as a beautiful Indian woman in a sari, and captured in countless works of art, Radha is rarely separate from her beloved Krishna, who is often depicted as blue, in contrast to her brown skin.

HOW TO INVITE HER INTO YOUR LIFE

Radha is associated with soulful yearning. She typifies a feeling we can well relate to when we yearn for that one special love—love that is deep, profound, all-encompassing. It was yearning that compelled Radha to leave the safety of her home and seek out her beloved Krishna. This yearning—which, for each, can only be quenched by the other—is the invisible spiritual thread that helps soulful lovers find each other and keeps them together. Nurture your longing to be with your true soul mate by embracing it—don't think it is a feeling to be overcome or avoided, or a void to be filled. Just imagine *he* is out there somewhere, and he's feeling it too. Trust that he yearns for you just as you yearn for him. And feed your longing using some of these ideas.

1. **Read poetry that depicts sacred yearning.** In *The Gita Govinda*, Krishna sends a message to his beloved Radha to meet him. It's a telling glimpse of the depth of his longing that can inspire all women. Your Krishna is out there too!

   Yes, Lady! In the self-same place he waits
   Where with thy kiss thou taught him utmost love.
   And drew him, as no one else draws, with thy look.
   All day long, and all night long, his cry is:
   Radha, Radha . . . like a spell said over and over.
   And in his heart, there lives no wish or hope
   Save only this, to slake his spirit's thirst,
   For Radha's love and Radha's lips,

And find peace on the immortal beauty of thy breast.

2. **Watch movies that tell epic love stories.** Movies can take us on a journey that shows us the power of yearning in action and the depth of feelings that men and woman can share. Movies can inspire our own inner knowing of what true love and higher loving can be like. You may also gain insight and inspiration from popular classic love stories. Watch whatever turns you on and makes you long for love! Every time your heart churns for the one who is meant to be yours, you are closer to him.

3. **Meditate and reflect on soulful, sensual love.** This meditation and reflection exercise will help evoke the essence of your desires. It asks a series of leading questions that address your yearnings and hopes, but also help you form inspired images and ideas of the kind of sensual, higher love you desire. You can sit with this meditation on your lap and spend time reading and then *reflecting* on each point in this meditation; or, if possible, make a recording you can play again and again. Listen to it as much as you can, review and reflect as much as you can.

SET THE MOOD. If reading it, play a piece of exotic yet soothing music, or even instrumental Hindu devotional music, to relax your mind. Light two candles—one for him, and one for you. This will illuminate your experience, and also shine a light to show him the way home...to you.

INCLUDE *EVERYTHING.* If you truly want a soulful lover, it is important that you imagine some of the sensual and erotic qualities you choose to experience with your love mate. Be as specific as you can, and include details on the physical, emotional, spiritual (and any other) dimensions of loving and lovemaking. Unless you are in a sacred relationship already, do not imagine a specific person. This is a very powerful meditation, and it's inappropriate to place spiritual expectations on someone who hasn't agreed to be intimate with you.

OPEN WITH AN EMPOWERING AFFIRMATION. Begin with this positive affirmation in the present tense: "*I am now cherished, loved, honored, and adored by the man of my dreams.*"

Now reflect on the points listed below. Give each point some time, visualizing and even *feeling* the responses with your body if possible.

- How do you feel when he looks you deeply in the eyes?
- Imagine how secure and loved you feel in his arms.
- Think of what he tells you as he holds you and strokes you.
- How do you feel about yourself as you experience being cherished, adored, and loved by the man of your dreams?
- Can you feel your heart opening? Can you feel your second chakra, the sexual center, opening? See that part of your body vibrating with orange light. Can you feel your throat chakra opening, freeing your communication—because you can tell him anything? See that part of your body pulsating in indigo blue.
- Imagine your anticipation of being with him in loving surrender, sharing the things you've only dreamed about before. What does it feel like, inside your body, when you think of opening to him and sharing your love?
- How does it feel to be loved by him? What's it like to be so in love?
- What does the scent of love smell like to you? Imagine the fragrance of your two bodies entwined.
- What does love sound like to you? The rhythmic beating of his heart, and yours, in harmony? The soft sound of his breath in your ear?
- How do you feel about life, about yourself, about your relationship when you are in his loving embrace? Let the journey take you deeper into your heart, to a place of awakening love—where the world feels so delicious and you feel so overwhelmingly

wonderful.

- What do you want more of when your bodies are entwined together? How open are you willing to be? How intimate do you truly want to be? How much do you want to give of yourself? How much do you want to receive?

- How does his skin feel when it's next to yours? And what does your flesh feel like against his? What is it like for you to feel him there, his physical being all around you . . . loving you . . . wanting you . . . and pleasing you?

- What are his kisses like? Does his mouth feel like your mouth, like you are the same person . . . as if you are not just sharing one kiss, but one mouth? What's it like to have someone there, always, kissing you and loving you?

- What does he say when he makes love? What words do you long to hear him tell you? How do you feel when he speaks them softly into your ear?

- Where is God when you make love? Where is the Goddess? Do you feel the divine energy of All That Is permeating your beings, making you each holy and whole, and uniting you in the God/Goddess force energy of pure love?

- Do you see the divinity in yourself through him; does he see his own God nature when he gives himself to you? Do you realize that this is the way it is meant to be—that we awaken one another to our own divine nature through love?

- What is it like to be a goddess, with your hero god, enraptured in divine love?

    CLOSE WITH THIS AFFIRMATION. Say it out loud and give it energy and life.

**I am cherished, loved, honored, and
adored by the soul mate of my dreams, now.**

GO TO SLEEP AFTER THIS MEDITATION AND AWAKE RE-FRESHED. Note how you feel in the morning and notice how people respond to you in the course of a day. This meditation can raise your energy so high that you begin to lift into your vision and live it more fully. Repeat it as often as you want. And send your wishes out into the universe to your true love, wherever he may be.

HOW TO KEEP RADHA WITH YOU

Get two jangling ankle bracelets. The Gopi cowherdesses are often pictured with dual ankle bracelets that jangle when they walk; the sacred dancers of India jangle in the same way. Wear your bracelets around the house and every time you hear their sounds mingle, think of your soulful lover and believe you can connect with him wherever he is.

Read her story. *The Gita Govinda* is the famous and beautiful epic Indian poem that tells of Krishna and Radha's longing for one another.

Surrender to the "aching" of Radha. It's okay to ache for love. Don't hide from it by drinking, overeating, compulsive shopping, compulsive "doing," or running around looking for ways to stay busy. It's okay to hunger for the embrace of your beloved. It will bring love even closer.

RADHA AFFIRMATION

"I am my beloved's, and my beloved is mine."

$\mathcal{I}$SIS

RESCUE YOUR RELATIONSHIP

*Love doesn't just sit there, like a stone, it has to be made, like bread;
re-made all the time, made new.*

—URSULA K. LEGUIN

WHILE THE IDEA OF LIVING happily ever after is what we all hope for, most of us will find that it takes some work; there is no such thing as the perfect partner or the perfect relationship. Our partner may be perfect for us, and we can even learn to see him as perfect just as he is, but even the most soulful and loving couples will have to slay a few "relationship dragons" as they travel the trail of true love together.

Eventually, as we put our energy toward striving to perfect our ability to love—instead of trying to "fix" our mates and ourselves—we will reap the rewards of a solid partnership. Our relationships will become our homes, and we will live as two against the world, instead of one. That home is a foundation upon which we can build our lives.

A good relationship must be created and nurtured over time. In the process, it is guaranteed that the person you love most will also challenge you, press your buttons, remind you of one or more parent, drive you nutty with the mirror he holds up in your face when you least want to look . . . and enfold you in arms that feel safer than any you have ever known before. A powerful way to keep your relationship sacred is to nip problems in the bud in a mature and loving fashion. Whether you are facing a major disagreement or an irksome miscommunication, it is important to make time for an immediate rescue—rather than wait until your relationship needs extraordinary measures and resuscitation.

Call upon Isis when it comes to demonstrating commitment to a partner and doing what it takes to make a relationship work. She helps us maintain extraordinary intimacy and divine relationships while still living in the real world. She represents commitment in the long haul, devotion, and keeping relationships sacred.

WHO IS ISIS?

She was the personification of the female creative power that conceived and brought forth every living creature and thing. She used power not only in creating new things but in restoring what was dead.
—*ANTHONY S. MERCANTE,*
WHO'S WHO IN EGYPTIAN MYTHOLOGY

Isis (*I-sis*) is one of the earliest and most important goddesses of ancient Egypt. Her worship, still active today in goddess religions, was a major part of Egyptian culture just over two thousand years ago; from there it spread to Greece, Rome, and elsewhere in the world, making her a universal goddess. Her image abounds on the walls of temples and tombs in Egypt and in museums worldwide. Because her powers and skills are so vast and all-encompassing, she's referred to as the "goddess of ten thousand names." She was known as healer, physician, enchantress, magician, patron of women in childbirth, mother, and devoted wife. Together with Thoth, scribe to the gods, she taught mankind the secrets of medicine. She represents both the maternal nurturing spirit and the ultimate magic of restoration and resurrection.

One of the most striking aspects of her story is her eternal relationship with her beloved Osiris—her brother, husband, lover, and co-ruler. Isis and Osiris shared the same soul. Along with siblings Set, Nepthys, and Horus (later known as Horus the Elder), they were nurtured in the womb of their mother, Nut, until it was time for their birth. Isis and Osiris ruled the rich lands of Egypt and taught their people agriculture, arts, and literacy. Their brother, Set, was jealous of Osiris and devised a plan to kill him—twice. Isis revived Osiris and brought him back; but after the second time he was never the same again. Isis was able to get pregnant with their son Horus, and raised him to seek vengeance for his father and claim his rightful place. Osiris became King of the Underworld and Isis the Queen of Heaven; together they ruled. She is often seen as a young mother suckling the infant Horus or as a trim Egyptian woman with dark hair, wearing formfitting gowns and elaborate jewelry. Her headdress is a throne or a solar disk with horns. She is sometimes seen with wings.

HOW TO INVITE HER INTO YOUR LIFE

Although we are unlikely to encounter *exactly* the same circumstances, woman can relate to the trials Isis had to endure to save her relationship. The first time Set killed Osiris, he tricked him into stepping into a coffin made especially for him and cast him upon the Nile. Isis was out of town delivering babies at the time. When she came home and found her husband missing, she threw on some raggedy clothes to disguise herself, and in emotional agony she combed the earth for her beloved. She asked everyone she saw about him, tracking every lead that might return her to her partner and best friend. She refused to let him go. She knew that if she kept looking, somehow Osiris would hear her and return. In *The First Love Stories*, Diane Wolkstein relays the call of Isis to her beloved as she searched for him:

My tears flood the land.
They burn my face.
Do not forsake me, Osiris.

When Isis finally found him, she had to turn herself into a winged goddess so she could fly and flap her wings above his body to fill his nose and mouth with air to revive him. It worked. Relieved, she hid Oriris somewhere she thought was safe. But when Set learned about Oriris's revival, he found him again, this time cutting his body into fourteen pieces and tossing them all about. Isis was able to gather every part of him except for his penis—so she made one out of wax and gold. She mounted him to conceive his heir, Horus, who would claim his father's kingdom on earth.

Isis and Osiris are together still, but Osiris is now in a different realm. Through his gates the dead must pass, if they are to be allowed into the afterlife. Isis has become the guardian of Osiris and of their sacred relationship—she loves him dearly, though he has changed.

To the human consciousness, it would appear that Isis is separated from her beloved by the veil between the worlds. But in truth, he is just a shout away. They are in many respects a working couple—she the Queen of Heaven; he the Lord of the Underworld—and they represent "as above, so below." As a working couple, each has separate responsibilities—just as you and your beloved get wrapped up in your jobs, your friends, your stress, and your fears. Sometimes, when enough time goes by, even people who adore one another can become distant and feel disconnected. Having truly been severed from her beloved, Isis knows how important it is to reconnect as soon as possible. Here is a loving, conscious way to share some time, clear the air, and reunite.

1. **Try this "Isis and Osiris renewal ritual for couples."** Before you begin, say a prayer to Isis—with or without your partner present—and ask her to share with you her great gift of

resurrection and rebirth so that you may be empowered to do this ritual with your own beloved. As a thank you, you can place an offering of incense, a loaf of bread, and two glasses of wine or juice for Isis and Osiris. Leave it on your kitchen table. When the ritual is complete, you and your honey can have a snack, on behalf of the God and Goddess. (Or, if your beloved may be resistant to a heart-to-heart ritual of reconnection, make a fabulous dinner and introduce the ritual as a fun idea that you hope might end with even more fun "making up.").

If you find yourself in unhappily-ever-after land, assess the situation and bring healing to any rifts, distances, or arguments. Perhaps you're rehashing an ongoing issue or you've both been working too much to spend time together. Find a quiet time and create a setting that will let you both decompress from the everyday stress of life and the stress of any relationship issues. Use this simple ritual to diffuse tension.

BRING IN LIGHT. Begin by lighting a pink candle, symbolizing the light of love.

GET INTO A LOVING MOOD. As a gentle meditation and attunement, close your eyes and "remember" love. This is an easy way to connect— or reconnect—if you've been feeling separate or distant from your beloved. Both of you can picture in your mind's eye a time in which you were completely in love with each other. Doing this will help set the intention for the ritual as well as create a feeling of being openhearted.

RECONNECT. Once you both feel centered, open your eyes and look deeply into the eyes of your beloved. Smile. Giggle. Feel whatever you feel, yet keep your eyes connected. It is especially potent if you hold hands as you hold eye contact. This is an effective way to look right into the soul of the one you love and to reestablish that soul connection.

TALK TO EACH OTHER. After a time of soulful connecting, open the floor to verbal communication. Each partner should have a designated period of time to speak—especially if there is a crisis or challenge in the relationship. For that period (ten to thirty minutes each) there should be no interruptions, comments, or excuses from the other side—just listening to what the beloved has to say. After that, the partner listening has a chance to share his or her views and experiences on that topic— or whatever is on that partner's mind and heart.

COMMUNICATE RESPONSIBLY. Take time to discuss needs, using "I" statements: *"I really need this"* or *"It would support me if I could have that."* Make a strong effort to never accuse or blame each other by using "you" statements, such as *"If only you would. . ."* or *"You never . . ."* Each partner should take responsibility for expressing needs, without an expectation of them being fulfilled by the other person. This gives both the space to say what they really want, without putting pressure on the other partner. Sharing pent-up feelings will take the steam out of them. Being able to do that with your partner, without retribution or shame, creates great freedom: an opening for giving and supporting one another.

BE PRESENT FOR EACH OTHER. This process helps couples reconnect to one another and to the power of their relationship, on an emotional, physical, intellectual, and spiritual level. You can use it any time. But when you really need time out together, it's useful to find a completely private, quiet place—ideally a hotel room—to hide away from all the distractions for a day or two and focus on being in the moment, together. It clears the mind, and the sinuses, as this ritual can lead to a wonderful "make up" intimacy.

It is helpful, after sharing individual needs, to reiterate your commitment to each other and to the ideas, projects, and experiences you want to create and share. There are many ways to reaffirm love and express the joy you feel. You can also do this as a separate ritual.

2. **Renew your vows or create a new intention for your relationship.** If you are married, you might want to repeat your wedding vows to one another while maintaining direct eye contact and holding hands. If you are in an exclusive, committed relationship, but not ready for legal marriage, consider sharing "commitment" vows. You can recommit to one another in the most casual way, just by speaking your heart, and by letting your feelings for each other be expressed by touch, movement, and eye contact.

HOW TO KEEP ISIS WITH YOU

Wear matching ankhs. The sign of the gods and goddesses of Egypt is the ankh, meaning eternal life. Get matching ankh rings or pendants to symbolize your eternal love for each other.

Always speak to and listen to one another. While Isis scoured Egypt for her beloved, she continued to speak to him. Though separated, they were never that far apart. People in love have the ability to communicate on many levels. Keep the channels open.

Send text or e-mail kisses during the day. The distance communication takes to travel between the two worlds is simple for a god and goddess. As modern-day Isis and Osiris, you can use e-mail to send love messages, concerns, thoughts that might be hard to say in person—and kisses and hugs—at any time of day! (Just watch out for bosses and nosy co-workers who might read your honey's expressions of love.)

ISIS AFFIRMATION

"I am in you. You are in me."

Part 4
GODDESSES OF
FAMILY LIFE AND FRIENDSHIP

 THE GREAT GODDESS

TRANSFORM YOUR RELATIONSHIP TO YOUR MOM

What unites all people of all times, is not that we are all mothers,
but that we have all been born of a mother who was born of a
mother who was born of a mother . . .
—DONNA WILSHIRE, *VIRGIN MOTHER CRONE*

WE'VE ALL HAD OUR ROCKY roads with our mothers. For some of us, it's still tough to be in the same room with Mom and feel like a grown-up. Just the sound of her voice is a hypnotic cue that can cast us back into childhood, into that old sense of "being little." She can get on our nerves like no other person can, and yet there's no one we'd rather run to when we have a problem, or call when there's a success to be shared.

Odd as it may seem, it's a completely natural phenomenon to long for our mother and at the same time feel let down by her. One reason is that we tend to place impossible, goddess-like expectations on our mother, forgetting that she is only human.

The mother-daughter connection is a sacred bond like no other. Although the umbilical cord has long been cut, there's an invisible power line that will always pull us back home. We are tethered for life to the one who brought us into the world. Although you may have spent years rejecting her worldview, when you begin to explore the path of the Goddess, you may feel a yearning to be closer to your mother, and you may just find yourself seeking a deeper connection

137

to your female ancestry. When you realize *we all* come from the Goddess, things change greatly in your relationship with Mom.

Call upon the Great Goddess when it comes to embracing your mother as well as your longing for *The Mother*. The Great Goddess shows you the power of the feminine that connects you to your mother, all women, and all ancestors. She helps you accept your mother's love and devotion as it is offered, while accessing a higher love from the Goddess of All That Is. She represents unconditional loving, nurturing, and positive parenting.

WHO IS THE GREAT GODDESS?

In the beginning people prayed to the Creatress of life, the Mistress of Heaven. At the very dawn of religion, God was a woman.
Do you remember?
—MERLIN STONE, WHEN GOD WAS A WOMAN

The Great Goddess is the Great Mother of all things, the source of all that is. She has been worshipped from the beginning of time and her worship continues today, by practitioners of goddess spirituality, Wicca, and other earth-based religions. She is the earth we stand on, the air we breathe, the fire we cook with, the waters of life that sustain us, and the spirit that lives inside us and all around us. She can be found in the history, mythology, sacred texts, spiritual practices, and folklore of every culture. The stories have many common elements, yet she is known by many names. In the beginning she was Inanna, Ishtar, Isis, Astarte, and Gaia; in modern times she's come to be known as Mother Nature. She is the very energy of a planet filled with life; she is life itself. She is fertility, death, and regeneration; we experience her through the flowers and trees, the moon and the ocean, the cycles of life and nature. Known in so many diverse forms—fluid like the ocean, strong like the ground, light as air, angry as the hurricanes, gentle as the first sign of spring—she is capable of adopting any role.

The earliest artifacts of goddess worship date back over thirty thousand years, and many believe that the first deity worshipped was a woman. She is often depicted as a full-figured female with a round, fecund belly, or as the earth herself.

HOW TO INVITE HER INTO YOUR LIFE

Like our own mother, the Great Goddess has always been in our life, but her presence is not always acknowledged or announced. Just as our mom is *there for us*, the Great Goddess has stuck around— through all our rejections, tantrums, fits, and taking her for granted. Understanding her role in our lives can connect us more deeply to our own mother. You may have concluded that your mother comes from another planet, but in truth, she hails from the same source as you—and all women.

1. **Reflect on these insights to help you with Mom.**

    MOTHERS ARE HUMAN. One of the reasons we become disappointed by our own mother, or feel that she isn't all we want her to be, is that we have a hard time accepting that she is human and imperfect. As babies we see Mommy as all-powerful; as kids we tend to see her as an all-knowing mother goddess who retains her power over all. She seems to be a master of the mysteries of life, and of healing. Yet being human, she has her flaws. She perhaps could never give us the kind of all-embracing spiritual sustenance we seek, or maybe she just is not as hip or with it as we'd like. It's humbling when we realize that Mom really cannot be all things to all people at all times, or always offer all the comfort we need. She cannot be the absolute everything that a deity is. You may even discover that while she may personify a mother goddess to you, she is not your "spiritual mother." And that's okay.

    WE CAN LEARN TO PARENT OURSELVES. As we grew up, our

mother used the resources she had to be the best parent she could be. But we cannot expect her to provide the magic and empowerment that the Great Goddess instills in us when we look to her to further our evolution. Ultimately, the Great Goddess shows us we can parent ourselves—the way we wish we'd been parented—and rely on ourselves. She encourages us as we strive for independence, trusts us to find our way in the world, helps us see the world as abundant and full of resources, and has faith that we can take care of our own needs. We may find that this leads us to a more authentic, relaxing, and enjoyable relationship with our mother: Mom doesn't feel she has to take care of us all the time, and we don't feel compelled to ask for help every time we get into a bind.

WE CAN EXPLORE MOTHER'S MYSTERIES. Our mother teaches us about the first mysteries of life, simple facts about how the world works, and also about sexuality, menstruation, and other landmarks of growing up. But the key to the "something bigger in life" goes beyond our one mom. Some religions and spiritual practices call out to the Goddess with the same reverence that other faiths call out to Christ, or Allah, or Buddha. We have many options for connecting with her in ritual, in celebration, and through nature.

2. **Reunite with your mother.** Many ancient religions focus on honoring the ancestors as a way of healing family relationships and rebirthing ourselves. You grow closer to your mother when you honor the source of who she is—and own it as the source of who you are. This exercise helps you connect to your mother through your family roots.

HONOR YOUR MOTHER AND FEMALE ANCESTORS. Ask your mother to help you in a special project to honor family roots by creating an "ancestor table." This will be a special altar table in your own home, featuring pictures of women in your family—your mom, grandmothers, sisters, aunts, and relatives from Mom's side—and special heirlooms or reminders. Also include a childhood picture and a more recent shot of you and your mother. The purpose of this ancestor table is to give you a visual link to your past, get in touch with the humanity of your family, and yet connect with the great power of the feminine that the ancients believed connected us to the Great Goddess, mother of us all.

SHARE SOME GIRL TALK WITH YOUR MOTHER. Get Mom talking about family history—the basic background as well as any scandals and wild tales, especially stories that highlight the special traits of female relatives. Was there a warrior queen or a preacher in your background, a farmer or a burlesque dancer? Go back as far into the family tree as possible. Especially try to find out if the women in the family had any particular strengths (*physical strength, the breadwinner, great cook, could drive a tractor, a healer, a loving person, took a leap of faith and left home and family to get married*, and so on). Take notes. Look for what was special about your relatives. And use this topic to gather a little more insight about your mother. Listen especially to how she talks about her mom; therein lies the key to how she learned to be a mother to you.

LOOK AT FAMILY PHOTOS TOGETHER. Get your mom to pull out the family photo albums and as you look through them, get her talking some more about the womenfolk. Pick at least one picture of each relative who will be on the ancestor table. Assure her you'll have copies made if she doesn't want to give up the originals. Realize that as you gather up the pictures you are embracing the special energy of the feminine that birthed your mother before you, her mother before her, and so on.

PUT THE PICTURES IN BEAUTIFUL FRAMES. If the originals are tiny, enlarge them through the magic of photo scanning or photo quality copy machines. Have your mom come over (if possible) and help you arrange them on the ancestor table.

ADD FAMILY HEIRLOOMS TO THE TABLE. If you have a piece of

jewelry, a hankie, or special item passed along by any of the relatives, include it on the table.

REPRESENT THE GODDESS USING THE ELEMENTS. Add the energy of the Great Goddess to the table by placing items that represent the four elements: air (a feather), water (tap water in a small cup or bowl, preferably one that belonged to your mom or grandmother), fire (a candle), earth (a pot or bowl of earth, preferably from your mother's backyard or neighborhood).

PICK OUT THE BEST FAMILY TRAITS. Review your notes about the special strengths of the women in your family. Type or inscribe them on a beautiful piece of paper like a scroll and title the list "The Strengths of Our Womenfolk." Buy two identical frames. Send one framed copy of the "strengths" to your mom for her home, and place one on your ancestor table.

VISIT WITH THE WOMENFOLK. Sit with them every day for a spell. Bring flowers, or favorite candies, or a special offering to the ancestors. (For example, if your grandmother grew corn, bring a stalk to her; if great-grandmother raised cows, bring a glass of milk; if she loved to sip tea, bring her a cup.) When you are having rough or confusing times (with your mother, your path in life, or your comprehension of the Great Goddess), ask the womenfolk to help soothe and improve things. When you are feeling low, read the list of family strengths and know they are in you as well. If you connect to the source of who you are, your relationship with your mom will naturally begin to improve and transform. Pray for what you need in the presence of your ancestors and ask for their help:

> **Ancient mothers and ancestors, please guide me, for you see what I cannot yet know. Let me take on your strengths and your spirit as appropriate to help me in daily life. Let me find my way in the world and still stay close to my own mother. Ancient mother, ancient spirit, please guide and protect me.**

3. **Heal misunderstandings with Mom.** Give misunderstandings to the Great Goddess for healing. If your relationship with your mother is strained or troubled, if you have trouble communicating, or if your mother has passed on and you feel incomplete in your relationship, it is important to try to heal it spiritually. Write down everything that is upsetting you. Roll the list up like a scroll and leave it on the ancestor table, with a prayer to the ancestors to help. Take another copy to a place where you can bury it in Mother Earth—a park, a backyard. With a little prayer of thanks to the Great Goddess, bury your list of concerns and pray that the Goddess take them into herself and transform them, giving your relationship with Mom a rebirth when the time is right. The Great Goddess takes things into her body—the earth—and returns them renewed. Ask her to bless both you and your mother with a happy resolve. Then do something nice for your mom. You might have a tree planted in her hometown or wherever her family roots are. Or make a donation to her favorite charity.

4. **Connect to the Great Goddess in prayerful chant.** In the practice of ancient earth religions, people gathered to ceremonially honor the Great Goddess and affirm their connection to her. They acknowledged themselves as her children. Today, many practitioners of earth religions and goddess spirituality sing her praises in brief repeated chants, sung over and over. These simple statements, such as the traditional "We all come from the Goddess" chant, connect us to the Mother of All Things. The following words were composed and are copyrighted by Z. Budapest.

> **We all come from the Goddess,**
> **and to her we shall return.**
> **Like a drop of rain, flowing to the ocean.**

HOW TO KEEP THE GREAT GODDESS WITH YOU

Hug your mother whenever possible. Reach out. She is a living link to the Great Goddess. In your life, she is the *first* mother of all things!

Keep a portrait of the Earth. An image from space of the planet we call home can remind you how precious and beautiful our Universal Mother is.

Spend time with Mom Nature. A walk in the park, a talk on the patio, a hike up a mountain, a moment gazing at the full moon, a swim in the sea—all will bring you closer to her.

Praise her in song. A wonderful way to stay in touch with the many traditions of the Great Goddess and to honor the divine ancestry of your mother is with the CD *Ancient Mother*, by On Wings of Song with Robert Gass. It's a wonderful collection of classic goddess chants from many traditions, performed by traditional singers and priestesses.

THE GREAT GODDESS AFFIRMATION

"We all come from the Great Goddess."

PELE

CHANNEL ANGER AND HEAL HOSTILITY

Holding on to anger is like grasping a hot coal with the intent of
throwing it at someone else; you are the one that gets burned.

—BUDDHA

FOR SOME OF US, NOTHING can stimulate anger like an
afternoon at a family function. Weddings and funerals are
notorious for stirring up the fires of family hostility and upset; a
simple holiday gathering can do the same in some clans. Much as
you love 'em, these people somehow know how to push all your
buttons. There are certain family members, and even close friends,
who do it to us every time. The result is often the same—we end up
getting angry and we express that anger outwardly or, worse, we turn
it inward because we don't want to upset others.

Some of us are like volcanoes ready to pop—fiery, angry,
permanently pissed off, and not afraid to show it and shout it.
Others need some inspiration to spew out some of the feelings
that are activated by family members; we also need help learning
to protect ourselves from the wrath of others. Anger can be useful
when acknowledged and utilized to propel self-development and
change for the better in family life. But anger unchecked makes
us sick, literally: excessive unexpressed rage will raise stress levels
so high that blood pressure can boil over. Yet if we express rage

excessively and live angry lives, we fare no better. We need a middle ground for acknowledging the pain that anger often masks, and for healing the hostility that is sometimes generated by unresolved and unexpressed issues with family and close friends.

Call upon Pele when it comes to dealing with anger and hostility. She expresses her rage without holding back, and yet she is a natural equalizer of anger. If you blow your top too easily, Pele can soften your temper; if you never quite express yourself, she helps you find your voice. She represents the power of fiery anger and hostility, passionate self-expression and responsibility over rage.

WHO IS PELE?

Pele is often thought of as a cruel goddess. This is untrue. Yes, she has a temper and possesses the power to vent her anger in a spectacular fashion, but her worshippers accept this as part of her nature.
—SCOTT CUNNINGHAM, *HAWAIIAN RELIGION AND MAGIC*

Pele *(PAY-lay)* is the ancient goddess who lives on the Big Island of Hawaii, in the famous Kilauea volcano, the world's most active. She was a pivotal deity in the ancient religion that reigned in Hawaii until Christian missionaries came and converted the native peoples in the 1800s. Her spirit and legends abound, and many consider the volcano her permanent temple; there is a long history of worship and sacrifice at her fiery altar. It is said that when Pele was a small child she did not like the water, as her sisters and brothers did. Eventually, as she came into her power, she shaped and formed her abode into the Big Island of Hawaii, where her red hot lava seeped down to the sea, creating lava rocks, jagged cliffs, and black sand beaches that still stand today.

The story of Pele's rage reflects the love-hate relationship between sisters. It speaks of sibling rivalry and, ultimately, forgiveness. When she was young, Pele met Lohiau, the young chief of Kauai; they fell in love and promised themselves to one another. But Pele missed her fiery home and headed back to her volcano. Soon she pined for Lohiau and realized she could not do without him. So she sent her trusted sister, Hi'iaka, on the perilous journey to the neighboring isle of Kauai to get him. As the two traveled back, her sister fell in love with the handsome prince. In anger, Pele killed him, *twice*, and Hi'iaka revived him. Pele spewed her angry lava to and fro and banned her sister from her island.

Her sister had stolen her beloved, and she expressed her anger without apology. It took some time but she eventually simmered down and forgave Hi'iaka. Having a new lover, Kamapua'ua, whose temperament matched her own, helped quell her jealous anger. Pele is pictured as mistress of the Kilauea volcano. It is considered her center, while the lava is often seen as her red, flowing hair.

HOW TO INVITE HER INTO YOUR LIFE

You can tell when Pele is pissed. Yet beneath the surface of her fiery eruptions is a great, bright light. Pele lives in the spirit of fire, a glorious element that brings warmth, excitement, passion, healing, and a sense of the sacred. But fire also burns. It can ravage and ruin our lives if it is not handled responsibly; its fierceness must be respected and carefully monitored. Many times over the years, people have watched in awe as the goddess's fiery temper destroyed everything in its path during volcanic eruptions. The same is true of our anger. When we direct anger at others, our words can slice and wound them. If we are the recipients of someone else's anger, we may be hurt in that same way. Words of anger can destroy our relationships, friendships, and opportunities. Yet anger and hostility that is unexpressed, unacknowledged, and unhealed can burn away at our insides and cause all sorts of emotional, physical, and spiritual health issues. The great sages of all time have warned: *Master anger or it will master us.* The ancients made offerings to Pele to appease and please her—and to settle her fury. It is important that we too offer up our anger to Pele so we can learn to utilize it, channel it appropriately, and heal its consequences in our lives.

Identifying and Understanding Anger

1. **Know thyself—and who pushes your buttons.** If you get queasy, nervous, or moody right before a family function, or before a designated time to be spent with certain family members or friends, chances are you are reacting to anticipatory stress, based on memories of family gatherings, and traumas, of the past. You may know exactly who and what gets your goat when you are with your family—or it might just be a dull ache somewhere that gets activated around certain people. It is essential to demystify the things you feel angry about and sort out why you feel so angry. Look at each situation from all angles and pick it apart until it is no longer mysterious or frightening. Treat the next family gathering as a research project and gather information:

   CLEARLY IDENTIFY YOUR HOT SPOTS. Don't feel bad about admitting who makes you angry. List the family members you have issues with and how you feel about them. Be real. *Does Mom drink too much and get nasty? Is your grandmother overcritical? Do siblings get on your nerves?* Get in touch with *what they do* that triggers unsettling emotions in you. This is the first step to transforming your reaction to other people's behavior.

   NOTICE YOUR OWN REACTIONS. So what do you do when you feel trapped? Overeat? Drink? Shop? Get lost in online chat rooms for hours? Do you fall asleep, withdraw, go unconscious and essentially avoid hot spots? Do you cry, whine, get cranky and have tantrums like a child? Do you explode inappropriately with anger? Or do you desperately want to flee but feel sentenced to family hell—and finally go home feeling drained, unhappy, or depressed?

PRETEND YOU'RE A REPORTER. Your assignment is a documentary on dysfunctional family gatherings. Pull back for a moment and become an observer in your own mind and memory. See if you can make a connection. For example: *When Mom drinks and gets nasty, I feel like I want to leave, but I can't get away, so instead I overeat to protect and comfort myself.* Or: *When my brother tries to hit me up for money, again, I resent him and I scream at him and we end up fighting all afternoon.* If you consciously map out some of the "cause and effect" behaviors that trigger anger and hostility in your family, you might be able to discern some specific behavior dynamics. Once you identify the dysfunction and the reaction to it, you are closer to healing yourself and bringing healing to your family.

2. **Leave a peace offering and memorize a prayer.** The ancients made the ultimate offering to Pele: they gave her the remains of their loved ones, utilizing her fire as the funeral pyre. They also gave her pigs and other gifts to quell her anger and keep her at peace. If you feel that the volcano of rage may be stimulated in you or a family member, try to neutralize the energy in advance with this simple ritual.

ASK FOR PELE'S LIGHT AND FIRE TO GUIDE YOU. You can also evoke Pele by lighting a candle, then ask her to support you through difficult family gatherings and issues, and help you to deal with anger—yours and other people's.

MAKE A PEACE OFFERING. Leave a flower on your altar for Pele and one near a photo of yourself, to energetically cast a peaceful, natural vibe on the day.

SAY A PRAYER. Do you have an anger problem with someone? Say your own version of this prayer, naming whatever fits your needs.

Pele, goddess of the fiery volcano, lady of the light:
I give to you my anger at _____ [name the person].

> **I give to you my fear of _____'s [name the person] anger.**
> **I give to you whatever keeps me angry.**
> **I give to you whatever keeps me from expressing how I feel.**

Then tell her *"mahalo"* (Hawaiian for "thank you").

MEMORIZE A SHORT PEACE AFFIRMATION. Speak it to yourself, in your own head, over again on your way to a family event. It can be as simple as this: *"Pele, queen of molten lava, this is too hot for me to handle. I surrender this to you."*

3. **Manage your emotions.** Historically, Pele is believed to have poured her wrath out in the form of volcanic eruptions. Some of us have personalities like that—or relatives like that! You can't change someone who is a rageaholic, but if you're the one raging uncontrollably, it's time to get a grip. When you feel you may fly into a rage because family members are aggravating you so much, you have to step back, assess the situation, and answer these questions truthfully: *Is someone in your family really being an offensive idiot? Or are you feeling out of control because something's been said or done that has touched a nerve or exposed a vulnerability in you?* Sometimes we try to defend our raw spots with a warring spirit in order to hide our truer feelings. Sometimes we go on automatic pilot and, quite predictably, get reactivated by someone else's hostility. We must learn to assess a situation and take ourselves out of it when we need to.

OBSERVE RATHER THAN PARTICIPATE IN FAMILY DRAMATICS. The Kalapana Safe Viewing program in Hawaii provides a safe place for observation so that you can experience Pele's eruptions without having to give yourself over as a sacrifice. Use the same principle to distance yourself and protect yourself from anger-charged situations. If you withdraw your energy from the situation, the fire will die down. It will take the charge off your emotions, and it won't give argumentative relatives anything to work with.

Try this three-step breathing exercise to help you hang in there.
a) Take a moment to breathe deeply before you say a word or
react in any way: just pause, even if all hell is breaking loose.
On that first exhale, choose to let go of confusion and illusion
so you can see the problem rationally and clearly. Think: *What
is really going on here?*
b) Breathe in again fully. When you exhale again, hold the intention that you are breathing out the agitation you feel. Make
a choice: instead of getting reactivated—which just perpetuates
the problem—you will simmer down through breathing.
c) Inhale again and imagine you're flipping a switch inside you,
turning on your internal cooling system, an air conditioner for the
soul. Feel the fresh, delightful cool air come on, making the heat
of anger die down. Relax. Stand firm in your sense of calm.

Repeat those steps as needed as you learn to use your breath to
center yourself. If you find that "breathing through it" isn't working,
change the energy and location. Take time out. Take a walk, go to
the store, leave the premises—and detach from what is going on.

4. **Release yourself from pent-up anger.** Some of us store anger in
   our bodies and turn it into illness and self-hatred. It can simmer
   or smoulder for years, and eventually erupt—either inside us,
   or onto others. Anger keeps us attached to people who make
   us angry in an unhealthy way. Holding on to it means we must
   keep anger in our hearts. Not a good idea! You can heal anger,
   hostility, and rage by expressing it responsibly.

IN GENERAL, WHENEVER POSSIBLE, TAKE ISSUES STRAIGHT TO
THE SOURCE. If you conquer anger at its source, it will not conquer
you. Tell the person the truth using "I" statements, rather than
blaming or accusing, then let the chips fall where they may. The
person will either "get it" or not. Sharing it honestly, when possible,
is a way to release pent-up anger so that it doesn't come out in

inappropriate ways. Sometimes, just having the courage to try to clear the air is enough to clear the air—for you.

LET OFF SOME STEAM. Not everyone can go to the source and tell people directly how angry they make us. But we can take the edge off anger in ways that aren't self-destructive. To chill out after a family gathering or other triggering interaction, get physical:

a) Run, go to the gym, swim, play basketball, or take a long walk.

b) Go home and hit some pillows.

c) For heavy-duty pent-up anger, try kickboxing or learning to (safely) punch a punching bag.

d) Dance to your favorite music.

5. **Share the story of your anger in a safe space.** Pele has always made her wrath a public spectacle; at the very least, she communicates her feelings. It helps to share and let others bear witness to your pain and anger. Group therapy or a professionally supervised spiritual group is a good start; Twelve Step recovery programs are always an option. There are many emerging online communities as well. Find a group that will treat your sharing as sacred and honor you in whatever place you are at in your healing process.

6. **Sing out your shame and give it over to Pele.** Musical prayers and songs take the shame out of us, deliver it into the hands of the divine, and uplift us so we can be healed. Hawaiian music that evokes the spirit of Pele can be very soothing, even if we don't understand the words. The people of Hawaii still sing and chant for Pele and Kilauea. Try this simple ancient chant.

E ola mau, e Pele e! 'Eli'eli kau mai!
(Ee-o-la-mao e Pay-lay ee! E-lee-e-lee ka my!)
Long life to you, Pele!

You might also want to chant whatever else comes to mind— even if it's gibberish. Chanting can release pent-up hostile energy and disperse negative feelings that may arise when you inventory your history of pain and anger.

HOW TO KEEP PELE WITH YOU

Meet her in her Hawaiian homeland. Pele's home, the Big Island, is one of the most breathtaking of the Hawaiian Islands. You can visit the island as a tourist and get ever so close to her, standing in the volcano crater itself and watching aspects of her fiery, smoky nature.

Gather her special tools. It's said that Pele had a magic *pa'oa* stick to help her find fire at her new home, and that her mother gave Pele a magic egg. Pele won't like it if you take sticks or rocks from her own beaches, but why not try to find a piece of driftwood and an egg-shaped rock at a beach near where you live? Imbue them with a Pele blessing and keep them near.

Name a star after one who's passed on. If you're holding anger mixed with love in your heart for someone who is deceased, try healing it from high above. Give that person a place in the eternal cosmic dance, a place where the soul knows no anger. It is said that Pele followed the northern star and found Hawaii; perhaps you can follow a star and find deeper healing. Contact the International Star Registry to have a star named for that person; you'll soon have the paperwork showing that you've devoted a part of the heavens to someone you cared about. Maybe from that perspective you can sense that the person is watching over you—and will never hurt you again.

PELE AFFIRMATION

"My fiery spirit is a healing force."

ALI

DANCE WITH THE HUNGRY GHOSTS OF YOUR PAST

If you cannot get rid of the family skeleton, you may as well dance with it.

—GEORGE BERNARD SHAW

EVERY FAMILY HAS ITS DARK secrets. And we all have our "elephants in the room"—the issues that are so obvious but are never acknowledged, discussed, or healed. Many of us have lives shaped around dysfunctional family backgrounds, and we tend to try to disassociate from them as we get older. It's a good idea to grow up and leave the past behind. But if we don't examine the pain of the past and try to heal it, we will drag it with us through life—and the hungry ghosts of our past will plague us.

We tend to think of ghosts as "supernatural" beings who haunt and taunt us and somehow chain us to our fears. They make a racket and loom around us so threateningly that we feel we must do something to quiet them down. Our very survival seems to be at stake. But what is scariest and most unsettling about a ghost is that we don't really know what it is: lost spirit or fiendish monster of our own mind? All we know is that there is a presence that somehow holds a power over us; we may not even know why. They may not be Hollywood poltergeists, but family members and others in our past with whom we share unresolved issues can haunt us just as surely.

154

Whether they're our flesh-and-blood living relatives, the deceased, or others who've moved on from our lives, hungry ghosts can insidiously haunt our daily lives—until we make a decision to set them free.

It's a human impulse to run from the darkness. Yet when you understand the truth about the shadow cast by hungry ghosts, you won't feel the need to run. Learn what they've come to teach you by making all that racket in your life—and then say "Boo!"

Call upon Kali when it comes to stepping into the darkness to heal the past and defuse the power of hungry ghosts and haunting family history. She helps adjust our attitudes so we can laugh in the face of fear and dance away our shadows and shame. She goes into the darkness to swallow our sins, worries, and concerns. She represents embracing the shadow, facing fear head on, and radically transforming your life.

WHO IS KALI?

In Mahakali there is an overwhelming intensity,
a mighty strength, a force to shatter all obstacles . . . sometimes she
assumes a frightening form and sometimes a benevolent form.
—AJIT MOOKERJEE,
KALI: THE FEMININE FORCE

Kali *(KAA-lee)*, also known as Kali Ma and the Black Mother, is the powerful Hindu goddess who presides over darkness, death and regeneration. She is the foremost of the tantric wisdom goddesses known as the *Mahavidyas*. Some fear her because she is so fearsome looking, but Hindus love and adore her as their Great Mother Goddess; she manifests power that is fierce, potent, healing, and loving. She is *shakti* (female energy) incarnate and the manifestation of primordial power. As the darker consort of Lord Shiva (who is also paired with the milder Parvati), she is often pictured dancing wildly with his form beneath her feet. She brings life and death, regeneration and rebirth. Her haunts are cremation grounds. She slays the evil demon known as the ego and beheads it; she eats pain, despair, and the secret shadows of our lives. Kali eradicates worn-out thoughts and beliefs that no longer serve us—and not always gently, as she uses a machete-like sacred sword to quickly do the job. She is a wild-eyed goddess, usually seen with skin that is black or blue to represent the darkness she takes out of humans. Her jewelry is a garland of men's skulls around her neck. Her tongue sticks out of her mouth, and she has four arms, a symbol of domination over the world. In one hand she holds a head dripping blood; in the other three she wields sacred weapons. One of her hands removes fear and grants bliss.

HOW TO INVITE HER INTO YOUR LIFE

Kali is the universal mother who can swallow all your sins and hack away the handcuffs that keep you shackled to the hungry ghosts of your past. She goes with you into the darkness—for you must see it, know it, and own it to be free of it. Kali enters it for you, represents you, and eats away at the darkness that is eating you. There comes a point in the process when you must surrender fully to her healing powers and let her bring you back cleansed, transformed, whole.

Keep in mind that this may not be an easy journey, as it requires you to own up to your darkest secrets and the parts of your life you have worked to keep hidden from others. In addition, some of us tend to get attached to our life problems as well as our personal ghosts. They are often people we love, know, or have known well, and it's not easy to let them go. We have grown accustomed to them, and are intimate with the way they go bump in the dark night of the soul. They scare us, but they are familiar and we may fear what life may be like without their racket and disruptions. These thoughts, prayers, and exercises will help you connect to Kali.

1. **Try this "Cosmic Talk Show" meditation.** Daytime television, reality TV, and online videos that peek into people's lives have become a contemporary arm of the goddess Kali, leading us through the dysfunctions of family life and digging up the old bones long buried in the backyard. And they can give us all a chance for catharsis and release. The father who drank, the mother who gambled, the uncle who abused, the brother who drugged, the cheating spouse—all have become talk show icons, parading their problems across the screen and showing us that we all have "issues," and there is always someone who is worse off. Crazy as some of these people may seem, they all reveal a part of us. They showcase their dramas and traumas on our behalf.

    In this exercise, you'll take on the task of freeing yourself from pain and shame by sharing it the way many people do these days: going on TV! Your TV show will be in your mind, and your studio will be entered through a meditation. You'll need a black candle, a TV set, and some time alone. (Note: This is not a task for the meek-hearted; it's suggested only for those who are ready to confront the hungry ghosts of the past.)

    SIT DOWN FOR THE SHOW OF YOUR LIFE. Take a seat in front of your TV for inspiration, but don't turn it on. Think of talk shows and reality shows that focus on people working through bizarre problems. Then, in the theater of your mind, create a composite talk show—*The Kali Show*—with a host who embodies the goddess's qualities: harsh when she has to be, honest to the bone, and willing to take your hand, lead you into darkness, then stand close by to pull you out when you've had your fill.

    BEGIN WITH PRAYER AND PRAISE TO KALI. Thank her for her help and for inviting you to *The Kali Show*. Hindus praise Mother Kali in many ways. She is considered the great, all-powerful *Devi* (Sanskrit for goddess), the dark destructress and the rebirther of the new you. Call to her in this *Shloka*, or prayer to Devi (from

Hindunet.com).

> **O mother, who is present everywhere, who is embodiment of Universal Mother,**
> **O mother, who is present everywhere, who is embodiment of Power and Energy,**
> **O mother, who is present everywhere, who is embodiment of Peace,**
> **I bow to thee, I bow to thee, I bow to thee.**

LIGHT A CANDLE TO THE SHADOW OF SHAME. Before you begin, light a black candle to shine a beacon into the darkness. The candle represents Kali Ma—the dark goddess—and it contains your shame, pain, and fear; your depression and sadness. Whatever happened in your childhood is past, yet there may be incidents that your mind won't lay to rest. Like a video that never ends, your mind replays them again and again: they may be so embedded in your psyche that they run your life without your realizing it. Even if an incident was brief, even fleeting, you must take your time now to honor your own process of discovery and gain insight. As the candle burns down, it melts the darkness in you so you can see the light of any given situation. Imagine that Kali is taking in all the blackness, so you no longer have to.

IN YOUR MIND'S EYE, SEE YOURSELF ON THE KALI *SHOW.* Sitting comfortably with your feet on the ground to anchor you, take three cleansing breaths and close your eyes. Imagine you are backstage at *The Kali Show,* waiting for the goddess to introduce you. Feel any nervousness you may have about going on TV to tell your family secrets. See Kali walk onstage to audience applause. Notice that she isn't as big or scary as you imagined. She seems tough yet kind. Trust that she will help you through this. Know in that moment you will be able to lean into Kali, for she is the cosmic talk-show host who can expose the dark root of your problem. She is the Great Mother who will nurture and protect you in the process.

TELL KALI AND THE WORLD THE TRUTH ABOUT YOUR PAIN.
Kali calls you from your backstage cocoon, and you stride out onto
national TV. The studio audience sits waiting to hear your dark
secrets. Millions of people will watch this show, including the people
you may talk about. But Kali assures you that if you get it out of your
system, you'll be fine: expressing your pain out loud is the first step to
healing it. She urges you to take this opportunity to inventory every
horrible thing you hold against your family, and against yourself. Own
your own darkness. *Why do you feel so wounded? What happened in your
past that caused you greatest pain?* It's time to tell them how they've hurt
you. Notice the feelings that course through you. Are you afraid to tell
the truth, or is it liberating? Whatever the feeling, keep following Kali's
instructions. Know that you are safe, you are grounded.

WHO ARE YOUR HUNGRY GHOSTS? Kali, Queen of the Cremation
Grounds, demands now that you identify the hungry ghosts of your
past: name the relatives and loved ones who haunt you. They can
be dead or alive. Be honest. *Who do you blame for your wounds? Who
has hurt you, betrayed you, messed your life up in some way? Who brings
tears to your eyes; who has scarred your soul?* Kali asks you to name
them one by one, and then asks you to look into the camera and talk
to them. She places a warm hand on your back for comfort and says,
"Go ahead, look them in the eye and tell them how they hurt you."
The camera zooms in for an extreme close-up and she encourages
you to feel the depth of pain, to relive the initial trauma. There's no
place to hide: it's time for the shame to be laid bare. The audience
starts chanting your name, encouraging you to address your ghosts.
You feel fear welling up inside—and also words that want to be
released. You try to hold the words back; you feel them burning
in your throat. Then you realize you can't keep the ghosts safe for
one moment longer. They must be exposed. And you realize that all
these years you've been hurting yourself trying to protect the people
who hurt you. Big hurts or little ones, you've turned them against

yourself. Kali is showing all four arms, and you feel them on you. "Go ahead," she urges, "Tell them now, and you'll never have to tell them again."

TELL YOUR "SHAMEFUL" SECRETS. Blurt them out. *Dad, you bastard, you ruined my life . . . Mom, you made me hate myself . . . Sister, you stole my attention . . . Brother, you broke my heart . . . Grandma, you never loved me . . . Uncle John, you took my innocence.* Whatever comes up, let it hurl. And hurl it right into Kali's open arms. She is ready to take on your pain and more. Don't be afraid. Let it out of you until there is nothing left to say. Then allow a moment of silence and even allow the audience a moment of shock. Then watch the shame disperse.

DANCE WITH DARKNESS. As a surprise, Kali has brought all the people you have just vented about to the studio. And somehow, when she brings them onstage, they don't seem so scary. They seem small, weak, tired, and powerless. The parts of them that frightened you once suddenly seem deflated. They can no longer hurt you. Kali begins the wild dance of death and regeneration. She begins to dance with your hungry ghosts and suddenly they are smiling. They are no longer ghosts who drain your battery and steal your life force. They are people. Regular people. They have no power over you. Kali teaches you to dance with the darkness; no longer will it feed your fears or shame. Music is playing and you dance like a wild woman— with Kali, and with all the hungry ghosts. You dance away darkness and shame. Your heart is lighter.

And when you are ready, you feel an interesting feeling wash over you—forgiveness!

2. **Surrender to Kali.** If you are in deep pain about your past and truly yearn for liberation, surrender it in its entirety to goddess Kali. There comes a point when we must allow *her* to decide how to handle things because we are clueless and emotionally paralyzed. Sometimes in order to gain everything, we must lose everything

and then build our lives anew. We live in fear of the transition period—in which all seems lost. We are too preoccupied with fear and guilt to see our way clear. Surrender your problems and fears to Kali. She'll return them in a transformed and perhaps unrecognizable form, and your life will be forever changed in an empowering way. Here is a releasing exercise to help you give over your issues to Kali:

- Anytime you feel anxiety, stop in your tracks and imagine that Kali is standing in front of you, ready to catch anything you want to surrender her way.
- Think of your problem or feeling of the moment—feel it, and then forcefully blow that feeling out of your body through your mouth.
- Catch it in your cupped hands as if it's a small ball of energy.
- Extend your arms and your cupped palms as in a gesture of holy offering. Hold the ball of energy in place for a moment. Bless it. Thank it for the lessons it has taught you.
- Then when you are ready, look at Kali Ma standing before you, a loving presence, and toss her all your cares.
- Thank her.

HOW TO KEEP KALI WITH YOU

Surrender unto her. Any time you feel haunted by hungry ghosts of the past, call to Kali and ask her to hold you close and take the emotional toxins from you.

Keep her image near. Place it on the inside of your front door as a symbol that this home is protected by Kali. This way it will shield you from negative energies coming from the outside as well as any generated inside the home.

Get a spiritual tuneup. When you sense a resurgence of hungry ghosts, Kali can help you put life in perspective. Call to her with this salutation (from kalimandir.org): *"To the Devi who abides in all beings in the form of intelligence, Salutations to Her, Salutations to Her, Salutations again and again."*

KALI AFFIRMATION

"My truth shall set me free."

$\mathscr{S}$AINT LUCY (LUCINA)

BRING LIGHT AND VISION TO YOUR FAMILY

> She would rather light a candle than curse the darkness.
> —DAG HAMMARSKJÖLD, ABOUT ELEANOR ROOSEVELT

$\mathbf{P}$ERHAPS YOU LOVE YOUR FAMILY, but you realize that they need a little work. No family is perfect, and not every family is as conscious as we might wish, but there is hope. You can be the bringer of light in your house, the lamp-bearer who tries to bring healing to the tribe.

Oftentimes, in family situations, we harbor ancient hurts and injuries and use the pain of the past to build a wall between us. But the wall can be breached. It just takes one person willing to boldly go where no family member has gone before, to try to heal family rifts and establish a little more "awareness" within the fold.

First, we have to open our own eyes and see our family members in a different light. Rather than accusing them of *this* and *that* and holding history against them, perhaps we can see them as who they are in the world. Open your mind to their whole being, but remember that there's no guarantee of a new perspective. Sometimes our greatest awareness about certain people and situations is that we can do nothing to heal them; that we must move on, let go, and focus that light on healing ourselves. An organic benefit of self-healing is that it's sometimes catching, and as we allow our light to

163

shine, it touches others and inspires them to let a new light shine through as well.

Call upon Saint Lucy (Lucina) when it comes to opening our eyes and shedding new light on old situations. She has the ability to see with spiritual eyes, and she teaches you to do the same. She represents bringing the light and seeing things as they are, and as they can be.

WHO IS SAINT LUCY?

Santa Lucia,
Thy light is glowing,
Through darkest winter night,
Comfort bestowing.
Dreams float on dreams tonight,
Comes then the morning light,
Santa Lucia, Santa Lucia.
—*ITALIAN DEVOTIONAL SONG*

The popular Saint Lucy was a medieval martyr who fought religious oppression and insisted on a life of light-bringing and devotion to Christianity and humanity. Alleged to be resistant to marrying and reportedly tortured in hideous ways for her belief in Christ, she is the heroine of the famed devotional song "Santa Lucia." One of the losses she suffered—if only temporarily—were her eyes, or her sight. Many believe the genesis of Saint Lucy can be found in the mythology of two Roman deities: Lucina, goddess of birth and light, who merged with the mother goddess Juno. Juno protected the people of Rome and was a special patron to women in matters of marriage, fertility, and all aspects of pregnancy and childbirth. Lucina was the deity of birth and light; she brought good things to light—like babies—and a baby's first sight. When merged as "Juno Lucina," she became a more full-bodied divine female, responsible for opening every new baby's eyes to see the world for the very first time. Also known as the Mother of Lights, she was celebrated in a festival of torchlights and bonfires in early December.

Similarly, Saint Lucy's feast day is December 13, and early celebrations included "the fires of Saint Lucia." Because the number thirteen is associated with the feminine, many practitioners of women's spirituality have adopted her as a patron of women. The tradition of honoring Saint Lucy seeped into the Scandinavian culture a thousand years ago, and to this day celebrations there include pageants of women dressed like the saint; activities begin December 13 and last for one month. In prayer cards, Saint Lucy is often pictured with her eyes sprouting like flowers, sometimes on a plate. On ancient coins, Juno Lucina was pictured with a child in her arms and two babies at her feet.

HOW TO INVITE HER INTO YOUR LIFE

There are many legends about Juno Lucina's successor Saint Lucy, and in all of them she stands as a symbol of light and hope. Her coming on December 13 marks a time of feasting, merriment, singing, and the spirit of friendliness and goodwill that lasts all through the holidays. Whether it's holiday time or not, it's a good time to *practice being nice to your relatives*. Even if you think they are lame, rather than insisting on always being right, consider seeing them in a new light. Having lost her physical sight, Saint Lucy found that her strong suit was her ability to see through spiritual eyes. Although her mythology suggests that her vision was magically restored, this can be seen as betokening a "new set of eyes," a new way of seeing, which can lead to a new way of being. By the same token, in opening a baby's eyes for the first time, Juno Lucina had the power to give a new soul a fresh start, innocent and wide-eyed. These are qualities we all need to bring home to our families.

1. **Shine a light of love.** Use an imaginary flashlight in this exercise: it's a powerful metaphor for revealing what was previously

unseen. Think of how your eyes can adapt to a dark night and become comfortable in the blackness. Suddenly a beam of light glimmers at your side—one that's especially powerful for illuminating what's right under your nose! By flipping a switch, you can turn a flashlight on and direct its light anywhere. Use your mental flashlight: it's a perfect tool for seeing your family, or particular members, in a new light. Just your *willingness* to try it will make a difference in those relationships you focus on. As we heal, they can heal too. Do these four flashlight exercises on your own, shining a light on those you love, and those with whom you have a love-hate relationship. Meditate or reflect on the following:

FIND AT LEAST THREE OF THEIR REDEEMING QUALITIES. Think of it this way: if you were to write a eulogy for this loved one, which of his or her positive qualities would you acknowledge and highlight?

THINK OF WHAT YOU NEED TO TELL THEM. If this person were gone from you tomorrow, what would you wish you had said, done, or completed with them? Shine a light on old grudges, miscommunications, and *missed* communications. For your own awareness, think of what you'd like to say "if you had the nerve or opportunity."

THINK OF ONE RISK YOU'D BE WILLING TO TAKE. Not every family member is receptive to healing old hurts, but what if they are and you just don't know it? What action or communication would you risk to find out? If you reached out and they reached back, how would you feel? Let Saint Lucy give you second sight to see where your efforts to patch things up will be greeted warmly.

LOOK INTO THE MIRROR THEY HOLD UP TO YOU. Often we are aggravated by our closest family members because they remind us of parts of ourselves, our history, our lives that we would rather not look at. Be willing to see where you, too, could use a little work and improvement. Fair is fair.

2. **Create a family-friendly ritual of thanks and love.** There are many ways to evoke a sense of warmth, joy, and light. Try some of these simple, generous gestures to bring closer the people you care about.

SAY GRACE. Whenever you are all gathered, hold hands and say a prayer of thanks over the meal. Even if your family has never said a dinner prayer in their lives, suggest one; or add this prayer to the customary grace that is said at dinner. Adapt it to your family's religious and spiritual beliefs:

> Mother, Father, God, Divine Spirit of All That Is, we thank you for this opportunity to gather together in one another's company. We thank you for the light you bring to this family gathering.
>
> Please grant us the vision to see the highest in one another, and grant us the opportunity to continue to be there for each other in good times, as well as not-so-great-times.
>
> Give us strength and fortitude to ride the tides of change, and empower us always to be nurturing and loving with one another. Open our spiritual eyes that we may see one another for who we truly are, and love one other in the same spirit.
>
> May sadness, disappointment, and anger be minimal; may happiness, positive thoughts, and good experiences together be bountiful. May we always cope, and hope, with each other with grace and love.
>
> We thank the Divine for this delicious dinner, prepared with love. May all consumed here tonight fill us with health and well-being. Amen. Dig in!

HELP OUT. Do things that assist with the ease of the gathering: come early, leave late, set the table, clean up, do the dishes, take the trash out. Or extend yourself in other ways, such as picking someone up from the train station or going for ice.

BRING SOMETHING SWEET. Bake a cake or a special dessert with your own hands and fill it with love and the secret prayer that everyone who tastes it will have sweetness and joy in their lives, if they so choose. Can't bake it? Then buy it and bless it with those sentiments.

CONTRIBUTE TO THE GOOD FEELINGS. Buy or locate a piece of music that is a family favorite, something that is part of your shared history and has good memories associated with it—Dad's big band music or Mom's Sinatra tunes. Play it after dinner as a special surprise. Music stirs the soul and conjures good feelings that can bring everyone together as they remember the good times. Even if there is no talking, the music will elevate the energy in the room. If you can't find a "family classic," choose any music that warms the heart and gets people in a good mood.

HUG A LOVED ONE. Showing physical affection and expressing appreciation in the form of authentic, loving compliments is a powerful way to bring light and smiles to loved ones. You might comment on someone's hair, outfit, or cooking, or acknowledge their sweet nature, kindness, generosity, brilliance, and so on. For example, you might just hug your sister and say, "I really love the way you cook" or "I'm so touched by the patience you have with Granny. You are so good with her!"

Hugging, along with offering a few kind words, is a warm expression that can do wonders. It will automatically raise the energy of the gathering.

3. **Random acts of kindness.** If you family lives far away or you don't have much time to socialize with them, stay in touch with simple gestures to let them know you are thinking of them:

- Call your dad, grandma, sister, or anyone in your family just to let them know you love them.
- Instead of complaining, send an e-mail sharing some good news that will bring smiles to their faces.
- Write a letter or card that acknowledges something you

appreciate about them.

- Send a book or CD you know will be helpful.
- Say a prayer for those you love whenever you think of them.

HOW TO KEEP SAINT LUCY (LUCINA)
WITH YOU

Wear a Saint Lucy medal to family functions. Icons and sacred jewelry abound in the church stores and Catholic boutiques. Get a medal and chain wear it as a sacred amulet.

Celebrate Saint Lucy's feast day. In Sweden and all Scandinavian countries, people celebrate Lucia Day on December 13. Usually the eldest daughter in the house dons a white gown with a red sash and a crown of candles. Saffron buns and gingerbread cookies are served. There are gatherings at schools and work places; there are pageants and parties.

The lights go dim and the Lucia maids sing the old song "Santa Lucia." Just light a candle and remember her!

See with new eyes. Practice seeing your family from a fresh angle— with new, spiritual eyes—at every opportunity.

SAINT LUCY (LUCINA) AFFIRMATION

"I see all with my spiritual eyes."

HE MUSES

CELEBRATE WITH SISTERS AND FRIENDS

The real muses that show up in our lives are usually found in our relationships. —ANGELES ARRIEN, *THE NINE MUSES*

OUR BEST GIRLFRIENDS, AND OUR sisters, are our most intimate, important, and closest companions for much of our lives. They've been there for us through thick and thin, as we were trying to figure out boys, parents, school, and life. Female friendships and "girl talk" were even more important than those magical moments we spent in the presence of that special male person. Over the years we've seen—time and again—that while men and jobs come and go, girlfriends and sisters are always there for us.

Our friends have forever been our solace and strength; they are an informal board of directors to help solve the common problems, and there's nothing like being surrounded by a group of women who truly care about your life. It is with our girlfriends and sisters that we can get down and dirty, telling the truth of what's in our hearts, minds, and souls. We can be ourselves, and become more of ourselves.

Women need each other. We need to honor our sisters and "soul sisters" and make sure those relationships are nurtured and cared for as we get older and further from our daily identity as one of a "gaggle of girls." As we get busier, more successful, and more involved in our business or career, life in the real world gets more complex. The

170

bonds of female friendship, however, remain simple. Finding the time to spend together is usually the most challenging part of our relationships. A special gathering with our female cohorts can have power and meaning for all!

Call upon the Muses when it comes to gathering in small groups of women. Because there are nine, they represent various aspects of creative female power and possibility. They guide our gatherings with joy, merriment, mirth, and the bliss of being together. They represent joyful self-expression, sacred sisterhood, and the bonds that link women everywhere.

WHO ARE THE MUSES?

I believe that the moment I open to the gifts of the Muse, I open myself to the Creation. And become one with the Mother of Life Itself.
—*JAN PHILLIPS,*
FROM MARRY YOUR MUSE

Greek deities who presided over the arts, the Muses are among the most familiar mythical figures. Although their numbers varied with the legends of various regions, the classical period in Greece established them as nine. Their mother was Mnemosyne, goddess of memory, a Titan who was said to have spent nine nights with the top gun god, Zeus, producing nine daughters, all beauties with long tresses. Hesiod suggested that the Muses were the ultimate party girls of Greece, "their hearts are set upon song and their spirit is free from care." Taking great pleasure in merriment, good food, and celebration, they helped mortals lighten up and let their creativity flow. They were closely associated with the Three Graces, but each had her own distinct area of expertise: Calliope was muse of epic poetry; Clio, history; Erato, the lyre; Euterpe, the flute; Polyhymnia, hymns and mime; Terpsichore, dance; Thalia, comedy; Urania, astronomy; and Melpomene, tragedy.

HOW TO INVITE THEM INTO YOUR LIFE

The Muses gathered at Helicon, a mountain near the Gulf of Corinth in Greece. This spot was sacred to them and to their special cohort, the god Apollo, and sometimes his sister, goddess Diana. They found this place more pleasant than Mount Olympus with its hustle-bustle—and Helicon was also a temple of sorts, housing statues of the Muses. They often gathered there with poets, orators, creatives, and theater folk, and enfolded them in their joyous revelry, freeing their inventive spirits to soar.

Throw a Pajama Party with a Twist

Plan a meeting of the Muses: invite your favorite females for a spiritual sleepover and a creative ritual that gives you all the chance to feel like goddesses and make choices for the futures you want to invent. Make of a list of your best female friends and relatives and invite them for a pajama party with a twist: a*muse* us! The theme is "Come as your favorite Muse." Send an invitation that includes a summary of the Muses' special qualities—from sexy Erato to funny Thalia to brainy Urania. Encourage your girlfriends to dress up like goddesses—and you do it too!

1. **Have fun food and music.** Treat it like any party for girls, with yummy snacks and great music. But tell the gang that there will be a special "sacred circle" where you will all gather like the Muses on Mount Helicon and focus on instilling joy and creativity in your lives.

2. **Create a sacred circle.** Ask everyone to gather for the formal part of the evening and give everyone a chance to participate. The ancients knew how to call to the Muses and cultivate on-going relationships. In ancient societies, it was customary to first invoke the inspiration and protection of the Muses for all

creative pursuits. You can call the energy of the Muses to your gatherings with friends and sisters.

3. **Start with a prayer/invocation:**

    God, Goddess, All That Is . . .
    Let us feel your presence here with us.
    Reconnect us to our highest selves, our personal muses. Let us all be empowered as soul sisters
    and take the journey together toward prosperity, success, and creative self-expression.

4. **Bring light to the gathering with this candleburning ritual.**

    Light an eight inch taper and place it on the center of the coffee table or table closest to where you are gathered. Speak the following.

    Let us light a candle to shine light on this gathering of goddesses . . .
    To inspire the light of the Muse that lives within each of us.
    To fill our hearts and souls with brightness and glory.
    To heal the hurts of the past and to embrace forgiveness.
    To forgive ourselves for hurting other women in the past.
    To declare we are ready to allow the power of gathering
    to be part of our lives.
    To declare we are ready for satisfaction and balance in all areas of our lives.
    To agree that we support one another in being successful, happy, fulfilled.
    To acknowledge we are ready to help one another achieve our mightiest goals.
    To our fears, for making life an adventure, and to a new, improved, productive, relationship to fear.
    To all the Muses within us, and to allowing them to assist on our journeys.
    To everyone's personal truth and authentic self-expression in the world.
    To request special guidance for any of us in the room, and in the

world, who want spiritual assistance and still are not sure how to choose it, ask for it, receive it.

Let us light a candle to thank the Goddess of All That Is, and the Muses, for bringing us together, guiding us out in the world, protecting us, teaching us, moving us through our next steps, and helping us claim our birthright as daughters of the divine.

5. **Spend some time with the Muses.** Let everyone talk about their outfit and why they picked that particular muse. Explore the mythology of these divine, dancing sisters, and how important they were to every creative endeavor executed by the ancients. Discuss the ways they can help modern women improve their lives. If any friends didn't wear Muse costumes, talk about which Muse she *would have chosen*, if she had the nerve!

6. **Evoke the Muses.** Call them into the circle with you to bless your goals, dreams, and desires.

    We call to the Muses . . .

    Melpomene, Muse of tragedy, please deliver us from sorrows and grief and help us remember all that is good about ourselves and our world.

    Clio, Muse of history and the written word, please help us honor our history together and let us write a new chapter in our lives, beginning tonight.

    Euterpe, Muse of lyric poetry, make our lives like beautiful poems, full, rich, and sweet with wonder and grace.

    Terpsichore, Muse of dance and song, bring your joyous expression to this circle and let us dance and sing and enjoy one another, and the new lives we will be creating.

    Erato, Muse of love poetry, bring your sexy stirrings and wild imaginings to our hearts and loins and let us look forward to your presence in our lives.

Polyhymnia, Muse of sacred poetry, bring us prayers and soulful messages and help us live more sacred lives.

Urania, Muse of astronomy, show us all your stars and let us dance in the heavens and know the sky is not the limit!

Thalia, Muse of comedy, let us hear your jokes and wild ideas and bring us to the point of sidesplitting laughter and joy that we may smile and fully enjoy your presence.

And so it is.

7. **Give everyone a chance to make a wish.** Pass out tea-light candles that can be lit from the taper that's already lit. Have a large sturdy plate nearby to rest the lit candles on. Let everyone take a candle, light it, and then declare a special goal or desire. Have them think of something that they will initiate and would like to have happen soon in their creative lives—or their work, love, or home lives. For example, *"I will start on that book I've wanted to write"* or *"I will open my own business."* Encourage them to go for big goals, because this will set forth the possibility for a new reality. While each woman declares her goals, the rest of the group listens and holds the space of creation with her.

8. **Thank the Muses.** When everyone has spoken, thank the Muses, God, Goddess, All That Is, and your friends. Suggest that for the next thirty days they work in partnership with the Muse they came as tonight—or whoever is their favorite—to begin to move their goals forward.

9. **Ask the group to support one another.** Now that you have all heard one another's goals, see if there is willingness to support one another in attaining them. Be each other's Muse! Suggest phone and e-mail contact to help each other along.

After your sacred circle and ritual, eat, drink, and be merry! A new wheel has been put into motion.

HOW TO KEEP THE MUSES WITH YOU

Stay in touch with your Muse. Once you've identified your Muse, evoke her for every creative and business endeavor. Ask for her help. Keep her emblems around you—tools of her creative trade, such as pens or musical instruments; anything that represents her.

Be in touch with your human Muses. Look for ways you can help one another in the world.

Gather again. Keep the energy going with additional gatherings and candle lighting ceremonies.

MUSE AFFIRMATION

"My life is filled with muses who
inspire me in all ways."

$\mathscr{M}$ARY MAGDALENE

SURVIVE THE LOSS OF A LOVED ONE
AND OTHER ENDINGS

We are healed of suffering only by experiencing it to the full.
—MARCEL PROUST

LOSING A LOVED ONE IS one of life's most difficult and devastating transitions. It is never easy to say goodbye. Death, or any kind of separation from someone (or something) we love, is an experience that can rattle us to our very core and uproot us from the life we know. The pain of loss is often too unbearable for words; it leaves us dazed, dumbfounded, and shocked. Then suddenly, there comes a day when we wake up, see the sunshine and say, "Hey, there's a light at the end of the tunnel." It just takes time.

Loss is a part of life that we all must face during our time on earth. We will lose people we love and adore, people we feel close to in certain ways, and people we have come to know in the public eye. We will lose people we didn't even think we cared for anymore, and we will be shocked at the impact of that loss on our lives. We will grieve with our nation and the world for the tragedies and losses that reach universal proportions and affect all people. We will mourn the ended relationships and significant personal losses that herald the end of an era.

While each and every one of us will face mourning and grief in our own personal way, and in our own time, there is a universal principle: *There is no way over grief, only through it.* We must cry and feel the pain, as searing as it may be, and get to the end of it, the place we can surrender and let go. Grief is a project unto itself. It takes us through a time in life where emotions are unpredictable, erratic, and odd. One moment you are wracked with inconsolable sorrow, the next you laugh hysterically at a joke; in the next moment you're feeling reflective and filled with loving memories of the person who has gone on. It is a complex process, a healing journey. And we often carry grief in our hearts way beyond our initial "grieving process." Grief may never fully leave, but we can get better at embracing it.

Death and loss place us in one of life's most profound and challenging "classrooms." Somehow, in the loss, we ultimately can find a gain—in the form of lessons, self-awareness, completion, healing, and, very possibly, a new life. When someone or something significant dies, a part of us does as well. This ending births a new beginning.

Call upon Mary Magdalene when coming to terms with loss. When your heart is breaking and hurting so badly you can't imagine anything worse, no one will understand better than Mary Magdalene. She shows us the power of a woman's love, the challenge of the healing heart, and the willingness to go on in the face of deep mourning. She represents the right to grieve and the ability to survive and grow beyond any loss.

WHO IS MARY MAGDALENE?

There were three who always walked with the Lord:
Mary, his mother, her sister, and Magdalene,
the one who was called his companion.
—*GOSPEL OF PHILIP, GNOSTIC GOSPELS*

Mary Magdalene, also called "the Magdalen," was the first disciple of Jesus Christ. She was the disciple he was closest to and, as many believe, the one he loved most. In the Gnostic Gospels, Mary

Magdalene appears as a disciple, singled out by Jesus for special teachings. Although most of us were raised to believe she was a whore saved by Jesus, modern feminist theologians believe she was possibly his wife—rabbis of the day had to be married and she was his closest consort. "When she cried," it was said, "so did he." At the very least, she may have been his spiritual wife and soul mate. It was Mary Magdalene who many believe anointed Jesus with the spikenard from the famous alabaster jar, in what Jesus said was preparation for his death; this was a duty that fell to the womenfolk in one's family. Mary Magdalene has been called a whore, a hedonist, and a sinner; she has the rep of a *femme fatale*. Although it is said Jesus cast seven demons from her, there is nothing that confirms her "sins" were sexual in nature and there is no place in the Bible that actually identifies her as a prostitute.

And although we all know about the twelve apostles, we hear little about the posse of women who also traveled with Jesus, who funded his ministry, who ministered to him, and who were with him at his death. Mary Magdalene was chief among them and obviously had the family financial wherewithal to travel with him. She is credited with helping to keep the Christ crusade alive after his death, although some believe she was the silent power behind the more public apostles, first Peter, then Paul. She is the woman mentioned most often in the Bible. In art she is often depicted wearing desert attire; some portraits show her as sexy and seductive.

HOW TO INVITE HER INTO YOUR LIFE

If Mary Magdalene could somehow endure the unbelievable gut-wrenching pain of this loss, and go on to keep the work and spirit of Christ alive, then she can help you get over your pain, too. Sometimes death comes after a long, arduous battle and we are, in some ways, relieved our loved one is free of the physical body. Other times, people we love are taken from us suddenly, with no warning. Mary Magdalene could do nothing more than watch helplessly as her beloved died on the cross. A loss so devastating leaves us shattered, confused, stumbling about, wondering why, and trying to picture how we can possibly go on. Healing is a process that takes time, and you must honor all of your feelings. The following exercises can help you through the death of a loved one. They can also be helpful for those going through a breakup or divorce.

1. **Honor your feelings.** Denial, yearning, disbelief, anger, confusion, shock, despair, sadness, guilt—are all typical feelings associated with loss. The tricky part is that each one can hit you when you least expect it, affecting your life deeply as you go through the process of grieving. It takes time to fully absorb and heal from the impact of a major loss. You may never stop missing—or loving—a lost loved one or friend. Time does heal. The pain will ease and you will go on with your life. But you must give yourself lots of time. As much as you may want to believe that loss of love is a curveball tossed by fate, remember that love shared is love that exists in your heart forever. The love you once shared is as real in death as in life.

2. **Carry on.** Serious loss heralds a time of great transformation, sometimes as dramatic as the proverbial phoenix rising from the ashes. It gives us a chance to reevaluate our own lives. It makes us think: *If it were my last year on earth, where would I want to be? How would I spend my precious time? What would I want to say to the people I love?* Ask yourself those questions and answer them either introspectively, mulling them over; or proactively: taking action or communicating about your thoughts.

3. **Soothe yourself with water.** Take a dip in saltwater whenever you feel sad, overwhelmed, depressed. The ocean or any salty

body of water is a great natural healer—or use your own tub by filling it with sea salt and Epsom salts to restore the electrolytes stress takes from you. Take many warm baths, filling them with uplifting scents and bath bubbles and soaking in their soothing, calming effects. Or make the shower a temple for your tears. You can have a good cry as you let the water refresh and cleanse you. In addition to all else, make sure you drink lots of water; it will keep you hydrated as it washes you from within.

4. **Be part of a support community.** After Jesus died, Mary was with a circle of other women. They shared a common bond of loss that held them together as they plunged into the depths of despair. Do the same as you mourn: gather others to you informally, or join an existing grief support group. There are many online; you can also check with your local hospital.

5. **Build an altar to the one you love.** Create a memory table. Fill it with pictures of your beloved and objects that honor and recall his or her life. You can also create an altar for a deceased pet, or adapt this idea for a relationship that has ended.

LIGHT A CANDLE. Get a special beautiful candle, or a plain white one.

RESOLVE ISSUES. If you have an unresolved regret or issue, write a letter and leave it under the picture of the beloved.

SIT AND TALK WITH YOUR BELOVED, AS YOU DID IN LIFE. It may sound crazy, but simply imagine that the one you lost is not far away, just a shout off in the distance. Many believe that our lost loved ones are separated from us only by a thin veil.

WORK TOWARD CLOSURE AND FORGIVENESS. Embrace them wherever they are. Share any concerns. Tell stories about your life.

FEEL THE SAFETY AND SACREDNESS OF THE MOMENT. If you can bring yourself to go through this process, you will find it hastens your healing and helps you process grief and begin to approach a healthy closure.

DON'T HOLD ON FOREVER. Let go when the time comes. Pack up the pictures and the mementos and put grief away. A new day will dawn. There are many schools of thought that say excessive grieving of a loved one, or grieving to the detriment of your well-being, binds a soul to us in an unhealthy way. Let yourself come to trust that your loved one is safe and where he or she is meant to be.

6. **Honor the gifts of loved ones.** Many people come to know that they have received a great gift from a beloved who has departed. There are many who believe that the beloved soul of those we lose continues to watch over us. How warming that thought is! Ponder this: What is the gift that your loved one has given you? Thank her or him for the lesson and the opportunity.

7. **Take over the mantle of a loved one.** It has been said that when a loved one passes on, we can take over his or her mantle. How? One way is to look deeply at how this person has contributed to us, and the world, and see the part of that life that we are best suited to carry on. Mary Magdalene shared the ministry of Jesus Christ and helped develop it. As she helped keep his memory and mission alive, she went on, many believe, to play a huge role in the development of early Christianity.

HOW TO KEEP MARY MAGDALENE WITH YOU

Embrace your pain. Whenever you feel the pain of loss, or a broken heart searing through you, remember, the only way to heal the pain is to travel through it. It may seem like a tunnel of torture, but remember, "This too will pass."

Stay present in the face of death. It's been said that when a loved one dies, the doors of heaven open. When the loved one walks through, a little bit of heaven's winds sweep around those left behind. As sadness soaks you to the very core, you may experience a surreal sense of still feeling very connected to the loved one. If you let it, the winds of heaven will sweep through you and bring you peace and clarity.

Keep her symbol near you. To represent the masculine and the feminine, keep a beautiful picture of Christ's sacred heart and an alabaster jar near you.

Anoint your heart chakra with sacred oils. Mary Magdalene anointed Jesus with a healing unguent of spikenard. This herb is in the valerian family, which helps calm you.

MARY MAGDALENE AFFIRMATION

"I will survive."

ESTA

CREATE A PLACE YOU CAN CALL HOME

A woman must have money and a room of her own . . .
—VIRGINIA WOOLFE, *A ROOM OF ONE'S OWN*

WE ALL NEED A PLACE to call home. Whether we live with roommates or alone, whether it's our first apartment or the latest of many, home is a place that offers security and rest, solitude, and separation from the world. Whether home is a cottage or a castle, a studio or a duplex, it matters not. As long as you have a refuge, a room to call your own, you have a sense of stability and place in the world.

What makes a home? Celebrities build huge mansion fortresses because they have so little privacy. Their homes are a complete shelter, a place to throw up a curtain to the world. Nuns and monks live in cloisters so they can focus on prayer and sacred living, untouched by the stirrings of the outside world. Some people use their homes to entertain and gather with others; they may love having guests, animals, kids clamoring all day. Others revel in the quiet splendor of a moment alone. It's important to assess the kind of place that to you is a home. Then set about finding it, building it, living in it, and making the rest of life's dreams come true.

Call upon Vesta when it comes to creating a home that is a personal haven and sanctuary. It is Vesta who made Mom's house into a home, and she will bring her spirit to your dwelling place too. She brings warmth and *that personal touch* to the place you call home. She can help you find an apartment as well as pick the right furniture, art, and all the little niceties. She represents sanctuary and feeling nurtured and empowered in the place you live.

WHO IS VESTA?

[Vestal virgins] had the sacred duty of tending the sacred hearth of the state in the Temple of Vesta in Rome. On March 1, the fire was rekindled ritually by rubbing two sticks together; if the fire went out, it had to be lit the same way.
—LESLEY ADKINS & ROY A. ADKINS, DICTIONARY OF ROMAN RELIGION

Vesta (*VESS*-ta) is the Roman goddess of the hearth. Although she originated as a spirit of the home who tended the hearth, she went on to gain importance in the Roman pantheon as the goddess to whom prayers for a safe and happy home and home life were addressed. And although she was personified as a female, she was represented only by flame. In homes it was the fireplace or hearth that called forth her warmth and protection. The Temple of Vesta was fashioned in the round, as were the thatched huts of early Rome. Six virgins kept constant vigil over the flame of the goddess. No men were permitted to enter the temple, and, as sacred flame-keepers, the Vestal virgins had to obey strict rules of conduct. Roman families gathered daily to honor her and perform sacrifices in her name. In art, Vesta is primarily depicted indirectly as the fire of the hearth. Although the ancients never portrayed her representationally, modern renditions show her as an older gray-haired woman.

HOW TO INVITE HER INTO YOUR LIFE

To the ancients, Vesta's hearth magic transformed a hut into a sanctuary. How can you do the same for your home? Whip it into shape! Your first task is to clean house.

1. **Organize your home.** Before you can rebuild or recreate, you have to let go of that which stands in the way. Remember that very specific spiritual law: "Nature abhors a vacuum." Get rid of something, then something new can come in. If your life is too cluttered with stuff, if your house is messy or disorganized, it's very hard to feel connected to Vesta's warmth.

   TOSS. As a symbolic step, make an offering to Vesta in the form of one messy desk or bureau drawer. Clean it out. Toss old stuff away. Reorganize. It's a symbolic step toward a sacred and impeccable home. The pure energy of release will move you toward the next drawer, closet, or file.

   CLEAN. Once you've decluttered, it's time to scrub, wash, and make things sparkle. A house becomes a magical home when you clean up with love. Treat it as a sacred act, not just a grungy chore, and make it an offering to the goddess of the hearth.

2. **Create magical surroundings:**

   BUY CANDLES. Find candles that will burn safely, and choose safe places for them. Then keep one burning as often as possible in honor of Vesta.

   FILL YOUR HOME WITH THAT WHICH IS SACRED. This may mean holy icons and art—or pictures of movie stars. Whatever is sacred to you is fine. Surround yourself with things that feel special and spiritual.

   DOCUMENT THE GREAT TIMES. Surround yourself with positive memories, such as photos and mementoes of good times and good health. Trash unhappy reminders of ex-boyfriends, broken hearts, failed jobs, or bad experiences.

   BUILD INTO THE FUTURE. Create a home that reflects who you are, and also where you intend to go in life. Don't get pulled into the past with old furniture or family relics—unless you are in love with them. Choose household items and furniture that advance your life, not that keep you stuck in history or negative consciousness.

INCLUDE FUN STUFF. Find things that bring you joy and that are a pleasure for visitors, such as pool table or basketball hoop, a chess set or a large-screen TV. Home entertainment and enjoyment is just as important to Vesta as fire. It brings pleasure and joy into the abode.

3. **To find a new home:**

Let Vesta help. If you're looking for a new place to live, petition Vesta to help you get there.

CLARIFY. Make a list of all that you seek in a home. Will you rent or own? Where should it be? How much will it cost? How many rooms?

VISUALIZE. Cut out pictures or renderings of your perfect home and paste a photo of yourself inside the new abode.

FOCUS. Create an altar to Vesta with a special candle to serve as the flame of the goddess. For thirty days, go to the altar with an offering of bread or baked goods, light the flame, read your list, look at the rendering, and pray to Vesta to please bring it closer to you; to bring you closer to it. Snuff the candle out when you are done. Offer the baked goods to the birds when you replace them with fresher foods—so mother birds can bring food to their homes, too.

BELIEVE. Set a goal for yourself and trust it will come true. For example, buy a six-bar package of soap and affirm, with the flame of the goddess as your witness: "Before these six bars of soap have been used, I wish to have my new home lined up or have the lease signed."

TRUST EVEN MORE. If the goal is not fulfilled exactly on time, that's okay. Start again with another six-pack of soap! Honor the notion that, as Vesta seeks the perfect digs, there may be some delay.

CELEBRATE. When the goal is fulfilled, thank her and make sure you honor her in your new home.

4. **Honor Vesta at mealtime.**

COOK AND EAT DINNERS AT HOME. When you turn on your stove or light a barbeque, know that you evoke her nurturing energies in the fire. Let her cook a good meal with you.

Mix affirmations about your future into your dinner. If you cook, do so with intention, placing prayers into every step of the preparation. If you don't, take on simple food preparation tasks, such as crafting a beautiful salad or slicing up a bowlful of your favorite fruits. Pour in prayers for your "hearth's desire" as you mix. Talk into the food as if you are talking to the goddess, petitioning her for all your needs, or even just declaring your goals. *"I eat good and healthy food. I have more than enough space in my home. I enjoy giving parties and soirees."* And so on.

ADD PRAYERS TO ALL YOUR FOOD. If dining with others, begin with a dinner prayer whenever possible. Or quietly place the palms of your hands just above your plate and zap the food with good energy while saying a prayer of thanks to Vesta. If you take the time to radiate healing light and bless your food you will always slow down and eat in a healthy manner.

EAT ONLY HAPPY THOUGHTS. Never talk about anything negative or depressing while eating. If you do so during a meal, you literally eat these things and take them inside you.

HOW TO KEEP VESTA WITH YOU

Clean up the room you use most. Vesta comes to cleanliness, neatness, and order. She seeks the open space and sanctified environment as a temple for her warmth.

Celebrate her on her sacred day. Vestalia, the Festival of Vesta, was essentially a holiday for bakers and millers. The Romans honored Vesta with bread and other baked goods on June 9. You can too by baking (or buying!) a loaf of bread in her honor and breaking bread with female friends that night.

VESTA AFFIRMATION

"I feel safe and happy in my home sweet home."

Part 5
GODDESSES OF
WORK AND FINANCES

AURORA

DISCOVER YOUR TRUE PATH

Follow your bliss.
—JOSEPH CAMPBELL

NO MATTER WHAT KIND OF work we do in life, or how we choose to pursue it, each of us has a personal path that is uniquely our own. Most of us want to do work we love; work that's fun, interesting, financially rewarding, and personally fulfilling. Fame and fortune, success in business, and legendary careers are not in the cards for all of us, but each and every one of us has a calling, something we believe in, a mission that gives our lives a sense of purpose and meaning.

Some are already blessed with a sense of who we are and what we are meant to do in life; others are searching and muddling through. Many of us will have smaller jobs that help us pay the rent while we train and prepare for our "real" careers; others will be burning up the fast track right out of college. Some of us will decide, or be swayed by circumstances, to opt for a "good job" over a great career opportunity; others will find their way to a new career later in life. Regardless of what form of livelihood we choose, all work takes on a new dimension when we approach it soulfully and ask: *What do I truly believe in? How do I want to share my talents and my good works in the world? What inspires me most?*

A true path is as personal as a fingerprint. It's not about competing with others or following cultural trends; it's about being your best and calling forth your own talents, abilities, and methods. It merges all the practical aspects of developing a career or professional life with the unique expression of who you are as an individual and how you convey that through your work in the world.

Whether you find your true path is as a hairstylist who interacts with thousands of clients and brings all of them joy and a more positive self-image, or as an author who writes books that change people's lives, having a sense of mission in life is what inspires you to joyously get up in the morning and go to work. It will inspire you to work with dedication, even when the going gets rough. Honor your path in life, and you will always find your way back to work that gives meaning to your life.

For every transitional time in life—in between jobs or in between other opportunities—it's important to appreciate the time as both an ending and new beginning; it's a point of power for any journey. It may seem scary and unsettling not to know where you're heading, but this is where the magic of new beginnings lives. Like the night gently turning to day, each experience will organically lead to the next leg of the journey, urging you to become the woman you are meant to be.

Call to Aurora when it comes to defining your life's mission and finding your way in the world: she brings dawn through the darkness and represents proof that tomorrow *is* another day. She reveals your next steps as she "raises night's veil" and opens the door to possibilities not seen or known the day before. She represents the dawn of new beginnings, fresh opportunities, and new ways of seeing things.

WHO IS AURORA?

The goddess Dawn, rosy-fingered, arose to bring
the light to the gods and the mortals.
—HOMER, THE ILIAD

Aurora (*aw-ROR-ah)*, the Roman goddess of the dawn, is also known as "light." To the ancients, she was "the rosy-fingered dawn with the snowy eyelids bringing the first glimmer of the day." It was her job to lead her brother, Helios, the sun god, into the new day; thus every morning she rose from the ocean into the sky. Sometimes she traveled as a winged goddess tilting an urn from which fell the morning dew; sometimes she was mounted on Pegasus, the winged horse; but most commonly she was seen riding in a purple chariot drawn by two horses. Her husband was Tithonius, a mortal who was made immortal, but not given the antiaging powers of the gods and thus becoming a shriveled elderly man. Perhaps because of her "situation" at home, Aurora was notorious for chasing and seducing young men. Symbolically, her husband was the "old" she left behind in bed each night and the young men were the "youthful energy" that she chased like the new day. She is often pictured as a wispy, airy, beautiful woman in white, or barely any clothing; and she is sometimes seen on a chariot streaking across the sky.

HOW TO INVITE HER INTO YOUR LIFE

As you lay your head down for the night, Aurora rests in the dark skies and twinkling stars, preparing to fly once again and launch a brand new day filled with fresh possibilities for passion and aliveness. Aurora goes to bed with the sleepy night, but when she awakens, the world is thenceforth transformed. To meet the dawn and greet the new possibilities brought by Aurora, try this exercise when you're beginning your professional life, job hunting or starting a new job, during transitions, or anytime you feel stuck along the way.

Ritual for a New Dawn: A Personal Mission Statement

You'll do this ritual over a twenty-four hour period. It can be a regular day in your life, but on this day you'll tune in to Aurora's energies and declare a personal mission statement for your life and life's work. (Expect that over time you'll rewrite it and make adjustments; you may want to use this ritual repeatedly over time.) Begin the night before with a cleansing bath.

1. **At bedtime, take a warm bath and cleanse the body, mind, and soul.** First turn off the television, tune out the world, and plan for a silent bedtime so that your mind is clear and new insights can arise. Review the stresses of the day and one by one release them into the warm water. When the bath is done and you pull the plug, intend and imagine that all of the day's disappointments go down the drain with the water.

2. **Wish upon a star.** Aurora is also the well-known term for the spectacular display of northern and southern lights (*aurora borealis* and *aurora australis*), which Webster's calls "a luminous phenomenon that consists of streamers or arches of light appearing in the upper atmosphere of a planet's magnetic polar regions." These lights streak across the sky from horizon to horizon, like Aurora herself making her sky trek. You may not live in a part of the world where you can see the lights named after the goddess of dawn, but just imagine that she lives in all stars. Before you sleep, look out upon the starry night in whatever way you can—from a back porch or window, or in your imagination—and wish for illumination on the life path you are to pursue.

3. **Go to bed with a prayer to the goddess.**

   Dearest Aurora, goddess of dawn,
   please bring illumination in early morn.
   As you awaken at your twilight hour,
   let me feel your energy and power.

4. **Awaken gently, before the dawn.** It has been said that the day's greatest power lives in the moments between night and day. That moment varies with the time of year, but it is often around 4:30 a.m. This is when Aurora prepares for her streak from night to day, a time when little else stirs. It is the time when many writers awaken to write, successful businesspeople awaken to start their day, and monks rise to pray. Challenge yourself to awaken at this hour, when nothing else is stirring, and allow Aurora to come to you. Rising at this time as a practice helps instill discipline and gives you a chance to start the morning when a new day is truly breaking.

5. **Watch night turn into day.** From a window, porch, or stoop, revel in the experience of watching Aurora bring forth the dawn. Slowly the night relinquishes its hold on the skies and gently the daylight comes forth. Notice what it is like, how long it takes, and how you feel as it is going on. It is a natural transformational event that illustrates how simple it is to go from darkness into light in a matter of minutes; how easily nature takes us from *then* to *now*.

6. **Ask Aurora to help you define your path.** If you like to meditate, go to your favorite spot and use your favorite music to go into a meditative state. If you are not familiar with meditating, just sit quietly, close your eyes, take three deep breaths, and then let them out. Relax your body. Relax your mind. Ask Aurora to help you understand the path you must follow by revealing your mission in life and career. Just listen and see what guidance Aurora brings. When you feel ready, open your eyes and write down whatever thoughts and ideas are in your mind.

7. **Sit and listen to her whispers as she transforms night to day.** If you are a coffee or tea drinker, go ahead and make your morning brew. You might as well utilize your normal caffeine buzz in an

inspiring way. (Fruit juice is just as fine.) Sit quietly and sip. If you sit for twenty minutes as the new day dawns, sipping your beverage, a million ideas will flow to you. Jot down any inspiration or ideas that come to you.

8. **Pay attention to subtle messages throughout the day.** Remember, Aurora gently transforms night to day and brings the light ever so gradually. You may find that Aurora's awakenings come to you slowly and subtly throughout the day. You may receive a phone call, open a book to a particular page, see a street sign or hear something on the radio that offers a clue—or a cue— to help you take your next step and shape your mission statement.

9. **Write a mission statement for your life's work/career.** Every organization has a mission statement to serve as a guiding light, and you can too. Before the next day's dawn, ask yourself the questions: *What do I believe in?* and *How do I want to express myself in the world?* Formulate a mission statement for your life's work/career. Include qualities you want to experience, general goals you hope to pursue and achieve, promises about how you will conduct yourself. Make it as specific as you are willing, but leave room for evolution and give yourself permission to live a life that is a work in progress. Crafting such a statement can help establish a rhyme and reason to your life and help steer you along your true path. Your mission statement can look something like this:

I do work that I love in the field of publishing. I bring compassion and openheartedness to my work, even in the face of difficulties. I earn more than enough money. I am passionate, committed, and dedicated. I am grateful for my skills and all my success, and will not take rejection personally. I am building a body of work I can be proud of, and I write things that touch people's lives. People will know my name and recognize me for my contributions. I experience great joy in

the work I do.

HOW TO KEEP AURORA WITH YOU

Get a good night's sleep, in general. Aurora comes riding through the night with her fresh beginnings of each dawn. Solid sleep will prepare you for the fresh start she brings you with each waking day. Allow plenty of time for much-needed REM sleep, where dreamtime occurs: it will help you awake feeling more hopeful, and reduce stress and enhance mental alertness throughout the day. In general, sleep enables you to be rested and ready for new opportunities and creations. If you continue to rise early to meet Aurora as she awakens, make sure you go to bed earlier at night.

Pay attention to dreams. Secrets and signs that can lead you on your path may come to you in the sleep state. Keep a dream journal by your bed and write your dreams down first thing upon waking. Notice any continuing themes or messages.

Pay attention to life. We all have the ability to look more deeply, hear more acutely, tune in more sensitively to life. This kind of awareness helps you spot new opportunities and pick up the subtle signs and signals from the universe that there's something you should look at or a corner you should turn.

AURORA AFFIRMATION

"I travel my true path."

ARTEMIS

PURSUE YOUR CAREER GOALS

My aim is true.
—ELVIS COSTELLO, "ALISON"

LAUNCHING A NEW CAREER, PURSUING advancement, or taking on a new opportunity that will lead to professional evolution is a wonderful, juicy time in our lives. It is often a time when we exert our independence and capabilities, and when our sexual energies and urges to party get channeled instead into attaining an important goal or opportunity. It's a time of laserlike focus, creativity, and almost lustful desire to make something happen, careerwise—to make it come to life.

Taking a proactive approach to career building is a way to take charge of your professional destiny. It may be a little daunting to put yourself out in the world and try things you have not yet experienced in life, but it is the act of giving it your best shot, with all your heart and soul, that makes an experience so gratifying. Like taking a ski lift to the top of a mountain and stepping off the slope to ski for the first time, it's exhilarating, risky, and occasionally terrifying. You may or may not have all the training needed for the task. The trick is to approach it *as if* you can, and will, pull it off.

The pursuit of big projects and career goals requires much love, nurturing, and attention. There is often a period of time when a busy,

200

career-dedicated woman may want to ditch the rest of the world and focus only on her work. It can be a somewhat isolating and single-minded pursuit. It may leave little time for family functions, and less time for love affairs. Friends at work, people who can teach us and help our careers along, and work-related tasks will be of utmost importance. There will be plenty of challenges that will test your mettle, such as procrastination, inability to focus, fear of failure or fear of success, lack of self-esteem, low motivation, and the inevitable failures, mistakes, and setbacks. Embrace the things that don't work out well; they teach us lessons that bring strength. If you're willing to take risks, you can rise above any roadblocks to success. The key is to aim high—and be true to yourself.

Call upon Artemis when it comes to setting your sights on higher targets and passionately hunting your career opportunities and advancement. She's a free spirit who empowers your independence, showing you how to go after what you want with passion, focus—and no apologies. By choice, Artemis is no man magnet, so she is especially helpful in those times when you don't want to dilute your career focus with romance. She represents self-reliance and the ability to aim high and hit the mark.

WHO IS ARTEMIS?

I sing of Artemis, whose shafts are of gold,
who cheers on the hounds,
the pure maiden, shooter of stags, who delights in archery . . .
Over the shadowy hills and windy peaks she draws her golden bow,
rejoicing in the chase, and sends out grievous shafts.
—*HOMERIC HYMN XXVII*

Artemis (AR-*teh-miss*), Greek goddess of the hunt, was one of the first feminists of the Mount Olympus set. A virgin by choice and huntswoman by skill and divine profession, she was chief hunter of the gods, known as "Lady of Wild Things." Artemis was fiercely independent and would let no man have her, but she knew her territory well and had many friends to help her along the way. She spent her days in the forest with her posse of animal guides and virginal wood nymph companions. She was famous for *always* reaching her target with her golden arrows, which are said to have "moaned" as they sped toward her prey.

She understood the ways of the wild, the nature of beast and bird, and could gently speak the language of wild nature, yet she was fierce and a force to be reckoned with. She was not afraid to make the kill. With her nymphs and hounds, she hunted in the deepest wilderness, slaughtering stags and lions. For recreation she gathered with her brother Apollo and their favorite friends, the nine Muses, to sing and dance. She is often pictured as a young woman in a short toga with bow, arrow, and animal friends in tow.

HOW TO INVITE HER INTO YOUR LIFE

Artemis wanted nothing to do with men (except her brother Apollo, perhaps) and the penalty for getting a peek of the virgin goddess could be instant punishment or death. The centaur hunter Actaeon once stumbled—or deliberately sought out—the goddess while she was bathing naked in a stream. With a single word and gesture, the outraged Artemis turned him into a stag, then watched him turn into dinner for his hounds. Although she could be nasty at times with the very animals she protected, she generally was ruthless with anyone or anything who sought to injure her posse of forest friends. She had her own agenda! Artemis is an excellent source of inspiration when you want to put men (and most other distractions) on hold and channel all your energy into getting your career off the ground or going after *the big job* or project. Swiftly did her arrows fly. And yours can too.

Artemis had focus. She attuned her senses with the laser

sharpness of an arrow, and her hunting arrows were associated with light. Arrows also represent the piercing, masculine principle; they are virility and power. Although Artemis is a divine female, she largely called upon her male energy to accomplish her work in the world. You too may find that there are times when you operate more on "yang" than "yin" energy in order to accomplish a goal. Although Artemis was an expert archer who packed a weapon, your greatest weapon is your mind. Your thoughts and your intellect are as potent as golden arrows when you give them power, language, and life—and focus them in the right direction. Consider this: *Everything human-made that exists in the world began as a thought form in someone's mind.*

You can call Artemis to you by adopting her skills as a mighty archer and an independent woman! Try these methods to help you go after what you want in life.

1. **Create a career treasure map.** Visualizing the results you want to create in your life is a powerful way to make them come true. As they say, *if you can dream it, you can create it!* You literally replicate your goals by creating a "career treasure map" that then becomes a road map to your future.

   CLARIFY YOUR GOALS. Just as Artemis fixes her gaze on her target before she lets her arrow take flight, you must know your outcome before you take aim—otherwise you can end up exerting a lot of energy in the wrong direction and missing opportunities. Think as specifically as possible about what you want your career and work life to look like.

   MAKE A COLLAGE OF YOUR DESIRED CAREER. To begin, you'll need a big sheet of oaktag or posterboard, glue, scissors, and magazines—use ones you already have, or buy new ones that have lots of images related to the goals, projects, or advancements you are after. Now cut, paste, and create your career treasure map with your own hands, heart, and spirit. Clip out enough magazine images to fill the whole posterboard; just flipping through the pages and selecting pictures will heighten your visualization skills. Arrange the images as creatively as you like: angles and overlaps are fine. Have fun with it! Include anything that relates to your goals: images of success and professionalism, fun at work, financial security and prosperity— images that reflect the way you want to look, feel, behave, travel, and live. Include headlines, quotes, and sayings that give language to your thoughts: for example, *First class all the way* along with a photo of a businesswoman traveling by air. Or find your motivation in the famous Nike ad that heralded female power, saying "Just do it!" You might also find articles and pictures of people in the public eye who represent the kind of success you seek; it's fine to use their images as symbols. But make sure all the images truly represent what you want! They will act like visual prayers and arrows of light, sent out to capture your dreams!

DISPLAY IT PROUDLY. Your treasure map is a personal and sacred blueprint for your career goals. Place it where you can see it daily, even if just in passing. It will support your internal visualization by placing your goals, dreams, and hopes right in front of your face! It stimulates conscious awareness and goal creation, and it acts as a visual message board for the brain. Gently, it feeds images of your future success to your subconscious mind in a way that draws you closer to those dreams, and draws those dreams closer to you. (If you are an extremely private person and have a roommate, you can keep it low key and hang it in a closet, or create it on a smaller scale, in a notebook, for example.)

2. **Treat your efforts as a sacred act.** Devote yourself to following your treasure map and making it come to life. When you dedicate yourself so fully to creating something meaningful, doing it as if you're building something sacred, it's an offering to the goddess Artemis. The energy you put in will come back to you—plus some extra. Ask Artemis for her blessing: *That I may be as skilled*

and devoted to my targets as you are!

3. **Sharpen your focus.** Set a specific goal and keep your eye on it, never letting it out of your sight. Focusing your energy on what you want to create will magnetize it to you. When you envision the end result, all the steps that lead you to it seem more natural.

4. **Dedicate yourself to your most important goal or goals.** While you wouldn't want to turn into a work addict who has nothing else in life, at the crucial stages of development, any project of importance will require *all of you*. When Artemis disappeared into the forest to do her work, the rest of the world faded away. Be a workaholic for the time it takes to make a dream come true; pour all your energies into your special goal. Live, breathe, and sleep it until you nail it down. As with all aspects of life, there is a time and a season for this kind of focused devotion.

HOW TO KEEP ARTEMIS WITH YOU

Carefully craft your language. Your words are like golden arrows that can create thought forms in your own mind, and those of others. Aim these arrows to help you "sell" your ideas to the right people—bosses, supervisors, clients, and people you want to be working with. Communicate in a positive, forward-moving manner when talking about important projects. Avoid complaining and groaning about how tired or stressed you are; focus instead on the benefits and importance of what is being created.

Keep an arrow on your desk. To remind yourself to reach for your goals, keep an arrow on your desk—or an image or statue of an archer or even Artemis herself.

Enjoy the hunt. The greatest way to evoke the presence of the goddess of the hunt is to pursue it with passion, as she did, and enjoy every nuance of the experience.

ARTEMIS AFFIRMATION

"I take responsibility for reaching my goals."

RIGID

FIND YOUR INSPIRATION

Inspiration is the simple recognition of the spirit within ourselves.
—WAYNE W. DYER

SOMETIMES GOOD IDEAS ELUDE US or brilliant ideas get clogged up somewhere between concept and reality. It's too hard to get into a "creative mood," or we don't have enough motivation or support to get a project cooking and completed. Good intentions are sometimes thwarted by anxiety about starting—and finishing—a project. You may be used to accomplishing tasks through deadline-induced inspiration, fueled by adrenaline and panic. Maybe you need to learn how to open to divine inspiration.

Many of us romanticize creativity as a power we evoke only when spirit moves us, but the real world dictates that things get done on deadlines and according to contracts. While it is always nice to wait for divine inspiration to strike, we also have to learn to evoke inspiration and draw it to us—and to catch it and use it when it comes. The amazing thing about the creative process is that one moment we may be completely stumped, and then suddenly, as if a switch has been flipped, the light bulb in our brain turns on. The heart opens the mind, and anything seems possible. And so it is!

Every project, in every profession, has a creative element. It begins with a flutter of inspiration and it becomes bigger, greater, and more fully formed in our minds. But a woman cannot live on ideas alone! Once the flame of creativity is alight, an idea can easily grow wings and take flight and manifest as reality. We have to honor the process of creation, and yet continue to consciously fan its flame.

Call upon Brigid when it comes to creativity, self-expression, and bringing new ideas into the world and giving them life. When you're at a loss for stimulation and motivation, when you're tearing your hair out with anxiety, she lights the fire in your inventive soul with her creative magic. She will freshen your ideas and bring her fiery spirit to your life. She represents the passionate flame of creativity and inspiration.

WHO IS BRIGID?

Brigit, excellent woman; flame golden, sparkling.
May she bear us to the eternal kingdom; she the sun, fiery, radiant.
—*SEVENTH-CENTURY HYMN OF SAINT BRIGID*

Brigid (*BRID-jeed*) is the Celtic triple goddess known as keeper of the sacred fire. Her name means "exalted one" and she is sometimes referred to as a "bride." Goddess of poets, blacksmiths, brides, and childbirth, she watches over hearth and fire, fertility, creativity, and healing. As a triple goddess, she represents the three aspects of the Divine Feminine and three stages of a woman's life—maiden, mother, and wise woman—all in one. When Christianity took hold, she survived the fall of the "old religion" and was adapted as a Catholic saint with a slightly different spelling of her name. She was, and continues to be, the beloved Saint Brigit of Kildare, said to be founder of the first female Christian community and abbess of a large double monastery in Kildare during the Middle Ages. In today's Ireland, a perpetual flame in her honor burns in Kildare's town square.

Brigid is touted as midwife to Virgin Mary and has long been invoked by women in labor; she is viewed as a great supporter of birthing new ideas as well. As a goddess, Brigid is always represented as youthful and beautiful, all three aspects of her the same age; she's pictured with fiery red hair, often holding a flame as her symbol. In her incarnation as saint, she is seen with cattle, and is affiliated with dairy and milk especially. It is said her cows were milked three times a day and could fill a lake with milk. She is also associated with water and wells. There are still wells in Ireland devoted to her as sacred shrines.

HOW TO INVITE HER INTO YOUR LIFE

Brigid is the symbol of Eternal Light. Legend has it that in the days before Christianity in Ireland, priestesses would gather on the hill at Kildare to tend the flame of the goddess Brigid. This evolved into an early Christian tradition whereby nuns in the abbey she founded were considered guardians of the "fire of Saint Brigid." Starting and sustaining a perpetual fire, nineteen nuns each took a turn tending the fire and on the twentieth day, Brigid tended it herself. To the nuns it represented the light of Christ. After her death, it is said the fire burned continuously, and it took a great deal of wood, but the ashes did not increase. Eventually the church outlawed the practice. In the spirit of the flame of Kildare, members of a worldwide organization called Ord Brighideach continue to maintain the twenty-day rotation schedule, keeping "Brighid's Flame" alive. You can too.

For Long-Term Projects

1. **Light her fire.** Just by lighting a candle we can evoke her energy and kick-start an endless flow of ideas and solutions. If you commit yourself to a twenty-day program of lighting a flame in honor of the goddess—a tradition with ancient roots—you

ensure twenty days of focusing on the creation of something important and you will have the chance to "work" with Brigid every day.

If you happen to have a fireplace, wood stove, or outdoor firepit, you can light any of these daily for twenty days in honor of the goddess. Candles are fine too: find either one large pillar candle that you light daily for an hour then gently snuff out until the next day, or twenty small candles. Votives will burn for about ten hours; tea-lights for about two to four hours. The color orange is particularly powerful because orange is the color of Brigid's flaming hair; it is also the color linked with the body's energy center for creativity and birth (known as the second chakra or sexual chakra).

PICK A TIME TO LIGHT THE FIRE EVERY DAY FOR NINETEEN DAYS. Try to keep to this sacred schedule, but if your timing is off, light the flame whenever you can daily. As you do, visualize the project for which you want her inspired blessings and say what it is, out loud if you can, as you ask for her help.

ASK FOR WHAT YOU NEED. Every day after lighting the flame, make your appeal in your own personal way, or use this prayer.

Brigid of the golden flame and fiery inspiration, I welcome you. Please bring me the inspiration and motivation I need to _____ [fill in your need]. On this day I pray that this sacred flame leads me to your light. Amen.

SNUFF IT OUT WITH A CANDLESNUFFER. After an hour, snuff the flame rather than blowing it out (which, spiritually, could suggest blowing the intention of it away). Thank the goddess for being with you on that day, and always.

FEEL THE ENERGY OF INSPIRATION BEGIN TO SIZZLE WITHIN. You may notice it within a few days of starting the daily ritual.

Pay attention to it. Seize it, ride its wave, and get your work done! Brigid's gifts will come naturally, in the course of each day. By the twentieth day, you may find yourself in especially good spirits, as you have had almost three weeks of intimate communion with the goddess of inspiration. On the day that Brigid is believed to tend the flame herself, approach the lighting of the fire with great reverence and thank her for every small gift she has given you in these twenty days. Recount every idea, inspired moment, creative experience, and finished project in that time frame and thank her for her part in it. When you acknowledge divine co-creation, you build a bridge of gratitude that can lead to greater confidence in the creative process as well as continued inspiration.

For Short-Term Inspiration

1. **Let her waters inspire you.** Because of her affiliation with sacred waters, you can also call Brigid to you with the help of water. Any time you can get out and sit by a lake or the ocean, your mind will clear and ideas will flow. If you can't spend time around a body of water, try a home water fountain. Sometimes called tabletop fountains or feng shui fountains, they are widely available in chain stores and online. Set it up in a part of your home or office that is not in your direct working area. When you need a little inspiration, you usually need a little relaxation. Turn on the fountain and sit and gaze at the running water; it is hypnotic. Let the sound take you on a relaxing journey, and as it does, imagine the goddess Brigid washing over you with her sacred, cleansing, healing waters. Ask her to help you with whatever you're working on. When you feel refreshed, turn off the fountain and go back to work—or symbolically let the inspiration flow by leaving the fountain on and flowing.

2. **Ask her to bless your handkerchief.** It is an old custom to leave a white cloth out on the table for the goddess to bless (at her holiday, Imbolc). To this day, people continue the tradition of honoring her with pieces of cloth that hang near her shrines and springs, such as the Well of Saint Brigit in Fouchart, Ireland. Keep an "inspiration hankie" handy. When you need a little help with a project, leave the white hankie on your table at night and, with a little prayer of thanks, ask the goddess to help with your need. Be specific. Then take the hankie to work with you the next day. Take it with you into any meetings or keep it by you at your desk. Anytime you feel the need, hold it in your hands and visualize that whatever you are trying to create or work through is done, completed.

HOW TO KEEP BRIGID WITH YOU

Keep the flames of Brigid's inspiration flowing. Light candles when you want to get in touch with Brigid. This invites her not only to visit, but to stay with you.

Find a Brigid Cross for home or office. Often made of straw and uniquely shaped, these are widely available and affordable and can be purchased at most Irish-American gift shops, or you can make one at home.

Listen to Celtic music. Tunes from the homeland of Brigid's birth will evoke her energy in your soul. New Age tunes and anything from Enya can call forth her warm and inspiring spirit.

Partake in her annual celebration. Brigid is honored with fire and prayer on the eve of February 1, known as Candlemas, and the day of February 2, Imbolc. It's a time to acknowledge her light and the increasing power of the light of day, and perhaps the first seedlings of spring. As she blesses nature's potential to bloom, we ask her to bless our creative ideas and ventures. This holiday of Brigid was precursor to Groundhog Day, the predictor of the coming spring.

BRIGID AFFIRMATION

"Inspiration fills me.My creativity flows easily."

$\mathcal{L}$AKSHMI

INCREASE YOUR INCOME

A girl needs cash.

—JOAN PERRY, FINANCIAL ADVISOR

IN ORDER TO FULFILL OUR dreams and create a life of our own choosing, we need the financial wherewithal to get there. Some of us are talented and savvy in the areas of saving and investing. Some of us are cluelessly living paycheck to paycheck, easily seduced by the next fabulous pair of shoes or financially devastated when an emergency expense comes up. Spending on ourselves is an act of self-love that we are all entitled to, but we need to make sure it doesn't create unmanageable debt or a sense of helplessness when suddenly we don't have enough money to pay the rent!

We may think that one of our biggest problems around money is *not having enough of it*. But the real issues often run deeper. We may not feel worthy. We may not feel capable of earning or managing it. We may tend to zone out when it comes to money, and feel afraid of attending to and nurturing our financial lives. Money is one of those highly charged issues! How does a person evolve from someone who lives paycheck to paycheck to someone who lives her dreams? It requires taking full financial responsibility. It's a growth process, to make the transition from someone who still can't balance a checkbook—all those quick debit card withdrawals make it so tricky—to someone who doesn't really *have to* balance it meticulously because there is always more than enough in the account. To create a situation of constant cash flow in our lives, we have to face our financial demons and adopt a prosperity consciousness. Or, in this case, let's call it "Lakshmi Consciousness."

Call upon Lakshmi when it comes to money. We need all the help we can get in surrendering poverty consciousness and increasing our income. But before you ask for that raise or promotion, or even before you consider underselling your services *just to make money*, ask for Lakshmi's help. She grants and delivers good fortune in material and spiritual realms. She represents abundance, plenty, good fortune, and beauty.

WHO IS LAKSHMI?

I invoke Sri (Lakshmi), the blissful goddess, who is sweet-smiling, who lives in a hall of gold, who is full of compassion and drenched with it from the heart, who is resplendent at the seat of the lotus, is lotus-hued, and who bestows all pleasures to her devotees.
—*SRI SUKTA, FROM THE RIG VEDA*

Lakshmi (*LOCK-schmee*) is the Hindu goddess of good fortune and beauty. She is actively worshipped around the globe by millions of Hindus and interfaith practitioners of goddess spirituality, and personifies abundance, prosperity, and wealth. It is said that three millennia ago, Lakshmi was born, fully grown, on a pink lotus that rose from the milky sea. She was immediately bedecked, bejeweled, and worshipped by the gods and sages. They prayed that she would come to their abodes, and to their worlds, because they believed that where Lakshmi is, one finds riches and fulfillment. "Believers" of all faiths trust that praying to the goddess of fortune brings all things good to life. Her eternal consort is Lord Vishnu, known as the Preserver, and her cohort is Ganesh, the elephant-headed Lord of Obstacles. Lakshmi, like many Hindu deities, is often pictured as a beautiful Indian woman with big dark eyes and with four arms. Most Hindu shopkeepers and business people keep her image in their place of business because they believe she brings them luck. With a sari-clad form that is very feminine and full, she sits or stands on her lotus throne. She usually holds two lotuses in her two hands at the back. Her front arms offer blessings and what are known as "boons" or favors from the gods. Her ability to enhance good fortune is symbolized by the gold coins that you see pouring from her hands back into the ocean of life.

HOW TO INVITE HER INTO YOUR LIFE

Lakshmi will work *with you* to increase your income—when she feels welcomed. But first she asks you to do your part to make your life and your financial situation a welcoming environment for her magical touch.

1. **Clean up and organize your living and work space.** The first step to inviting Lakshmi is to clean up your home environment and remove excess clutter. Lakshmi is attracted to cleanliness. Before the Hindu new year of Diwali, which falls in October or November, women clean their houses the night before the new moon to help attract Lakshmi. On Diwali they light oil lamps to invite her; she is drawn to the sparkling cleanliness and the glowing lights. She can more easily bring good things to us when our lives are organized, or at least when we are *trying* to be more organized! Declutter and create order in your desk area and your files, and get on top of financial records. Even if you can't pay all your bills, know what you owe and put a system in place for being financially accountable.

2. **Praise her and pray to her.** Before people of the Hindu faith ask for Lakshmi's assistance, they evoke Ganesh, Lord of Obstacles,

and ask for his help in removing barriers to the success Lakshmi can bring. You can do this by saying:

Om Ganesh, Om Ganesh, Om Ganesh.
O elephant-headed Lord!
Remover of Obstacles,
the bestower of happiness,
salutations unto thee.
Please open the path to prosperity.

Then praise Lakshmi's powers and attributes, and petition her for help:

Dearest MahaLakshmi (Mother Lakshmi), who resides in the pink lotus, who wears a red sari, and who is gifted with great beauty, please come into my life. Brilliant Lakshmi, who is loved by Vishnu, the gods and the sages, please bring your light into my life. Generous Lakshmi, who has four arms, who carries two lotuses, who wards off evil, and who pours forth the abundance of the universe, please bless me with your bounty and help me increase my finances, now.

Then end with a mantra that will bring this to you easily and peacefully (*shanti* means peace):

Shanti. Shanti. Shanti.

3. **Start a Lakshmi Prosperity Bank.** Lakshmi is attracted to her own image and she's honored when you place her picture or icon in your home. Get a small statue or postcard of Lakshmi (widely available online) and build a small "bank" in honor of the goddess of fortune. Your Lakshmi bank will be a mini-shrine, a place where you will commune with the goddess, and, ideally, the place where you will organize and honor your financial life in her presence.

CHOOSE A PLACE FOR YOUR BANK-SHRINE. It should be positioned so that you can see it every day, and have an area designated for paying bills and dealing with finances. No matter where you place it, it should be easily accessible to you. If you must stash it out of sight, place it in a southeast closet or room and visit her frequently.

GET A CLEAR GLASS VASE. This will be your Lakshmi bank and as you fill it with coins, you will see your prosperity grow.

PLACE LAKSHMI'S PICTURE OR ICON NEAR YOUR BANK. If you don't wish to use her picture, simply view the bank as a vital essence of Lakshmi's prosperous energy and dedicate it to her.

START YOUR BANK WITH FOUR SHINY NEW QUARTERS. These represent Lakshimi's four arms; symbolically the new coins will initiate financial flow. Taking the time to quiet yourself and feel relaxed, offer the coins to the goddess as if you are giving a divine gift. People often make offerings to Lakshmi using the right hand. But you can also make offerings by prayerfully using both hands, cupped, and gently spilling the coins into the bank. As you do so, thank her *for all the good fortune that she is now pouring into your life, and for all areas of your financial life that she will empower and help you develop.*

ADD FOUR QUARTERS DAILY FOR THIRTY DAYS. If you don't have four quarters every day, use the coins you do have. Just make sure you share your good fortune with the goddess daily. Spend a moment of sacred silence every time you drop a coin in and acknowledge the increasing finances. The sight of your money growing and the sense that *you are growing it with your own hands* with the goddess's help will instill you with greater confidence and inspiration.

DO ALL YOUR FINANCIAL TASKS AT THE BANK-SHRINE. As you add money to it, it adds power to your financial life, so it becomes a sacred space in which to handle all your money-related tasks. Write your checks, pay your bills, and review your credit card records in front of Lakshmi. If you don't have a checking account, start one now—and fill out the application forms in front of the bank-shrine. (You should also have a savings account!) When you're feeling brave, balance your checkbook. Get in the habit of evoking Lakshmi in all things financial.

WHEN THE BANK IS FULL, REMOVE THE MONEY AND COUNT IT. First, following the spiritual law of tithing, put 10 percent aside for a worthy cause that you would like to support. Put the rest in a savings account and dedicate it as an offering to the goddess Lakshmi.

WATCH YOUR MONEY GROW AGAIN! Have fun filling up your Lakshmi bank again (and again). At the end of each thirty-day cycle, add more money to your savings account.

HOW TO KEEP LAKSHMI WITH YOU

Keep things clean. Lakshmi revels in cleanliness and order—and you will too! You may start out keeping your home, your head, and your finances free of clutter in an effort to attract her support and energy, but in the long run you'll be doing it for yourself. Your financial life will be so much healthier!

Wear gold and precious jewelry. Lakshmi loves things that sparkle and shine. Beautiful jewelry will draw her to your being— and make you feel like a goddess!

Eat healthy foods that symbolize Lakshmi. If you like yogurt, honey, and milk, eat, drink, and be merry in the name of Lakshmi, because these are the offerings made to her as part of worship. Every time you partake of one of these foods, imagine she is nurturing your very being with foods that sustain life; and that you are taking in the empowering energies of beauty and good fortune.

Experience a Lakshmi puja. Hindu people honor Lakshmi with a worship service known as a *puja*. Anyone of any faith can attend, at a Hindu temple, or have a Hindu priest perform one in a private home. Prayers are uttered repeatedly during a Lakshmi worship service and devotional songs are sung. Celebrate her during the Hindu holidays of Navarathri (usually in October) and

Diwali (November new moon). You can also request a *puja* online at saranam.com. They perform the worship service in India and send you blessed materials from the temple. Keep in mind that the prices will look high because they are in rupees, but when you order it is translated into USD and other currencies.

LAKSHMI AFFIRMATION

"My life is rich in so many ways."

$\mathcal{N}$EMESIS

EMBRACE YOUR INNER SABOTEUR

No one can make you feel inferior without your consent.
—ELEANOR ROOSEVELT

MANY OF US HAVE A "nemesis" at work. Perhaps it's a co-worker who makes our blood boil. Or an incompetent colleague who charms her way into the good graces of the powers that be, edging in on our territory. Or a boss who takes our ideas and presents them as her own. If you haven't come across this person yet, you likely will someday—because even the nicest of us will, at some point, work with someone we don't like or who does not care much for us.

If you do have such a nemesis, how many lunches with friends, phone calls with loved ones, or happy hours with office pals have you spent trashing the person you consider the bane of your professional existence? How much have you complained, and yes, whined, about the one person who is always impinging on your territory, treating you like crap, pulling power plays, sabotaging you behind your back, making you do more than your fair share of work, stealing your ideas—and generally turning your office life into a living hell?

One of the most difficult steps in healing our hearts and lives from the offenses and attacks of people we work with is to recognize this: often they are holding up a mirror to us, a mirror that reflects something we need to look at in life. Usually it has to do with how we

221

sabotage ourselves and sometimes destroy our own good work, good fortune, and opportunities. It's a hard mirror to gaze into, because it spotlights self-hatred and wounds you may not even know are there. It's human nature to tend to see problems as defects in others, but because you may be stuck with your office nemesis for some time, it is important that you work on yourself. Your archrival may be reflecting your own worst behavior—or your own worst attacks on yourself—and pushing you to evoke your power in a way you never have before. In many cases, this person represents a classic case of "Your problem is your best friend."

Call upon Nemesis when it comes to dealing with confrontations and conflicts with work associates. She helps us recognize when someone in front of us is reflecting something within us; she helps us heal self-sabotage. She represents the internal mechanisms of judgment, retribution, and revenge and how they can backfire on us if we do not have a clear concept of "so within, without."

WHO IS NEMESIS?

Goddess of Righteous Anger (Justice, Unhappiness). She is a primordial deity who emerged from Chaos. She's an avenger because she takes away happiness if she thinks her sister Tyche has been given too much.
—MARTHA ANN AND DOROTHY MYERS IMEL,
GODDESSES IN WORLD MYTHOLOGY

Nemesis (*NEM-eh-sis*) is the Greek goddess of retribution, revenge, and moral indignation for evil deeds and undeserved fortune. She was in charge of putting "evildoers" in their place and kicking butt in the event of arrogant and unscrupulous behavior. She was not at all big on letting people have what *she viewed* as excessive wealth, happiness, or even self-confidence. Her name means one who distributes or deals out retributive justice, and that's what she did for the ancients: anyone who tried to get one over on her was eventually under her thumb. Nemesis was somewhat of an "instant karma initiator"—you stole, you hurt another, you committed a crime, you ended up with something you did not deserve, and she was on you. She was the daughter of Erebus and the night goddess, Nyks. She is said to have had a rip-roaring affair with the king of all gods, Zeus, which produced the beautiful Helen of Troy; but some stories say she only laid an egg containing her daughter and then refused to nurture it, leaving the hatching to someone else. Nemesis was represented, often in tragic art, as a serious and thoughtful young woman, sometimes seen with wings or a sword and whip. She is sometimes depicted as a griffin.

HOW TO INVITE HER INTO YOUR LIFE

The American Heritage Dictionary points out that Nemesis's name has come to symbolize "a source of harm or ruin, an opponent that cannot be beaten or overcome, and one that inflicts retribution or vengeance." Nemesis is like the proverbial pebble in your shoe. But consider this: She's not out to get you. She's there to guide you. Your enemy at work is this goddess's vehicle for teaching you more about your "inner nemesis." She sees the people who criticize you, bully you, and frustrate you as catalysts for your transformation. Nemesis holds a mirror to us so we can uncover our own dark side and heal ourselves. We can't change the people around us—and it's not up to us to do so—but we can expand our understanding of a frustrating situation, and we can change our own reactions and behaviors.

1. **Become aware of Nemesis—and yourself.** As tempting as it may be to fantasize your retaliation for any perceived or actual wrongs, leave that to Nemesis. The first thing to do when confronted with a difficult person at work is look inward, honestly. If you're dealing with someone who's angry, arrogant, competitive, resentful, manipulative, nasty, sneaky, deceitful, paranoid,

or emotionally unbalanced, you must assess whether there's anything in that person *that is also in you.* If you're interacting with someone who leaves you feeling bad about yourself, you've got to identify the mechanism for how that occurs. Even if you're a very nice, caring person, there may be something in this person's behavior that agitates you for a reason other than the obvious; you might even find yourself being uncharacteristically nasty and defensive. Often, our challenges with difficult people stimulate a form of trauma reenactment, where we literally recreate the difficult experiences of childhood in our adult lives. This can serve to show us a side of ourselves that is buried in the unconscious. From a spiritual perspective, it is designed to bring up old wounded parts of us that need healing.

2. **Create a Nemesis Awareness Chart.** On a plain sheet of paper, make three columns. At the top of the first column, write the name of your own "nemesis" at work. Write your own name at the top of the second, and write "Family" at the top of the third.

LET IT ALL OUT. In the left column, write down all your complaints about this person: for example, she or he is nasty, arrogant, a liar, manipulative, backstabbing, and so on. Let loose! Even the act of discharging some of your pent-up feelings on paper will be helpful.

IS THIS ME? Next, ask yourself honestly if you can relate to any of those qualities. Do you see them in yourself? If the person you take issue with is overly competitive, envious, intentionally covert, could it be that you have any of those traits too? If so, write them down in the column under your name, beginning with "I am . . ." and owning up to the quality.

CHECK THE FAMILY TREE. Then, in the third column, note whether there's anyone in your family who exhibits the kinds of behaviors you find so problematic with your work nemesis. Maybe you had a parent who was very critical and judgmental. Perhaps you had a sibling with whom you had a great rivalry, or who was always vying for attention and taking it away from you.

REVIEW YOUR LISTS. Take a deep breath and ask Nemesis to guide you as you go over the completed three-column chart to seek clarity and illumination. See if you can identify all the specific ways you feel attacked and aggravated by your work nemesis; and also search for any corresponding behavior in you or someone in your family.

DON'T BE SHOCKED! Most everyone will find a little bit of their work nemesis in themselves and their families; some will find more similarities than others. The chart helps us see that our situation at work may be just the icing on the cake; it may simply be triggering painful or disturbing behaviors we developed or were exposed to in childhood.

Healing these wounds is a process, and the first step is to illuminate them and begin to notice what sets off the difficulties at work. For example, as a child perhaps you felt out of control at home, and today you have a very dysfunctional boss. Every interaction with the boss may include not only the current drama the boss is creating, but also the reactivated old dramas and traumas you grew up with. In many ways, these difficult work situations cause us to regress and feel like children again—and it's hard to put in a decent day's work when you feel three feet tall!

3. **Keep doing a self-sabotage reality check.** Use the chart as a launch pad for getting to know your patterns and your emotional, psychological, and spiritual make-up a little better—and for exploring the family history that may affect you at work. There are many ways in which you may be repeating or reacting to family patterns at work. Or you may have a family that didn't empower feelings of worthiness, and thus Nemesis may show up like a bully in the workplace who challenges you to own your power. Be gentle with yourself as you muster the courage to sort all these issues out.

4. **Identify where you are your own worst enemy.** The darkest aspect of Nemesis is that she also represents the part of us that is lacking in self-esteem, self-appreciation, and self-love. Nemesis is sometimes pictured with a sword and whip to emphasize her power to punish misbehavers. How often do you use that sword and whip, metaphorically and emotionally, to punish yourself? How often do you retreat into a critical self-image when someone at work gives you a hard time? How often do you judge yourself and take the blame when it's really not yours to take? How many times have you compulsively tried to "fix things" and "make things better" at work with people who mistreat you? And how often do you berate yourself for how *you* respond to difficult people, or for any ill feelings you may have toward them for being mean to you? Ask yourself: *If someone were physically beating me up the way I beat myself up, wouldn't I fight back?* If so, it may be time to take on the challenge of Nemesis and begin to free yourself from her grip. She only wants you to stop being cruel to yourself!

5. **Purge some of the negativity.** Cleanse other people's negative energies, and your own, every day after work. Take a warm, saltwater bath in kosher salt, sea salt, and a cup of Epsom salts; it will help relieve aches and restore electrolytes when you are stressed. Dunk your entire body—hair too—at least nine times, and as many times as you feel you need to. With each submergence in the water, feel negativity washing away. Make an offering to the goddess at every bathtime; surrender to her one negative quality that you have discovered within yourself that you would like to heal. Feel free to have a good cry and let your salty tears fall into the water, which represents the salty, healing water of the sea. Release, release, release into the water. Say a prayer:

Nemesis, I surrender _____ to you [name the quality you wish to release]. Please help me learn the lessons of this situation and move on. Please help me find balance at work and peace in my heart. Please bring the right remedy to me now. Please heal this situation, heal me, and all involved, for the highest good. Amen.

HOW TO KEEP NEMESIS WITH YOU

Limit self-judgment. When you are critical with yourself, you are often critical with others. This puts people on the defensive and they may reflect criticism back at you. Try being gentler with yourself and see whether it is also mirrored in your world.

Give up the ghosts of past betrayals. If you have been fired, pushed out of a job, hurt by an alleged friend, skipped over for a promotion, given a smaller bonus than a co-worker, you have felt the sting of Nemesis trying to get your attention. Obsessively focusing your energy and thoughts on how you were stung in the past is not productive; in fact, it might add to creating more of the same. Try to use disappointing experiences to grow and learn how you can improve yourself.

Seek professional support when needed. Counselors and therapists can help you through the rough spots. It's always good to get an emotional tune-up when you're in a work situation that is seriously depleting your energy.

NEMESIS AFFIRMATION

"I can choose my actions and reactions to all things."

DURGA

DRAW YOUR BOUNDARIES

A very important part of being kind to ourselves is learning how to say no, and how to set, and be able to defend, boundaries.

—ROBERT BURNEY

RAMA, DYSFUNCTION, ASSORTED CRISES, AND just plain "bad energy" generated by difficult people can drive a sane woman straight to the bar after work if she doesn't stay balanced and grounded. Some businesses seem to thrive on a constant state of chaos and emergency. Perhaps you work with a perfectly nice but slightly "emotional" or "creative" crew of people who are big on drama. Or maybe you're just having one of those days where you're barraged by a series of activities that, in the course of a day, begin to wear you down: The boss is in a bad mood and barking at you; your co-workers have brought their personal problems along to the office; people keep interrupting you with annoying questions; the phone is ringing off the hook; your team needs more hand-holding than you can manage.

When people are getting in your face, and into your space, it's tough to draw the line and limit their access to you. You need a strategy for staying focused and strong; a way to avoid getting dragged into other people's dramas and any other shenanigans that drain your energy and disrupt your productivity. Office politics, imbalances, or chaos can turn an eight-hour workday into a prison shift—unless you know how to draw your boundaries and keep a healthy distance from the craziness.

Call upon Durga for those days—weeks, extended time periods— when people are getting on your nerves, intruding on your space, draining your battery, and giving you a hard time at work. Durga helps you define and create boundaries—physical, psychological, and spiritual. She shows you how to psychically protect yourself from intruders and ward off anyone who does not wish you well. She represents valor, the warrior spirit, and the ability to be mistress of your environment.

WHO IS DURGA?

The demon threatens even the might of the gods, who call
upon Durga to save them from the chaos it represents.
By slaying the demon, Durga restores order to the cosmos.
—FROM THE ANTHOLOGY OF SACRED
TEXTS BY AND ABOUT WOMEN

Durga (*DUR-gah*) is the Great Mother and warrior goddess of the Hindu tradition who symbolizes strength, valor, and protection. Worshipped by millions over the world, she is a particular patron to women, who regularly direct their morning worship and daily prayers to her attention. She is the first personification of the Divine Female in the Hindu pantheon, having emerged from the cumulative powers of all the gods, who called her forth—and conjured her, some say, by breathing fire— when they could no longer fight Mahisasura, the Buffalo Demon who threatened the world. Brandishing the weapons given to her by the gods and representing their fiercest forces of good, Durga set off on her lion to find and destroy him. With her eight arms and numerous weapons, ornaments, and apparels, she was the only one who could reach the nasty demon and stop him. (Her name, in Sanskrit, means "a fort," or a protected place that is difficult to reach.) In addition to being a slayer of evil, she is also the Great Mother, a nurturer, comforter, and loving protectress. Durga is typically seen as a beautiful Indian woman with eight arms (sometimes ten); dressed in a sari, she rides a lion and sometimes a tiger, each hand holding a weapon or poised in a sacred stance.

HOW TO INVITE HER INTO YOUR LIFE

Durga embodies the very powerful warrior aspect of the Divine Mother, yet she is also the all-powerful, very nurturing mother who wants to safeguard her children from harm and look after their well-being. She unifies the male and female principles, embodying both the ultimate divine power of the feminine, called *shakti*, and the energies and attributes of the divine male. She protects the universe, and *is protected by* the universe, therefore, when you come under her auspicious shield, she's got you covered!

Durga has the very special power of being "unreachable." With her help, you can keep negative people, vibes, and happenings out of your personal space, or at least deal with them in a way that lets you feel more in charge. Bring Durga to work and let her be your fort.

1. **Call her to you with a special mantra.** For thousands of years this mantra has been used to evoke the goddess's help and protective power. It can be your secret weapon at work!

Om dum durgayei namaha
(Om-dum-dur-gay-nam-a-ha)

Memorize it, chant it out loud when possible, keep it in your head— or write it out on a sticky note and post it on your computer, your phone, or your desk. Anytime you feel your boundaries being impinged upon, start chanting it over and over in your mind. Repeating this mantra will enhance your own strength and help you endure difficult situations. It will call her energy to any situation. It means essentially: *"Om and salutations to that feminine energy which protects from all manner of negative influences, and for which Dum is the seed."*

2. **Pray to her.** The Hindu tradition is rich with prayers, odes, and devotional songs to Durga. These hail her powers, exploits, and traits. You can recite this ancient ode from *Durga Mata* to offer praise and ask for her attention to your needs. Since people typically leave offerings at Durga's feet in temples, you might also copy the prayer and tape it underneath an image of her, or rest it under the frame, beneath her feet.

> **Oh mistress of the universe, whose nature is the world, filled with all powers. Save us from dangers. O goddess Durga, praise be to you.**

3. **Keep Durga's image on your desk.** In Hindu culture, an icon or image of the goddess brings in her energy. The image of Durga with eight arms, packing all those weapons—yet with such a sweet and beautiful face, and with a lotus in one hand— is a wonderful visual reminder of warring power, woman-style. Although she is generally pictured riding a tiger or lion, and often portrayed stomping on the Buffalo Demon, her demeanor is peaceful. It is believed that having her image handy helps you focus on her powers and enlist her in your aid. If you cannot keep her picture on the desk, keep one in your wallet instead and place a miniature toy tiger on your desk to represent her. It helps to understand the spiritual significance of Durga's awesome arsenal of weapons. She lovingly holds one hand out, decorated palm facing outward, to ward off negative vibes. The rest of her accoutrements are sacred objects that represent aspects of divine protection. Her bow and arrow represent the male and the female; her sword symbolizes wisdom and the battle against ignorance; her three-pronged trident, an attribute of the god Shiva, stands

for the three faces of the divine as Creator, Protector, and Destroyer; her snake symbolizes the eternal cycle of time and immortality; her conch shell, an attribute of the god Vishnu, is a musical instrument used to ward off demons (with the spiraling of its shell representing infinite space); the wheel she spins on one finger represents life and death; and the lotus is a powerful symbol of beauty, fertility, happiness, and eternal renewal; it is the throne of all the gods and goddesses. It is important to note that Durga packs a lot of good in those weapons, so her assistance serves everybody for the highest good!

4. **Imagine her as your force field.** Durga's weapons physically put space between her and opponents, and they can *spiritually* put space between you and yours. Having a rough day? Need some time and space to get work done? Put "the spiritual seal of Durga" on your door and around you. Call in her divine protection by visualizing yourself surrounded in pure white light; then use your imagination to visualize her powers creating a wall of protection between yourself and others. Try it out some day: imagine she is stationed at your office or cubicle door, weapons poised; she sits on her tiger. She will not let anyone too near you because you have work to finish, or because your moody boss is bumming you out too much. Imagine that she makes sure any bad moods or vibes bounce off you. This is the divine version of: "Talk to the hand."

5. **Keep a bell on your desk.** In Hindu temples, priests ring bells during worship to eliminate distracting sounds, concentrate the mind, and to acknowledge worship of a deity. Bells are also used to "clear energy" because they can change the focus. When things are tense in your office, or if people are stuck in a fruitless debate or a creative struggle, why not ring the bell? You can even become the co-worker known for ringing the bell to cut the tension. If your office is too stuffy or corporate for that, ring the

bell in your mind. Hear it ring out! Secretly you will be calling Durga to the rescue.

HOW TO KEEP DURGA WITH YOU

Burn sandalwood incense at home. In the evening, unwind with a scent that is used in temples and conjures the energy of Durga, as well as spiritually cleansing you after a challenging day.

Get a Durga yantra. This is a mystical diagram and mandala that represents the invincible goddess. It is often seen on postcards and posters, or beneath the foot of the animal she rides. It represents power, strength, and victory over obstacles. You can get one from an image of the goddess, or buy a yantra in shiny brass or as an amulet. It is used for protection, as if the goddess has her eye on you.

Visit her in a temple. Most Hindu temples have an icon of Durga, or one of her sister goddesses, that you can visit during normal temple hours.

Experience a Durga puja. Durga is celebrated during the Hindu holiday of Navarathri, which honors the Divine Mother. For nine days, usually in October, people honor the goddess with *puja* and washing of her icon. In India, huge icons are taken to a body of water and immersed—returned to the source—in honor of Durga. You can experience this holiday at any local Hindu temple.

Be a warrior princess. Durga's multiple arms symbolize her ability to defend herself and all people in all ways, and to bring enlightenment and transformation at the same time. Imagine that she is your backup and your partner in business battles.

DURGA AFFIRMATION

"I am a one-woman army when I choose to be."

$\mathcal{S}$AINT TÉRÈSE

GET THE JOB DONE

Live every moment as if you are building a temple.

—SRI RAM

W E ALL HAVE OUR GRUELING days at work, those times when we must complete a project, honor a responsibility, or follow a directive that makes us want to run screaming from the office. You know the kind: It feels *so* difficult and *so* unpleasant that the mere thought of it makes your skin crawl. Sometimes we simply cannot conjure the energy and enthusiasm needed to complete a task, or we get annoyed at having to do menial labor that seems to have nothing to do with the career path we are pursuing—like fetching something for a boss, spending all day making copies, or tracking down information for a super-dull report.

If you're a procrastinator by nature, typically, when confronted by an unpleasant task, you enlarge it to epic proportions in your mind, creating lots of drama. Then you do your darnedest to avoid it, dance around it, and make excuses for not having it done—and you suffer the consequences for delays. Unfortunately, not every step on the career path is graced with a bed of roses, yet you can learn to smell the flowers anyway! Wouldn't it be nice to have the inspiration to approach even the most mundane and annoying tasks as if they are an act of love for the divine?

Call upon Saint Térèse when it comes to completing even the most boring tasks in a simple manner without a lot of conversation about whether we like it or not. She was known for her knack of approaching everything she did in life as an offering to God. She represents the power to do many small tasks with lots of love—and to give up complaining as a temporary sacrifice or offering to the divine.

WHO IS SAINT TÉRÈSE?

Instead of becoming discouraged, I said to myself: God cannot inspire unrealized desires. I can, then, in spite of my littleness, aspire to holiness . . . I want to seek out a means of going to heaven by a little way, a way that is very straight, very short, and totally new.
—SAINT TÉRÈSE OF LISIEUX, THE STORY OF A SOUL

One of the most beloved of Catholic saints, Térèse (teh-*REHZ*) of Lisieux, a.k.a. "The Little Flower," is a very cool spiritual heroine for women of all faiths. She is not a goddess, but in the Catholic faith she is widely prayed to and revered. She advocated conducting all of one's life as a simple devotion to God. Born in 1873 to parents who yearned for religious life but instead had a brood of children, Saint Térèse had the fervor in her blood from an early age and had many spiritual ambitions. In childhood, she had a vision of the Blessed Virgin that was said to heal her; as a girl she wasn't wild about domestic tasks but spent hours kneeling in contemplative prayer. After an emotionally vulnerable childhood, she prayed to be stoic and insisted on becoming a nun; she was finally accepted into the Carmelite order. She learned to flow with the rigors of convent life and give herself over to quiet obedience and devotion. In her eloquent biography, *The Story of a Soul,* she noted the pleasures of performing small tasks as opposed to striving for major feats or thinking that greatness lies only in big accomplishments. She reveled in God's small graces. She died at age twenty-four, yet saw her impending death as yet another blessing in the wheel of life. She is most often pictured in her nun's habit and yellow cloak, clutching a bouquet of roses and a crucifix. (Early photographs are also available of this modern-day saint.)

HOW TO INVITE HER INTO YOUR LIFE

Térèse's popularity transcends religion. Although she spent her young life in mystical communion with Christ and addressed her prayers to the Virgin Mother, you do not have to devote yourself in the same exact way—or become a nun, for that matter—in order to benefit from her approach. She didn't label one task more important than another; all were equal in significance. Life becomes a living grace when you allow each action to bring you closer to the divine. Evoke Saint Térèse for especially tedious projects that make you *emotional*. Life unfolds with far more ease when lived in a state of gratitude. Your energy level will change dramatically if you say thanks to the divine throughout your day, for every task you accomplish—from morning shower to going to bed at night.

1. **Evoke her with scent and smell the roses.** Legend tells us that if she agrees to help, Saint Térèse will send you a rose. Many have claimed to smell the fragrant flower after praying for her intercession. So why not *invite her* with a rose. When faced with a daunting task, see if you can take a moment to get to a florist and buy a single red rose as an offering for Saint Térèse. For those times when you can't get a fresh rose, keep a small bottle of rosewater or essential rose oil around. Dab some on your wrists to symbolize that you are reaching out to the Little Flower for her help. You can tune in to her energy from anywhere and let her guide you. Once you get past your self-imposed limitation, she is like "cosmic coffee," urging you to get things done...and with a big smile on your face.

2. **Take three steps forward.** Imagine that you are moving from your complaints to a state of grace. This physical expression, accompanied by a declaration to Térèse, will create a shift in energy:

> Saint Térèse, I take this step into the day that has been given to me and ask you to give me the ability to see all tasks as equally important. Saint Térèse, I take this step into the day that has been given to me and ask you to empower me to do my best. Saint Térèse, I take this step into the day that has been given me and I ask you to step forward with me.

3. **Say a little prayer and count your blessings.** When faced with a nasty task or a dull duty, saying a little prayer of thanks can never hurt. In addition, if you make it a point to start blessing everything you do, you might find buried in the most hideous tasks the divine inspiration to do a good job and move on. While completing a task, bless each aspect and express gratitude (Try these: "*Thank you for this functioning copy machine. Thanks for the nice weather so I don't get rained on while I'm out job hunting.*")

4. **Keep it simple, stupid.** Simplicity was Saint Térèse's approach to life. And "K.I.S.S." is the motto of many Twelve Step programs, where people with addictions learn, among other things, how they complicate their lives by dramatizing and blowing things out of proportion. Dissect any task into its simplest components, identifying them from beginning to end. Approach it systematically and with the intention to *just get it done.*

5. **Complete everything.** For inspiration, post this "Thought for Today" from Brahma Kumaris World Spiritual University next to your desk. "A task left undone remains undone in two places—at the actual location of the task, and inside your head. Incomplete tasks in your head consume the energy of your attention as they gnaw at your conscience. They siphon off a

little more of your personal power every time you delay. No need to be a perfectionist, that's debilitating in an imperfect world, but it's good to be a 'completionist.' If you start it, finish it . . . or forget it."

HOW TO KEEP SAINT TÉRÈSE WITH YOU

Always keep a rose on your desk. One lone flower will call to mind the Little Flower and make you feel better every time you catch the scent or look at it.

Celebrate her traditions. Her feast day is October 1. There is a nine-day Saint Térèse novena that you can get online or at most Catholic churches. It will explain how to commune with her and request her help according to her tradition.

Get closer to her. Around the country you will find shrines to the beloved saint and, since she was a living heroine, you can also view her relics. You can purchase a Saint Térèse medal in any Catholic gift store.

Light a Saint Térèse candle. Yellow is her color: consider lighting a yellow candle in her honor.

SAINT TÉRÈSE AFFIRMATION

"I approach each task, big or small, with grace, gratitude, and love."

Part 6
GODDESSES OF PLAY
AND LIGHTHEARTEDNESS

AST

BE PLAYFUL AS A PUSSYCAT

You have to sniff out joy, keep your nose to the joy trail.
—BUFFY SAINTE-MARIE

SOME OF US KNOW HOW to enjoy life. We're good at making plans to party, setting up "play dates" with friends and making sure that our calendars are filled with fun things and fun people. Then there are those of us who are so locked into an "all work and no play" ethic that we even bore ourselves! And somewhere in between the wild party animals and the *no-party* animals are professional women who are so anxious to "make it in life" that we forget it's supposed to be fun along the way!

If you work too many hours, worry about too many things, spend all your non-office time at work-related events and find yourself grumpy and stressed when the weekend finally rolls around, you are literally disabled by lack of playfulness. If you barely have any personal time and don't know how to use it when you do, it's time to lighten up. It's playtime!

Call upon Bast when you're ready to come out and play. A goddess who is revered through having fun, she brings out the pussycat in you. Felines represent the feminine, and they are sacred to Bast. She represents surrendering to pleasure, fun, and seizing all of life's opportunities to *meow!*

243

WHO IS BAST?

Bast became an important national deity about B.C. 950, and her festival was among the most popular in Egypt. Vast numbers of men and women were in attendance . . . There was singing and dancing, people clapped their hands, or played castanets.—*WHO'S WHO IN EGYPTIAN MYTHOLOGY*

Bast (*BAHST*) is the Egyptian goddess of play and pleasure, frolic and fun, music, dancing, and partying. Also known more formally as Bastet, she was the ruler of Lower Egypt's holy city of Bubastis, which was devoted to all of those playful qualities—and to cats. Almost everyone in Bubastis had a cat, and they all knew how to party! Bast was so cherished by her people that cats were considered sacred creatures, bejeweled in life by their owners and mummified like humans in their death. In addition, many of the Bubastic temples bred sacred cats that lived like royalty inside the temple and were worshipped as the personification of Bast here on earth.

Her feast day was celebrated with unbridled enthusiasm each October 31, as thousands of Egyptians came from near and far on barges to pour into her city to party, drink wine until they dropped, sing, and often dance lewdly. It was a religious festival with lots of cutting loose and letting down of hair. Partying and gaiety were rampant. In addition to fun and felines, Bast was a noted patron and protectress of pregnant women—and cats—and watched over female fertility, which linked her with the moon. At the same time, she was a noted sun goddess. Bast originated as the lion-headed goddess Sekhmet, who represented the raw power of the sun and presided over healing. Sekhmet, a powerful goddess in her own right, is now considered the fierier, fiercer aspect of Bast. Bast is often depicted as a female with a cat's head, often holding a *sistrum:* a famous musical instrument of ancient Egypt that was said to drive away evil spirits. She is also quite often pictured as a black or gold cat with a beautiful jeweled collar.

HOW TO INVITE HER INTO YOUR LIFE

When it comes to playfulness, the cat goddess of Egypt is a kitten to be reckoned with! She began as a lion goddess whose image grew tamer over time—as will you, when you connect with her wonderful energy. Bast wants her celebrants to be light, happy, self-expressive. Where there is a party, or celebration, there is Bast. You can evoke her just by singing in the shower or dancing to a snappy beat, by adding a kitten to your home—or by acting like one. Bast was revered through the act of having fun and relishing life's pleasures. She is still present in all forms of good, old-fashioned enjoyment!

1. **Observe playtime with the experts.** If you're not feeling like the life of the party, or your playtime skills are rusty, try observing and partaking of life's simplest pleasures to learn how to have fun again.

   WATCH CHILDREN PLAY. One of the best ways to remember how to play is to watch how kids play. They *just do it*—no agenda, no schedule, and nothing to do *but* play. Kids never want to leave the park or stop the game, even though many games have no goal other than the act of playing itself. They explore, trip, fall, get up, throw a ball, chase a butterfly, make mud pies in the sand—and love every moment of it! If we can connect to playing through the eyes of child, we will have a new sense of the purpose of playfulness. Just as kids need to play—to blow off steam and be entertained—we need to play, and honor the part of us that wants to be part of a fun game or a goofy moment!

   OBSERVE A CAT AT PLAY. If you can't get to a park, watch a cat a play. The playful nature of a kitten is a sight to behold! Cats have an amazing frolicsomeness; just look at how much fun they have with a simple item or the imaginary objects they chase around the house. They are also very tuned in to you; *they* can tell *you* when you're not having fun. Cats can help you monitor your moods. They can mirror and act out your inner feelings. If you're jumpy, a cat might poke around mischievously or run back and forth wildly for no apparent reason.

2. **Be nice to cats.** Try these cat-friendly ideas.

HONOR YOUR CAT. Bast comes to life in all felines, so if you already live with a cat, she's close by. Cats were sacred to Bast, and were treasured and treated like royalty by the Egyptians. Cats were among the first domesticated animals, kept as pets and beloved family members, and also served as official family destroyers of pesky snakes, mice, and rats. In ancient Egypt, snakes especially were a threat in the home, so the family cat could be a lifesaver as a household guardian. Cats were considered demi-gods because they also protected the royal food supply from vermin.

ADOPT A CAT. If you don't have a pet and are ready to care for one, Bast will award you even more brownie points if you find your cat at an animal shelter or rescue it from an environment where it is not cared for. Good homes for all cats are a priority for her; she weeps over the fact that there are more cats than good cat homes to go around.

FILL YOUR HOME WITH CAT KNICK-KNACKS. The Egyptians were big on cat *tchotchkes*. In any museum with an Egyptian collection, you'll see many cat-shaped amulets, ornaments, and statues in honor of Bast. (Cat mummies were big as well!) Today, you can shop anywhere and find cat items to accessorize your home and body. Wear cat earrings, necklaces, and pins; enjoy cat statues, art, and feline gear such as fancy feeding bowls.

TREAT YOUR CAT LIKE A GODDESS. A cat calls the shots in your house, as a goddess should. She strikes just the right balance of affection and aloofness, with an air of aristocracy we can learn from. If you treat your cat like a goddess (or god), you'll more likely treat yourself as one, for you'll be the mother of a divine being! Make sure your cat has elegant dining bowls, healthy food, proper shots, and veterinary care, and a nice warm place to sleep, be it on your pillow or next to your bed.

3. **Fill your life with joy.** Look at your schedule to see how many fun things you've planned that you're looking forward to. And how many play dates have you scheduled? If your schedule is a mix of work, play, romance, and family life—congratulate yourself for achieving such balance! If it's filled with meetings and work appointments, begin to pencil in some play. If there's nothing much happening at all, decree that you are ready to play and find the things that fill you with joy.

4. **Expand your play options.** If you had no limitations of time, money, or energy, what would you do with your life? To get your imagination going, start by listing whatever sounds like great fun: travel widely, take singing lessons, try ballet, get a summer beach house—whatever your dreams of play, dare to list them! Put all your secret fantasies on the list. It's for your eyes only.

5. **Find good playmates.** One of the first ways to invite playful Bast into your life is to begin to liberate yourself from people who bring you down. While you may not want to ditch old friends (and relatives) entirely, you can opt to spend less time around them and more time with people who empower the joyous spirit in you. Make it a point to develop friendships, alliances, and social contacts with people who are positive, joyous, and share your interests.

6. **Enjoy some good old-fashioned fun.** Are you finding you're less interested in noisy clubs and more drawn to the fun you can have at home? Arrange play nights for groups of friends and pull out some classic games. The big hits are board games such as Trivial Pursuit, activity games like Twister, and charades—either

the miming or the drawing variety. Serve some snacks and have
a blast!

7. **Play outdoor games.** If you're one of those people who like to
strategize on everything, you might find it hard to just *play*. You
might need a more planned approach. Look for courses that
offer structured play—such as Outward Bound, which has a
super-fun outdoor ropes courses, or paintball or other skirmish
games. Or plan an outing with friends to a ballgame or other
sporting event.

8. **Fill the air with the sounds of music.** The sound of joyous music
echoing through your home is a form of reverence to Bast. Play
your favorite tunes every moment you spend in your abode. Find
music that makes you want to belly dance, or inspires you to move
your body in some way. Remember, too, that even when you're
not feeling playful, music can take you on a journey through
pain and lift you high above it. It can easily and immediately put
a smile on your face.

HOW TO KEEP BAST WITH YOU

Take care of your cat. Daily care and playing with your feline pet
will honor Bast and keep her present in your life. And if you have cat
allergies, you can get a beautiful stuffed cat.

Wear cat jewelry. No animal is more revered in modern jewelry
design! Find a cat ring, necklace, or any cat trinket to keep Bast with
you; you can even buy an Egyptian-style replica of the cat goddess.

Get a cat suit. Not only will it give you that sleek feline look, it
will make you feel playful and free, ready for fun!

BAST AFFIRMATION

"I love to play!"

$\mathcal{U}$ZUME

BURST OUT IN LAUGHTER AND SUNSHINE

Turn your face to the sun and the shadows fall behind you.
—MAORI PROVERB

WE'VE ALL HAD THOSE DAYS when everything that can go wrong does go wrong. When the check *isn't* in the mail, the dog pees on the rug, and the dry cleaner loses your favorite shirt, it's very easy to get bent out of shape and lose your sense of humor. There are plenty of things in life that can lead us down a bumpy, grumpy path. But there's always one thing that can snap us out of it in a nanosecond: laughter. You can do it with anyone safely, it's mess-free, it's drug-free, and it doesn't require a condom. A good laugh, like a good orgasm, alleviates tension and makes you feel alive all over.

Laughter is like medicine. Studies have shown that when we laugh, it is physiologically impossible to be depressed or sad. Like a quick fix of fun, an easy-to-access mood elevator, laughter helps uplift us and heal us. Even if you're not in the mood to laugh, *the act of laughing will make you laugh some more.* Then you can see that there's an entire world around you just waiting to give you a good hoot, and to point out the hilarity of being divinely human.

We all need comic relief, time out from tragedy and challenge. We can help heal ourselves—and our friends and family—with humor and laughter. If you, or anyone you know, are suffering from humor deprivation, it's time to have a good laugh. It costs nothing yet helps you gain a new attitude and perspective. Laughter brings sunshine into your life. No matter how awful things may seem, your world can change with a simple twitch of your facial muscles—a flicker of your lips that starts as a smile and grows into a big, loud, hilarious laugh.

Call upon Uzume when it comes to helping yourself, and others, see the hilarity in life. She shows you how easy it is to laugh, and how it can change the world, returning us to sunshine and smiles. She represents the power of lightening up and having a good guffaw.

WHO IS UZUME?

The Playful Goddess Ama No Uzume would dance by the entrance of the cave, making notions and faces that would bring such a laughter from those who watched Her that curiosity of Amaterasu would be aroused enough to open the door and peer out.
—*FROM ANCIENT MIRRORS OF WOMANHOOD,*
VOLUME II, MERLIN STONE

Uzume *(a-ZOOM-may)*, the bawdy Shinto goddess of merriment and mirth, also has the role of shaman—a role with an important place in traditional Japanese culture. Also known as Ama No Uzume, she is loved as a joyful exhibitionist, wild and wacky in her ploys to get a good laugh—as her legend will show! Uzume is closely linked with the sun goddess Omikami Amaterasu, still the supreme female deity of the Shinto faith in Japan and elsewhere. Their destinies were entwined and their friendship sealed when Uzume helped Amaterasu through a dark time and healed her—and the world—with laughter.

Amaterasu's name means "Great Shining Heaven" and it's said that rice cannot grow without this "queen of all *kami*"—the earth's natural forces. She is considered mother to all the emperors of Japan; all royal families trace their roots to her. Shinto temples honor her with beautiful large mirrors through which her spirit can enter for ceremonies and blessings. Her holiest shrine in all Japan is the huge sacred mirror at the Ise Shrine of Amaterasu Omikami, a humble wooden temple on the bank of the Ise Wan. In art, Amaterasu is depicted as a goddess with a calm, regal, yet soft demeanor (when she isn't represented as a sacred mirror). Uzume, on the other hand, is portrayed as voluptuous and scantily clad, dancing wildly. How did these two opposite personalities become so closely linked for all time?

The Day the Sun Went Away

A famous Japanese myth tells us about the day the sun goddess, Amaterasu, went away. That's when Uzume, literally, showed her stuff.

It all started when Amaterasu's brother Susano-O, the wind god, got drunk, acted like a jerk, and defiled her temples and rice fields. She pleaded with him to stop making a mess, but he refused. Upset, Amaterasu withdrew to a cave, and the world was plunged into darkness and cold. All her sibling gods and goddesses pleaded with her to bring the sunshine back; the world was a mess without it— but Amaterasu wouldn't budge. So they asked the wild and bawdy Uzume to intervene. As a shaman, she was unafraid to dance into the darkness; as a goddess of merriment, she would do anything for a laugh. So what did Uzume do?

First she stripped naked, covering herself with only with a few flowers and leaves. Then she turned over a washtub, hopped up, and did a lewd dance, simultaneously pounding the shaman's healing drum beats with her feet atop the tub. In her fervor of divine ecstasy, she lifted up her flowery garb and exposed herself. All the deities in the vicinity laughed hysterically—so loudly that Amaterasu, hearing the wild cheers, hoots, and hollers, finally couldn't resist. She peeked out from her cave and couldn't help smiling at the sight. A mirror had been placed behind Uzume, and when Amaterasu saw her own beauty for the first time, she was dazzled. Laughing hysterically with the rest of the cosmic crew, she vowed never to go away again.

HOW TO INVITE HER INTO YOUR LIFE

To evoke the energies of Uzume, you have to understand the great power of a good laugh, especially shared by friends. Uzume's power was that she literally brought back sunshine with her ability to make others laugh. So try these ways to do the same with your own friends.

1. **Share laughter and light with friends.** You don't have to be as outrageous as Uzume. Friends can share a laugh over the most mundane and silly things. Whether we live in midtown Manhattan or on a farm in Montana, we can always gather with a friend or two to enjoy a new day's sun and share the absurdities of our lives.

SHARE A MEAL. Just one breakfast meeting a week with people of a similar sense of humor is great medicine for the soul. Order your meal, say thanks for a new day, and celebrate by sharing laughs, cracking jokes, and being goofy. You can have joke contests and funny storytelling fests. If you're not natural joke-tellers, buy a joke book and practice on each other. Stay in touch with your friends during the week by e-mailing each other the best Internet humor you can find.

START A GOOD MOOD VIRUS. If you long to be the ultimate fun bunny, the favorite friend everyone wants to be around, take responsibility for spreading good cheer. Uzume didn't just get Amaterasu laughing—she had all the deities in stitches first. When we allow ourselves to feel good and filled with joy, we radiate. Just as our bad moods can be contagious, our good moods can pave the way for many miles of smiles. If we smile, people smile back; if we laugh, they chuckle too!

LAUGH LIKE CRAZY. When Uzume did her wacky dance, she wasn't wondering, "What will the other goddesses and gods think of me?" She was focused on bringing the sunshine back. Outrageous and out there, she got everyone laughing—and you can too, without lifting your skirt (unless you want to, of course!). If you're with a small group of friends who aren't feeling too peppy, or even if you're with just one bummed-out buddy, and you want to break the bad mood: start laughing. (You wouldn't want to try this at a funeral—just in a non-emotionally charged situation where the room, and people in it, need a blast of fresh energy.) It's up to you: break out in laughter! Start slowly, with a straight face, so they don't even know what you're up to. Then formulate a smile . . . then turn it into a chuckle . . . then build into a contagiously happy laugh. They'll think you are insane at first, until they can resist no more. The laughter will sneak up on them and out of them. Just keep laughing like crazy, and see if one person can resist the allure of that wild laughter. It will fill the room with a burst of giggles and sunshine!

2. **Create a deck of "Happy Cards."** Buy a pack of plain index cards and some magic markers and on each card write a funny saying, quotation, or joke that cracks you up. Keep them in a special box or a decorated coffee can, and reach in any time you need a laugh. When friends come to visit, offer them as treats like brownies—have each friend draw a card from the can. Yes, it's silly! That's the point!

3. **Let's go fly a kite.** Kites are one of Amaterasu's emblems, and of course belly laughs are the trademark of Uzume. Just imagine the great laughs you and a friend will have as you attempt to get a kite up in the air—especially if you haven't tried it since childhood. Make sure that as it flies, you send your wishes to heaven. *Pray for a life of sunshine that is filled with the sound of laughter!* Even if the kite dives, you will have set forth a positive intention and seasoned it with a laugh. (Of course, if you're a serious kite flyer, there may be fewer laughs, but there will be plenty of joy.)

HOW TO KEEP AMATERASU
AND UZUME WITH YOU

Keep smiling. Every time the sun fades, lift your mouth into a smile. Remember—you cannot be sad, depressed, or cranky when you're smiling.

Share a feast of Japanese food. It's healthy, it's light, and it comes from a culture that holds the Goddess as part of daily life. Invite friends out to eat in your favorite Japanese restaurant and share jokes and good spirits as you enjoy a meal in honor of Uzume.

Honor the goddesses on the solstice. Amaterasu is honored on December 21, at the winter solstice. It is a celebration of the birth of light, and the reemergence of the goddess, once again coming out of her cave to warm and brighten the earth. Uzume is part of the essence of that celebration because, remember, Amaterasu would never have emerged were it not for the wacky shaman goddess who made her laugh!

UZUME AFFIRMATION

"A good laugh a day keeps the darkness away."

IRIS

CATCH A RIDE ON A RAINBOW

And then, in the blowing clouds, she saw a band of faint iridescence . . .
She looked for the hovering colour and saw a rainbow forming itself.
—D.H. LAWRENCE, FROM *THE RAINBOW*

WE ALL GET THE YUCKIES, those times in life when things feel dark, drab, and dreary. They might hit us during rough spots—a loss, a challenge, a sad mood—or they might be precipitated by nasty weather, spending too much time cooped up at home, not having enough positive contact with other people, or even by just working under fluorescent lights at the office, day in and day out. Sometimes we just get so blah that the color seems to drain out of life.

Environmental factors can affect our moods and sense of harmony, especially if we're spending too much time indoors, out of touch with nature, or if our home is a bit dim or drab. Sometimes, just a little splash of light and color will bring on the cheer and help us refocus our vision on a brighter view of life. For example, yellow is a color known to be uplifting and sunny; green inspires feelings of abundance, rebirth, spring, and growth. Sitting by a window and letting natural light shine in can lift our spirits.

There is a time and a season in everyone's life for exploring and embracing the blahs, and then there are times when we simply need to brighten our life with a more eye-opening, uplifting approach.

Call upon Iris when it comes to chasing away the blahs and bringing color into your life. She brings her light touch to dark days, and raises your vision over the rainbow as she carries your hopes and dreams to the heavens. She represents hope, vitality, and the power of colorful communication with the divine.

WHO IS IRIS?

Homer calls her "fleet Iris of the Whirlwind Feet" and she travels so fast that all we usually see is the trail of her multicoloured passage across the sky.
—*FROM SHE: THE BOOK OF THE GODDESS*

Iris (*EYE-riss*) is the Greek goddess of the rainbow and divine messenger of the gods and goddesses of Olympus. Considered a handmaiden to Hera and close aide to Zeus, she ran messages to and from "the eye of heaven." A female counterpart to Hermes (Mercury), she too is winged, symbolizing swiftness, and carries a caduceus, a symbol of healing and divine communication. Her name means "rainbow" (or "an appearance resembling a rainbow") and the Greeks believed that any rainbow in the heavens heralded her arrival. She was known to travel over its arc, without a chariot, in a many-hued robe; she bolted so quickly that only the colors of her robe rushing through the sky were visible. She was daughter of two Titans, Thaumas and Electra, and by most accounts was considered the bright-eyed sister of the Harpies, who were notoriously dark and gloomy. Though she was sometimes called upon to deliver difficult news, she was known as a sweet-tempered goddess, with no enemies. This gave her an all-access pass to the universe, making her welcome in all corners of the earth and beyond. Iris's duties included the sacred responsibility of leading the souls of dead women to the Elysian Fields. To honor her in this role, the Greeks planted her purple iris flowers on the graves of the deceased. Iris is usually pictured as a golden-winged maiden in a long flowing garment that is colored like the rainbow, or as a rainbow itself.

HOW TO INVITE HER INTO YOUR LIFE

The rainbow is viewed in many cultures as a symbol of hope and vitality. As the embodiment of the rainbow, Iris helps bring color and cheer to our lives. On golden wings she takes our heartfelt desires to the Divine and brings glad tidings that help us lighten up and feel peaceful. She also represents the idea that a colorful existence is part of our birthright, and that color draws a bit of heaven to us here on earth.

1. **Experience her in rainbows.** A rainbow is one of nature's most glorious sights. The Greeks deified them because they believed they signaled Iris streaking the sky. Rainbow sightings may seem to require a bit of serendipity, but there are just three simple ingredients needed: showers, sunshine, and sight. Technically speaking, a rainbow occurs when light is refracted (or "bent") through millions of raindrops. The drops act like prisms, catching the sun and reflecting it back in vivid colors. While the bigger the drops of rain the more vivid the rainbow, you can find the rainbow goddess and her hues in even the tiniest drop of water. A willingness to seek her out will expand your ability to see the colors of life and to view life through new eyes!

2. **Place a rainbow crystal on your window.** Buy a multifaceted Austrian crystal, also called a feng shui crystal, and let the sun shine through, filling your home with a dancing spectacle of all the colors of the rainbow goddess. The principle behind rainbows also applies to the facets of a crystal: the sunlight refracts through them and scatters rainbow-tinted light.

3. **Bring more color to your abode.** If your apartment or home is drab or dark, try a splash of brightness.

PICK COLORS THAT SUPPORT THE MOOD YOUR WANT TO CREATE. Studies show that certain colors have specific effects on mood and attitude. Interior designers regularly consider these facts when creating home and office spaces. In addition, color therapy is an accepted modern mood enhancer; feng shui takes into account that colors have specific impacts on our lives: our goals, happiness, prosperity, and matters of love. The basic idea is to bring in the hues that offer the "right energy" to each room. For example:

a) **Purple** creates mystery in a room and can help you feel closer to the divine. It also represents royalty and wealth.

b) **Blue** helps you relax and feel peaceful; it makes a room seem cool. It also represents wisdom.

c) **Green** imparts the feeling of being in nature and is also healing. It also represents health.

d) **Yellow** cheerfully energizes and expands the size of a room. It also represents creativity.

e) **Orange** is also a cheery color, but it may make you hungry. It also represents creative expression and sexuality.

f) **Red** is the color of courage, daring, aliveness, and passion. It represents good luck.

g) **Pink** promotes affection and makes you think of love. It's soothing, and it also represents romantic relationships.

PAINT YOUR WAY TO HAPPINESS AND WHOLENESS. A fresh coat of paint can do wonders to change your outlook on life. The six colors of the rainbow are red, blue, green, yellow, orange, and purple. Use whatever hues empower you and make you feel good. Paint one room, or paint them all. Not up for a paint job? Then paint one small item as a symbolic gesture of colorful change.

CHOOSE COLORFUL HOUSEHOLD ITEMS. Curtains, shades, pillows, throw rugs, towels, and dinnerware in bright shades can all spice up your home. Plants and flowers can also give your home a new attitude and feeling. As you add more hues, your life will become more colorful.

4. **Create a message board to the goddess.** If you don't have the desire—or the wall space—for a full mural, try making a bulletin board into a communications center for uplifting messages and ideas. Buy a rainbow poster, place it at the bottom of the bulletin board, and leave room on the top—*somewhere over the rainbow*—for messages you'd like Iris to take to "the eye of heaven." Write little prayers, goals, hopeful thoughts—such as "today I move forward" or "I will have a divine time today"—and tack them onto the board. Add pictures, too: images of smiling people, of happy, vibrant women, of art that represents the colorful life you choose to experience. Consider them cosmic memos to the goddess. Gaze at it for a few moments every day.

5. **Counteract darkness with crayons, markers, and doodles.** Any time you are feeling low, out of sorts, or sad, you're more vulnerable to the dark energies of the Harpies, but you can balance it out by drawing, doodling, and coloring your way to a brighter moment.

KEEP A SET OF RAINBOW-COLORED MAGIC MARKERS AND WHITE PAPER HANDY. If you feel the heaviness or darkness of life creep close to you, pull out your art supplies and craft your way to a more colorful mood. Draw anything! Let the colors swirl, twirl, and fill the page. Write things that you *wish* you felt like saying: *I am happy, I am alive, Today will be so much fun,* and *Sunshine fills me.* Even if you don't feel those things inside, keep at it anyway: you can write or draw yourself out of a funk.

TRY YOUR HAND AT COLORING BOOKS. If you prefer a little more structure in your artwork, you may love coloring books for adults. They feature beautiful scenes from nature, goddesses, intricate mandala-like drawings, and many other mystical images. People usually use colorful pencils or skinny markers to work on these. Some people frame them and hang them up in their homes. They are lots of fun and are used to relieve stress by focusing the mind on a creative activity.

HOW TO KEEP IRIS WITH YOU

Let her bloom in your life. The iris flower was dedicated to the goddess because it blooms in all the shades of the rainbow. It has a long history of special significance. Irises look and smell beautiful, and come in many uplifting colors and styles that can bring happiness to your home.

Wear the colors of the rainbow. Dress in bright hues. Don clothing, scarves, shoes, and accessories that make you feel great. Purples, blues, yellows, greens, oranges, reds—wear Iris with you always.

Buy a new lipstick. Nothing cheers a woman like a new color— or two. Studies show that when women want to make a change, they begin with lipstick.

Quit complaining. Just for one day, don't moan, groan, or complain about anything, at all. See how you like it. If you do, then try it again . . . and again . . . and again. You might find you've developed a new habit that helps keep the Harpies away!

IRIS AFFIRMATION

"I can always see the rainbow past the storm."

UTTERFLY MAIDEN

COME OUT OF YOUR COCOON AND FLY

There came a time when the risk to remain tight in a bud was more painful than the risk it took to blossom.

—ANAÏS NIN

THERE WILL BE TIMES IN life when we find ourselves in a waiting period, a holding pattern. Such a pattern is often a transitional phase, one that prepares us for the next stage. Sometimes it feels as if we are incubating—like an infant in the womb being readied for life. Although we're still attached to the umbilical cord that sustains us, our birth is imminent.

One such change culminates in our adolescence, when we crawl from the comforting cocoon of family life and suddenly have the desire and ability to spread our wings. But even in adulthood, during any "inbetween time," we may feel cocooned, separated from the world, and as if nothing is happening. But in truth, a new possibility is being developed and nurtured as an old stage is being outgrown. For everything there is a time and a season.

Problems come when we find ourselves squished into a situation that we have definitely, without-a-doubt outgrown, yet we can't seem to leave it behind. It's become so familiar and comfortable that we don't want to budge. Some people call it the "fly in the garbage pail syndrome"—a fly has the great big world to traverse yet she swirls around the same garbage pail over and over. She may alight on your arm from time to time, she may buzz around your apartment, but when you open the window, she will not leave. She's stuck.

In order to grow, we are continually called to surrender a part of the life we have known, to shed our old skin so we can be born anew. We have to stretch beyond where we were before. It's as if a part of us must die to let something new and vibrant be born. Hopefully we struggle through it, the way a baby chick breaks out of a shell or a butterfly emerges from its cocoon; this is a natural process of growth. When the time comes to let go and fly free, it's a glorious moment of rebirth.

Call upon Butterfly Maiden when you're ready to emerge into your fuller state of being. She teaches you to gain strength from your struggles toward transformation—and then to surrender to nature's will when it's time to become the butterfly you're meant to be. She represents transformation, emergence, and taking flight in life.

WHO IS BUTTERFLY MAIDEN?

*Butterfly Maiden is the Hopi Kachina who
governs Spring. A Kachina is a Nature Spirit.
They are sacred spirits living in the plants, animals,
and female ancestors who link the human with the divine.*
—NANCY BLAIR, GODDESS FOR EVERY SEASON

Butterfly Maiden is a Native American fertility goddess who brings her pollen from one place to another, spreading transformation and new beginnings. Like the fresh breath of spring, she is witnessed on the wings and in the soul of a butterfly—the creature that can transform herself from a caterpillar to a flying work of art by following nature's simple calling to create a cocoon, inhabit it, and then emerge from it when the time comes. She is the spirit that moves the butterfly to produce the tiny eggs that will become larvae, and that allows the caterpillar to know when to fashion its cocoon and when its transformation is complete. The Hopis believed she pollinated the world of nighttime dreams, carrying the life force from dreamtime to reality; in essence, making dreams come true. She is a creative force, a symbol of rebirth and regeneration. Hopi legend says that the butterfly is the best messenger for making wishes come true and that they are taken to heaven on its wings, hence, Butterfly Maiden. She is pictured in modern art as a young Native American woman, dressed in or surrounded by butterflies.

HOW TO INVITE HER INTO YOUR LIFE

In the Native American culture Butterfly Maiden hails from, it is believed that each animal, plant, and insect has its own energy and spirit; the healing qualities in each are called medicine. "Butterfly medicine" is about our personal power and responsibility to renew ourselves. It requires us to skillfully understand and honor our own nature and rhythms; to know when to build a cocoon and when it's time to fly! When we follow the ways of butterfly medicine, we know that while growth is sometimes distressing, lack of growth is even more painful!

Learn from Nature

1. **Understand the natural transformation of butterflies.** Some of us might think that caterpillars are ugly, but they're obviously a required stage of the process. You might be surprised to know that the yuckiest-looking ones become the most beautiful butterflies! Caterpillars begin as tiny eggs left on a leaf by a mature butterfly. The eggs hatch into tiny larvae (baby caterpillars). These minute slinky things begin to chow down on nature's bounty and quickly grow into adults, eating until their skin is fully stretched. It is then that the caterpillar builds its shell-like home, the cocoon—also

called the chrysalis. For ten days the mystery of transformation quietly takes place. Then slowly, almost magically, the butterfly appears. These creatures are a miracle of nature. We too must allow ourselves the space to endure the less colorful caterpillar stage of life in order to grow more fully.

2. **Witness butterflies in flight.** It's considered auspicious to see these fluttering creatures; they always leave a sense of wonder in their wake. They stir the soul and inspire us to see that we, too, can aspire to move gracefully and freely from one place to another. They help us imagine that we can soar. Keep an eye out for them on a soft summer day and count your blessings if one happens by you. Or visit one of the many butterfly conservatories that can be found around the country. They offer an environmentally protected way to observe hundreds of varieties of butterflies in action, see cocoons, and learn more about them.

3. **Create a sacred ceremony to inspire personal transformation.** Are you in a holding pattern that has you a little stuck? Are you at a crossroads in your life, needing a spiritual boost to move you forward? Try this exercise *only* if you don't mind a short period of self-imposed darkness in which you will feel restricted and only if you can do this safely. In this exercise you will emulate a butterfly emerging from a cocoon.

GATHER SOME UNCOMFORTABLE ITEMS OF CLOTHING. Start this exercise dressed in undergarments plus a pair of shorts or leggings and a T-shirt. Now find some clothing items in your closet that are way too tight and uncomfortable, preferably items you can layer, including sweaters, gloves, and hats. Look for jeans that are too small, a bra that squishes, or even a panty girdle and tight skirt.

PREPARE TO SPEND SOME TIME IN A CONFINED, DARK SPACE. A small bed in a dark bedroom is best. Find a heavy blanket and plenty of pillows and lay out your items of clothing out on the bed.

PLAY MUSIC YOU LOVE. Set the tone with soothing music that makes you feel comfortable, safe, and loved. This will help establish a dichotomy: you've outgrown this place, but you feel too safe and comfortable to leave—yet.

OFFER A PRAYER OR INVOCATION TO BUTTERFLY MAIDEN.
I come in the name of new possibilities.
Butterfly Maiden, please join me, protect me, fill my heart with the power and inspiration of butterfly medicine.
Let me move forward now from my cocoon and answer Spirit's call to fly.
May I trust my heart.
May I grow lighter, wiser, and more skillful as I learn to fly higher.
I thank you. So be it.

SLIP INTO YOUR COCOON. Draw the shades or curtains, turn the lights out, let your special music play, and slide under the covers. Relax and let yourself feel soothed. Sink into the comfortable embrace of the bed and let yourself unwind with the music.

BRING ON THE DISCOMFORT. Once you're relaxed and feeling good, begin to add layers of clothing. In the darkness, pull them on over whatever you're already wearing—a tight bra over the bra you already have on, an extra shirt or two followed by sweaters, and tight pants or skirts over your bottom half. Then pull the covers up. Feel the snugness and let it get a little uncomfortable.

COMMUNE WITH BUTTERFLY MAIDEN. In the silence, dark, and discomfort, call to her and ask her to be your harbinger of transformation, to help you prepare to initiate changes in your life. Give some thought to what you would like to transform or "grow beyond."

NOTICE WHERE YOUR MIND GOES. You will likely feel the clothing get tighter, the bedcovers more restrictive, the darkness more repressive. Feelings of "wanting to get the heck out of here" will not be far behind. When you reach that point, whip off the covers, strip off the extra clothing, turn on the lights, open the window, and breathe in the fresh air! Notice the big difference between being confined and stuck—and feeling free.

DECLARE YOUR FREEDOM. Choose to get yourself unstuck from whatever situation has a hold on you. It's time for transformation! Think of one major goal that can truly change your life. Aspire to it. Hold it in your heart and mind. Let it take on life and promise.

CLOSE WITH THIS BUTTERFLY BENEDICTION.
Butterfly Maiden surrenders to the cycles of life, and she flies high when the time is right. I will too.
I choose to believe in myself.
To trust my own heart.
To walk my own path with wisdom.
To create new dreams and follow them.
To honor my abilities.
To be keeper of my own destiny.
And maker of my own life path.
Thank you, Butterfly Maiden, for guiding this ritual.

HOW TO KEEP BUTTERFLY MAIDEN WITH YOU

Grow a butterfly-friendly garden. You can keep her spirit close to home if you have a sunny spot in your garden and a green thumb. Find out what kinds of nectar plants attract butterflies and how to grow them in your garden.

Get a dreamcatcher. This Native American sacred object is a branch fashioned into a circle, and made with netting and feathers; it comes in many sizes. It's believed that if you place one by your bed, Great Spirit will catch all your good dreams and filter out nightmares and bad dreams. It will help you hold on to dreams of positive transformation.

Create a butterfly doll. The Hopi children were taught that the spirit of Butterfly Maiden lives in the kachina doll. They are often made of ceramics or straw but you can fashion one with clay and place a drawing or image of a butterfly on it.

BUTTERFLY MAIDEN AFFIRMATION

"My time has come. I have arrived."

$\mathcal{F}$AIRY GODMOTHER

BELIEVE IN MAGIC

Bibbidi bobbidi boo!
—THE FAIRY GODMOTHER IN DISNEY'S *CINDERELLA*

W E CAN ALL USE A Fairy Godmother. At any age, at any stage, in any situation involving the heart and soul, it's so reassuring to imagine a special being who's there just for you.

If you've lost hope in finding your prince or princess . . . If you're feeling you need a change in careers . . . If you're looking in the magic mirror and hearing, "You could use a little freshening up" instead of "You are the fairest in the land" . . . If you're finding that those fabulous glass slippers you got on sale are too darned hard to walk in . . . or if you've forgotten how to let your imagination run free and trust in the abundance of the universe—it's time to let magic back into your life.

Believing in magic is essential for creating a life of our own choosing. It helps us to remember that we live in an unlimited universe where anything is possible. It also makes life more interesting and fun.

We survive childhood by believing that magical intervention is just a wish away—from Superman to Santa, there's always someone to save the day. Girls, especially, grow up with the concept of a female being with magical powers who shows up when we *really* need her. It's her job to rescue us, help us escape a bad situation, and

269

assist us in transforming our lives; ultimately, she ordains that we'll live happily ever after. And that is simply the way of the universe . . . when we're kids!

As adults, our brains begin to bog down with rationalization and judgments that rob us of the magic available to us in real life.

As little girls, we see in the Fairy Godmother our first glimpse of a goddess-like being with special powers. As we get older, many of us continue to secretly wish and hope for a magical mentor to show up. Tucked away in our heart is the belief that someone wise and wonderful is waiting in the wings to step in and lend a hand—or a wand. Whether she turns a pumpkin into a coach, shows us our true beauty, or protects us from wickedness, she gives hope that a magical life awaits.

As time goes on, we come to realize that we are the ones who can create our own magic. The task at hand is to refuse to allow old disappointments and pessimism to sink our dreams. Our Fairy Godmother remains a symbol of the enchantment and bliss we once dreamed would be ours for the taking.

Call upon your Fairy Godmother when you are ready to remember the magic of believing. She helps us conjure faith and optimism and connects us to all the mystical and magnificent possibilities of the universe. Like the beloved grandmother or aunt with special powers, your Fairy Godmother is a spiritual heroine who helps us remember the magical divine powers that dwell in the universe and in our hearts.

WHO IS THE FAIRY GODMOTHER?

The Fairy Godmother is an enchantress, a holy sacred mother of the ancient mysteries. She ushers in what we think we do not know or cannot have or dare not express. She offers us gifts of the spirit: the gifts of inner guidance and universal love.
—*FROM INNER CHILD CARDS*

The Fairy Godmother is the wonderful, magical, mystical being who shows up in fairy tales just in the nick of time, wand in hand, to help the heroine make her dreams real and live happily ever after. The godmother's roots extend way past the Disney movies that have made her so popular, into the ancient religions. She is actually a composite of many feminine archetypes and magical beings. The concept of Godmother may be as old as goddess worship itself—the ancient belief in the protectress of the human family. Some trace her roots to the Fairy Queen, the top female in the kingdom of mystical beings endowed with powers of magic and enchantment (you remember them from Shakespeare's *A Midsummer Night's Dream*). Some Welsh folk ballads called fairies "the mothers" or "mother's blessing." The classic fairy tale by Charles Perrault was one of the first to name Cinderella's special helper in this way: "This godmother of hers, who was a fairy . . ." Sometimes this mystical female mentor character is presented as a sorceress who uses her powers for good, especially to guide her charges to healing and transformation. The Fairy Godmother is often pictured as an older, wise woman with a magic wand—as in Disney's *Cinderella*—or as a mystical "good witch" priestess such as Glinda in another classic movie, *The Wizard of Oz*. She can also be depicted as a stern but nevertheless wholly magical caretaker figure—think Mary Poppins—who brings healing to the whole family.

HOW TO INVITE HER INTO YOUR LIFE

Our Fairy Godmother is our metaphor, mentor, partner, guide. And she is one of the memorable ways in which the Goddess has stayed alive in our hearts: as the magical female who can do all things magnificent, as long as we do our part as well! Continue to believe in her, and she will stay alive in our hearts and lives!

1. **You must have a wand!** A wand is the magical tool of choice of all conjurers and witches—in fairy tales and in real life. In

fairy tales, a wand represents magical powers and abilities. Practitioners of Wicca and other magick-based religions use wands to harness magical powers and magnetize wishes. You can purchase a beautiful handmade wand with stones at the tip and other fancy trimmings, or buy a simple children's wand and keep it where you can see it. It is the emblem of magic in your mind. Owning one will make you feel magical.

2. **Keep fairy dust around.** It's a symbol of possibility that reminds us that life can be invented and created from nothing, and dreams can come true. It gives us hope. It also reminds us to "clap for Tinkerbell," to focus our attention to make magic happen. Use gold or silver sparkles, pretty confetti, or buy some packaged pixie dust.

3. **Receive her blessings.** Buy a Fairy Godmother figurine with a lovely wand. Place her nearby and at an angle that allows her to tilt toward you with special blessings.

4. **Read yourself positive bedtime stories.** Filling your mind with fanciful images and magical thoughts is so much healthier than the evening news! There's a vast array of material to choose from. Explore books that include Fairy Godmothers and similar characters. Select inspiring stories about magical lives—books that help you enjoy romance, royal treatment, and happily-ever-after endings. Notice whether you feel happier or more energized in the morning! You may find that you awake with a smile and an anything-is-possible attitude.

5. **Be inspired by magical movies and TV shows.** If you have children in your life, you may already own a few magical movies. You can also have fun researching new movies, television shows, and series to put on your watch list. Add those to your favorites, including the classics you enjoyed as a child. Any form of media

that helps you tune into magical memories and uplifting feelings is perfect to view whenever you need a lift. Enjoy watching and being transported into magical worlds.

6. **Listen to your Fairy Godmother's advice.** She has wisdom to share: learn to create your own magic and get yourself out of your own fixes!

TAKE "THE JOURNEY" TO WHOLENESS. While it would be nice to have her clean up our messes and issues with one wave of her wand, we must be willing to take the journey she invites us on. Even in fairy tales, we are asked to do our part in transforming our own lives. Before she waves a wand and snaps her fingers, she makes sure we learn a life lesson unlike any other. It's the journey of becoming more fully who we're meant to be that really leads us to the *potential* for happily-ever-after. Only after we take the journey—with all its scary twists and bumps and dark characters—are we ready for the leap of faith that leads us to the ultimate healing and transformation. So when you find yourself on one of those bumpy life paths, don't give up hope . . . remember that it's part of a process.

APPRECIATE HER SPECIAL SUPPORT. Our Fairy Godmother lets us tap into the goddess within by helping us believe in ourselves. The magical accessories are just to help us "fake it until we make it." The true gift is the boost of confidence. While it may seem that Cinderella's life changed with a mere twist of a wand, in truth, her Fairy Godmother was a real mother figure, a soul friend who reached out a hand to help her onto the next rung of life's ladder. By showing her some other options, she expanded Cinderella's ability to go after the greater things in life.

ASK FOR BIG PRESENTS, BUT ACCEPT WHATEVER IS GIVEN. The modern Cinderella might prefer a magical credit card with unlimited prepaid credit and a limo driver to take her shopping—and that's fine. But if you ask for the gold card and a chauffeur, and instead you get a department store gift certificate and cab fare, accept it gratefully. Our Fairy Godmother sometimes tests us before she delivers the goods. Our grace and gratitude in the face of disappointment help keep us humble when the big windfall occurs.

GET HOME BY MIDNIGHT. Our Fairy Godmother can be the internal voice that guides us and helps us keep our promises and enhance our integrity. She knows exactly when the magic of any given situation will wear off, and when to come home. Heed her guidance—it's always for your own good!

7. **Choose to dwell in a magical universe.** With *all* her magical cohorts, our Fairy Godmother opens our heart and our memory to the childhood pleasure and power of making things up. She is the light side of the Goddess—benevolent, hopeful, and healing. Fairies can also be mischievous and edgy (like Tinkerbell!); they need those qualities to protect and guard their charges and territories. There's a wide range of cousins and distant relatives to the Fairy Godmother that can also be called upon to help. Just opening our awareness to the enchanted worlds helps us invite enchantment into our lives.

GENIES. Arabic and Islamic folklore describe beings called *jinni* (a word Americanized as a "genie"). Although they have the power to do good *and* bad, they essentially follow a master's orders. They have power to grant wishes; think of the genie that popped out of Aladdin's lamp. When you need something fast, you can always rub a lamp, a teapot, or something brass and ask your personal genie to please bring it to you.

ELVES. In Germanic folklore, these fairylike little folks dwell in forests, the sea, and the air. They can be vengeful and mischievous, but also very helpful, like Santa's elves. Ask them to assist with all your gift-giving needs and more.

PIXIES. These are the playful spirits of the English tradition—

imps who like to fluster young maidens and lead travelers astray. If you lose your way on the road, or you can't find your car keys, tell the pixies to cut the pranks and help you focus on getting to where you need to go.

MERMAIDS. This mystical maiden of the sea has a beautiful face, shapely torso, and a fish fin lower half. Always put a prayer out to mermaids when swimming, to keep away the sharks—and creepy, swishy sea urchins—and to help you travel by water safely.

ANGELS. Among the most celebrated and popular channels to the divine, angels take many forms and have a variety of specialties. Many people keep their Fairy Godmother alive by seeing her as guardian angel—with wings and a halo rather than a wand.

HOW TO KEEP YOUR FAIRY GODMOTHER WITH YOU

Wish upon a star, every night. Or write one wish a night on a small piece of paper and slip it under your pillow before you go to sleep. Your Fairy Godmother and the cosmic crew are always listening.

Honor the magic in everyday life. Notice your Fairy Godmother in those synchronistic moments when fate and possibility create a miracle of sorts: You think of a person and she calls you at that moment. You're supposed to be somewhere, yet by running late, you avert a traffic accident. You run into someone you were destined to meet in a place you almost didn't visit, had it not been for the gentle urging of a voice within. Day in and day out, your Fairy Godmother shows you that there's really no such thing as a coincidence. The people and experiences you draw to you are all there for a reason.

Blow bubbles. Just like a kid, buy a bottle of soapy bubble liquid with a wand. Then find a place outdoors or by an open window and blow bubbles. As you watch them floating in the air, imagine they're carrying your wishes to your Fairy Godmother, who will grant those she deems worthy. Let your heart open as you continue to blow bubbles and call out your wishes. When you feel you have had your fill, dedicate the last batch to her. Thank her for touching your life and helping you believe.

FAIRY GODMOTHER AFFIRMATION

"I wish I may, I wish I might . . .
I wish and desire a magical life."

CLOSING THOUGHTS

In revisiting all the goddesses and spiritual heroines in this book I was overcome with a sense of hope. It was the same hopefulness I felt when I first researched this book and discovered there were so many goddesses to help us with all aspects of life.

I hope that the chapters you've read have introduced you to some new and wonderful spiritual mothers and sacred females. I hope they bless your life in a thousand ways. I hope they help you know the goddess within.

Take your time with them. Get to know them. Work with the one who calls to you the most, or with many at once, depending on your needs. It is also fine to simply see the Goddess as one Divine being with many facets, or to call to her by one name.

I believe that our Divine Mother, by any name, is always there for us. That she will not forsake us, even during the worst of times. She is closer than we even imagine, often just a breath away.

We need the Goddess to help us through life's challenges. And she needs us. Let us open our hearts to her divine powers and do our part to perfect our lives and uplift the world.

Blessings,
Rev. Laurie Sue

CHAPTER NOTES

Artemis

Epigraph: *My Aim Is True* was Elvis Costello's 1977 debut album.

"Who Is Artemis?" quote: Edith Hamilton, *Mythology: Timeless Tales of Gods and Heroes* (New York: Grand Central Publishing, 1999), "I sing of Artemis," from Homeric Hymn XXVII.

Some Artemis mythology adapted from Nancy Hathaway's *The Friendly Guide to Mythology* (New York: Viking/Penguin, 2001).

Aurora

Epigraph: "Follow your bliss" is a phrase made famous by Joseph Campbell in his legendary interview series with Bill Moyers, first broadcast on PBS television in 1988. The fuller quotation: "My general formula for my students is 'Follow your bliss.' Find where it is, and don't be afraid to follow it." Appears in Joseph Campbell and David Kudler (ed.), *Pathways to Bliss: Mythology and Personal Transformation* (Novato, CA: New World Library, 2004).

"Who Is Aurora?" quote: Homer, *The Iliad* (New York: Penguin Classics Deluxe Edition, 1998).

Edith Hamilton, *Mythology: Timeless Tales of Gods and Heroes* (New York: Grand Central Publishing, 1999).

Diana Apostolos-Cappadona, *Dictionary of Women in Religious Art* (New York: Oxford University Press, 1998). This source provided images and some insights into Aurora's mythology.

Bast

Epigraph: Sainte-Marie quote from "Daily Celebrations: Life Is a Celebration of Passionate Colors" at www.dailycelebrations.com/joy.htm.

"Who Is Bast?" quote: Anthony S. Mercatante, *Who's Who in Egyptian Mythology* (New York: Barnes & Noble Books, 1995).

Amy Sophia Marashinsky and Hrana Janto (illus.), *The Goddess Oracle: A Way to Wholeness Through the Goddess and Ritual* (Boston: Element, 1997; Stamford, CT: U.S. Games Systems, 2006). This source provided some mythology and inspiration on Bast.

Anthony Veggi and Alison Davidson, *The Book of Doors Divination Deck: An Alchemical Oracle from Ancient Egypt* (Rochester, VT: Destiny Books, 1994).

This source provided details on the history of honoring Bast.

Brigid

Epigraph: Wayne W. Dyer, *Inspiration: Your Ultimate Calling* (Carlsbad, CA: Hay House, 2007).

"Who Is Brigid?" quote: Amber K, *Candlemas: Feast of Flames* (St. Paul, MN: Llewellyn, 2001).

Information on the continuing ritual of the flame found at "Lighting the Perpetual Flame," County Kildare Community Network website, http://kildare.ie/community/notices/perpetual-flame.asp.

Flame-keeper history recounted at the Ord Brighideach International Order of Flamekeepers website, www.ordbrighideach.org/home.

Miranda J. Green, *Dictionary of Celtic Myth and Legend* (London: Thames and Hudson, 1992).

Michael Jordon, *Encyclopedia of Gods: Over 2,500 Deities of the World*, (New York: Facts on File, 1993).

Butterfly Maiden

Epigraph: Attributed widely to Anaïs Nin, writer and diarist; official website is at www.anaisnin.com.

"Who Is Butterfly Maiden?" quote and other information from Nancy Blair, *Goddesses for Every Season* (Boston: Element, 1995).

Clarissa Pinkola Estes, *Women Who Run with the Wolves: Myths and Stories About the Wild Woman Archetype* (New York: Ballantine, 1992).

Jamie Sams and David Carson, *Medicine Cards* (Rochester, VT: Bear & Company, 1988). This classic deck of divination cards and book provide priceless insights into the "medicine" of many creatures.

Facts and insights on butterflies drawn from American Museum of Natural History website, "The Butterfly Conservatory," www.amnh.org/ exhibitions/butterflies.

Discussion of butterfly habits drawn from North American Butterfly Association website, www.naba.org.

Durga

Epigraph: Robert Burney, in *Codependence: The Dance of Wounded Souls* (Encinitas, CA: Joy to to You & Me Enterprises, 1995).

"Who Is Durga?" quote: Serinity Young, *An Anthology of Sacred Texts By and About Women* (Fort Collins, CO: Crossroad, 1993): 298.

The mantra "Om Dum Durgayei Namaha" appears on the "Sanskrit Mantras and Spiritual Power" website, www.sanskritmantra.com/simple.htm.

Mistress of the universe prayer: Ne Dejih, *Durga Mata* (Springfield, VA: Diamond Pocket Books, distributed in the USA by Nataraj Books).

Kailas Nath Seth and B. K. Chaturvedi, *Gods and Goddesses of India* (Springfield, VA: Diamond Pocket Books).

Eva Rudy Jansen, *The Book of Hindu Imagery: The Gods and Their Symbols* (Diever, Holland: Binkey Kok Publications, 1993). This source provided descriptions of the gods' tools and symbols.

Eve

Rabbi David A. Cooper, *God Is a Verb: Kabbalah and the Practice of Mystical Judaism* (New York: Riverhead, 1997).

Rabbi Joseph H. Gelberman, *Kabbalah As I See It* (Self-published, n.d.). This interpretation inspires us to believe that Eve was meant to eat the apple; it was part of human evolution.

Naomi H. Rosenblatt and Joshua Horowitz, *Wrestling with Angels: What Genesis Teaches Us About Our Spiritual Identity, Sexuality, and Personal Relationships* (New York: Delta, 1995).

Carolyn M. Ball, *Claiming Your Self-Esteem: A Guide Out of Codependency, Addiction and Other Useless Habits* (Berkeley: Celestial Arts, 1995). Source of many insights into women's self-esteem.

Apple juice ritual adapted from "The Liturgy," in Rev. Jeannie Weyrick and the World Light Fellowship, *The Order of Melchizedek: Handbook and Study Guide for Ordination and Initiation* (Wappingers Falls, NY: World Light Fellowship Publishing, 2000).

Dianne Hyson, "An Apple a Day: Pretty Good Advice," on "Dateline UC Davis," www.dateline.ucdavis.edu, April 17, 2007. Hyson cites a twelve-week study of twenty-five healthy adults who drank apple juice and ate apples, with clear benefits after only six weeks.

Fairy Godmother

Epigraph: Incantation spoken by the Fairy Godmother in Walt Disney's film *Cinderella*, and on the 2005 CD in the song "Where Did I Put That Thing/ Bibbidi-Bobbidi-Boo (The Magic Song)."

"Who Is the Fairy Godmother?" quote and other historical background:

Isha Lerner and Mark Lerner and Christopher Guilfoil (illus.), *The Inner Child Cards: A Journey into Fairy Tales, Myth and Nature* (Santa Fe, NM: Bear & Company, 1992).

Freya

Epigraph: From the 1991 classic movie *La Femme Nikita,* DVD released by Vidmark/Trimark in 1997.

"Who Is Freya?" quote and background: Patricia Monaghan, *The New Book of Goddesses and Heroines* (St. Paul, MN: Llewellyn, 1997).

Ralph Blum, *The Book of Runes* (New York: St. Martin's Press, 1993). This background information helped in the development of the "sex runes."

Susan Bowes, *Life Magic* (New York: Simon & Schuster, 1999).

Micha F. Lindemans, "Freya," in "Encyclopedia Mythica," www.pantheon. org/articles/f/freya.html.

Time-Life Books, *What Life Was Like When the Longships Sailed: Vikings, AD 800–1100* (New York: Time-Life, 1998).

Gauri

Epigraph: Daphne Rose Kingma, "Seven Steps" excerpted from *Weddings from the Heart: Contemporary and Traditional Ceremonies for an Unforgettable Wedding* (San Francisco: Conari, 1991).

"Who Is Gauri?" quote: California State University Dept. of Anthropology web page "The Goddess Gauri," www.csuchico.edu/anth/mithila/gauri.htm.

"Hindu Prayer to Mother Gauri" appears on "The Hindu Universe," www. hindunet.org.

Meenal Atul Pandya, *Vivah: Design for a Perfect Hindu Wedding* (Wellesley, MA: MeeRa Publications, 2000).

Stephen Schuler, *Meeting God: Elements of Hindu Devotion* (New Haven, CT: Yale University Press, 2002).

Information on the Gauri Festival: "Indian Express" website, www.indian express.com/res/web/pIe/ie/daily/19990413/ile13143.html.

The Great Goddess

Epigraph: Burleigh Muten (ed.), *Return of the Great Goddess 1999 Engagement Calendar* (New York: Stewart, Tabori & Chang, 1997), quoting Donna Wilshire, *Virgin Mother Crone: Myths and Mysteries of the Triple Goddess* (Rochester, VT: Inner Traditions, 1993).

"Who Is the Great Goddess?" quote: Merlin Stone, *When God Was a Woman* (New York: Harcourt Brace, 1976).

Layne Redmond, *When the Drummers Were Women* (New York: Three Rivers, 1998). Source of much historical information.

Starhawk, "The Charge of the Goddess" in *The Spiral Dance: A Birth of the Ancient Religion of the Great Goddess*, tenth anniversary ed. (New York: HarperCollins, 1979, 1989): 90–91.

Green Tara

Epigraph: Widely attributed to Robert Leighton, www.worldofquotes.com/ topic/Jewels/1/index.html.

"Who Is Tara?" quote: Stephen Beyer, *The Cult of Tara: Magic and Ritual in Tibet* (Berkeley: University of California Press, 1978).

Some of the wisdom and research for this chapter was contributed by Rev. Victor Fuhrman, M.S.C., R.M., www.victorthevoice.com.

Hathor

Epigraph: "I Feel Pretty," with music by Leonard Bernstein and lyrics by Stephen Sondheim, is the ode to self-esteem sung by Maria in the musical *West Side Story* (played on film by Natalie Woods).

"Who Is Hathor?" quote: Wilson Pip, "Hathor: Egyptian Goddess of Sky—and Terror," *Wilson's Almanac*, www.wilsonsalmanac.com/goddess _hathor.html. Attributed to a "Hymn to the Goddess Hathor, Egypt, 18th Dynasty."

Time-Life Books, *What Life Was Like on the Banks of the Nile: Egypt 3050–30 BC* (Alexandria, VA: Time-Life Books, 1995).

Ellis Normandi, *Feasts of Light: Celebrations for the Seasons of Life,* based on Egyptian goddess mysteries (Wheaton, IL: Quest, 1999).

Alison Roberts, *Hathor Rising: The Power of the Goddess in Ancient Egypt* (Rochester, VT: Inner Traditions International, 1997).

Iris

Epigraph: D. H. Lawrence, *The Rainbow* (New York: Penguin Classics, 2007):

"Who Is Iris?" quote and other information: Linda Garland and Roger Garland (illus.) and Nigel Suckling, *She: The Book of the Goddess* (Cornwall, UK: Lakeside Gallery, 1998).

"Rainbow" article by Rachelle Oblack at www.weather.about.com/od/r/g/ rainbows.htm discusses the science of rainbows.

Ted Andrews, *How to Heal with Color* (St. Paul, MN: Llewellyn, 1994).

Isis

Epigraph: Attributed to Ursula K. Le Guin, author of realistic fiction, science fiction, and fantasy; cited at www.ursulakleguin.com.

"Who Is Isis?" quote: Anthony S. Mercante, *Who's Who in Egyptian Mythology* (New York: Barnes & Noble Books, 1995).

Isis's call to Osiris: Diane Wolkstein, *The First Love Stories: From Isis and Osiris to Tristan and Iseult* (New York: HarperPerennial, 1992): 10.

The "Isis and Osiris renewal ritual" exercise was adapted from a ritual co-created by the author with Richard Cohn, PhD.

Jean Houston, *The Passion of Isis and Osiris: A Gateway to Transcendent Love* (New York: Ballantine/Wellspring, 1995).

Anthony Veggi and Alison Davidson, *The Book of Doors Divination Deck: An Alchemical Oracle from Ancient Egypt* (Rochester, VT: Destiny Books, 1994).

Kali

Epigraph: "Inspirational Words of Wisdom/George Bernard Shaw Quotes," www.wow4u.com/george-bernard-shaw/index.html.

"Who Is Kali?" quote and other background: Ajit Mokerjee, *Kali: The Feminine Force* (Rochester, VT: Destiny Books, 1998).

"Prayer to Devi" from "The Hindu Universe," www.hindunet.org/ shlokas/7.html.

Elizabeth U. Harding, *Kali: The Black Goddess of Dakshineswar* (York Beach, ME: Nicolas-Hays, 1993).

John Stratton Hawley and Donna Marie Wulff, "Kali: Blood and Death Out of Place," in *Devi: Goddesses of India* (Los Angeles: University of California Press, 1996).

Kali Mandir, *Salutation to Her* found at the online cyber-temple to goddess Kali, www.kalimandir.org.

"Mother Goddess as Kali: The Feminine Force in Indian Art" (Article of the Month, August 2000), Exotic India Art Newsletter, www.exoticindianart. com, provided history and other background.

Kuan Yin

Sandy Boucher, *Discovering Kwan Yin, Buddhist Goddess of Compassion* (Boston: Beacon, 1999).

Some of the research and wisdom on Kuan Yin for this chapter was contributed by Rev. Victor Fuhrman, M.S.C., R.M., www.VictorTheVoice.com.

Lakshmi

Author's note: As a longtime fan of Maha Lakshmi, I have studied her history and worship since 1998. Some of this chapter is drawn from my years of observing ritual and *puja* in Hindu temples.

Epigraph: Joan Perry with Delores Barclay, *A Girl Needs Cash: How to Take Charge of Your Financial Life* (New York: Three Rivers, 1999).

"Who Is Lakshmi?" quote: Dipavali Debroy, *The Holy Vedas: Rig Veda, Yajur Veda, Sama Veda, Atharva Veda* (New Delhi: B.R. Publishing, 2006). From the "Sri Sukta," *Rig Veda*.

Ganesh chant: Sri Swama Sivananda, cited at "Ganesha," www.dlshq.org/religions/ganesha.htm.

Upendra Nath Dhal, *Goddess Lakshmi: Origin and Development* (Delhi: Eastern Book Linkers, 1995).

D. Debroy, *Laksmi Puja* (Delhi: Hindi Pocket Books, 1996).

Lilith

Epigraph: At the height of his career, Pablo Picasso is said to have made this comment.

Quote from *Alphabet of Ben Sira:* Norman Bronznick (trans.) with David Stern and Mark Jay Mirsky (eds.), *Rabbinic Fantasies: Imaginative Narratives from Classical Hebrew Literature* (New Haven, CT: Yale Judaica Series, 1998).

Linda Garland and Roger Garland (illus.) and Nigel Suckling, *She: The Book of the Goddess* (Cornwall, UK: Lakeside Gallery, 1998).

Raphael Patai, *The Hebrew Goddess* (Detroit, MI: Wayne State University Press), 1990.

Renée, *The Lilith Shrine: My Online Shrine to My Role Model as an Uppity Jewish Woman,* www.lilitu.com/lilith.

The Alphabet of Ben-Sira (Alphabetum Siracidis, Othijoth ben Sira) is an anonymous medieval text attributed to Ben Sira (Sirach), the author of *Ecclesiasticus.*

Mary

Epigraph: Edgar Allan Poe and Wilbur Stewart Scott (ed.), excerpted from

Edgar Allan Poe: Complete Tales and Poems (Victoria, BC: Castle Books, 2003): 777.

"Who Is Mary?" quote: Andrew Harvey and Anne Baring, *The Divine Feminine: Exploring the Feminine Face of God Around the World* (San Francisco: Conari, 1996), "Ancient Prayer of Protection," Andrew Harvey (trans.): 113.

Rev. Lawrence G. Lovasik, S.V.D., *Our Lady of Lourdes* (New York: Catholic Book Publishing Co., 1985).

Marist Fathers, *Novena to Our Lady of Lourdes*, from The Lourdes Center, Kenmore Box 575, 698 Beacon Street, Boston, MA, 02215.

Mary Magdalene

Epigraph: Attributed to Marcel Proust, found in Andy Zubko (ed.), *Treasury of Spiritual Wisdom: A Collection of 10,000 Inspirational Quotations,* newed. (Delhi: Motilal Banarsidass, 2004).

"Who Is Mary Magdalene?" quote: James M. Robinson (ed.) and George W. MacRea (trans.), *The Nag Hammadi Library*, revised ed. (San Francisco: HarperCollins San Francisco, 1990). Reading from *The Gnostic Gospels* section from "The Gospel of Philip."

Mary Ford-Grabowsky (ed.), *Sacred Voices: Essential Women's Wisdom Throughout the Ages* (New York: HarperCollins, 2002).

Susan Haskins, *Mary Magdalene: Myth and Metaphor* (New York: Riverhead, 1993). Source for history and feminist theology.

Carla Ricci, *Mary Magdalene and Many Others: Women Who Followed Jesus* (Minneapolis, MN: Fortress Press, 1994).

Mary Magdalene, An Intimate Portrait, V.I.E.W. Video, New York, shown on Lifetime Television for Women.

Some of the wisdom and insight for this chapter was contributed by Rev. Jeannie Weyrick, founder of the Reunification Church, formerly the World Light Fellowship (www.reunificationchurch.org).

The Muses

Epigraph: Angeles Arrien, *The Nine Muses: A Mythological Path to Creativity* (New York: Archer/Putnam, 2000).

"Who Are the Muses?" quote: Jan Phillips, *Marry Your Muse: Making a Lasting Commitment to Your Creativity—A Complete Course in Creative Expression* (Wheaton, IL: Quest, 1997).

Edith Hamilton, *Mythology: Timeless Tales of Gods and Heroes* (New York: Grand Central Publishing, 1999).

Nancy Hathoway, *The Friendly Guide to Mythology: A Mortal's Companion to the Fantastical Realm of Gods, Goddesses, Monsters and Heroes* (New York: Viking, 2001).

Nemesis

Epigraph: "Women's History/Eleanor Roosevelt Quotes," http://womens history.about.com/cs/quotes/a/qu_e_roosevelt.htm.

"Who Is Nemesis?" quote: Martha Ann Imel and Dorothy Myers Imel, *Goddesses in World Mythology: A Biographical Dictionary* (New York: Oxford University Press, 1993).

Diane Apostolos-Cappadona, *Dictionary of Women in Religious Art* (New York: Oxford University Press, 1998).

The American Heritage Dictionary of the English Language, fourth ed. (New York: Houghton Mifflin, 2000).

Nike

Epigraph: "Just do it" is the now-famous advertising slogan launched by the Nike corporation in 1988.

"Who Is Nike?" quote: From Pausanias, a Greek traveler and geographer of the second century CE, author of the *Description of Greece* [*Periegesis Hellados*], a tourist-like guidebook that remains a valuable text on ancient ruins. Cited by Maria Pretzler in *Pausanias: Travel Writing in Ancient Greece* (London: Duckworth, 2007): 105.

Aaron J. Atsma, "Nike" in *Theoi Greek Mythology: Exploring Mythology in Classical Literature and Art*, Theoi Project website, New Zealand, www.theoi. com/Daimon/Nike.html, copyright 2000–2008.

Diane Apostolos-Cappadona. *Dictionary of Women in Religious Art* (New York: Oxford University Press, 1998).

Oshun

Epigraph: Charlotte Rose, in *The Doctor Is In* (New York: Erotic Playgirl Romance/Masquerade, 1994).

"Who Is Oshun?" quote: Diedre Badejo, *Osun Seegesi: The Elegant Deity of Wealth, Power and Femininity* (Trenton, NJ: Africa World Press, 1996).

Kayode Afolabi, *Osun in Colours: Pictorial History of the River Goddess Osun* (Seattle: Booksurge Publishing, 2006).

Mirror exercise adapted from Laurie Sue Brockway, *How To Seduce a Man and Keep Him Seduced* (New York: Citadel Press/Kensington, 1997).

Caldeo Sookram, "Fruits, Flowers, Honey for Oshun," article on the Oshun Festival in Salybia, Nigeria, *The Express* (local Nigerian newspaper), "Today" section, Aug. 26, 2002.

Oya

Epigraph: Judith Gleason commented on her book *Oya: In Praise of an African Goddess* (New York: HarperCollins, 1992) in "The Awakened Woman" e-magazine, www.awakenedwoman.com.

Amy Sophia Marashinsky and Hrana Janto (illus.), *The Goddess Oracle: A Way to Wholeness Through the Goddess and Ritual* (Boston: Element, 1997; Stamford, CT: U.S. Games Systems, 2006).

Baba Ifa Karade, *The Handbook of Yoruba Religious Concepts* (San Francisco: Weiser, 1994).

This chapter's insights on an organized approach to change were adapted from ideas provided by planning technologies of change consultant Theodore A. Hagg, Ableman Management, New York City.

Pele

Epigraph: Attributed to Buddha in the journal *A Buddhist Perspective*, www.abuddhistperspective.org/journal/2007/4/4/like-a-hot-coal.html.

"Who Is Pele?" quote and other background: Scott Cunningham, *Hawaiian*

Religion and Magic (St. Paul, MN: Llewellyn, 1995).

Ancient Mystery, Hawaii: The Wrath of Pele, Fire Goddess of Hawaii, investigation of the 1983 eruption of the Kilauea volcano and supernatural powers believed to rule the island, video narrated by Leonard Nimoy, produced by Filmroos for A&E Network, 1997.

"Long life to you, Pele" chant is from "The White Moon Gallery Presents Pele, Goddess of Fire" website, www.orderwhitemoon.org/goddess/Pele2.html.

"Summary of the Pu'u 'O'o-Kupaianaha Eruption, 1983-Present,"

Hawaiian Volcano Observatory website, USGS: Science for a changing world, http://hvo.wr.usgs.gov/kilauea/summary/main.html.

Information on the Kilauea volcano can be found at the tourism website www.gohawaii.com/about_hawaii/explore/volcanoes.

Persephone

Epigraph: Marjorie Kinnan Rawlings, *The Yearling* (1938, republished by Aladdin Classics, 2001).

"Who Is Persephone?" quote: "Hymn to Demeter" in Homer, Nicholas Richardson (ed.) and Jules Cashford (trans.), *Homeric Hymns* (New York: Penguin Classics, 2003).

Brenda Shaeffer, *Signs of Healthy Love* (Center City, MN: Hazelden, 1986). Insights into what makes a healthy relationship were adapted from this book.

Radha

Author's note: I have also studied the story of Krishna and Radha since 1998, observing many worship services and *pujas*—source of some of the details in this chapter.

Epigraph: Emily Brontë, *Wuthering Heights* (New York: Bantam Classics, 1983).

"Who Is Radha?" quote: Jayadeva and Sir Edward Arnold (trans.), *The Gita Govinda* (Victoria, Australia: New Humanity Books, 1990). Segment on Krishna's longing for Radha, page 49.

John Stratton Hawley and Donna Marie Wulff, "Radha: Consort and Conqueror of Krishna" chapter in *Devi: Goddesses of India* (Berkeley: University of California Press, 1996).

Sophia

Epigraph: From the author's 1997 interview with Judith Orloff, MD, for *Women's News*, Westchester, NY, discussing her first book, *Second Sight* (New York: Warner Books, 1997).

"Who Is Sophia?" quote: James M. Robinson (ed.) and George W. MacRea (trans.), *The Nag Hammadi Library*, revised ed. (New York: HarperCollins, 1990). Reading from *The Gnostic Gospels*, excerpt of the ancient writing "The Thunder, Perfect Mind," p. 297.

Moses Hadas (introduction) and Edgar J. Goodspeed (trans.), *The Apocrypha* (New York: Vintage, 1989), excerpt of "Wisdom of Solomon,"

Apocrypha 6:12–16, pp. 188–189.

Robert A. Powell, *The Most Holy Trinosophia and the New Revelations of the Divine Feminine* (Great Barrington, MA: Anthroposophic Press, 2000).

Willis Barnsone and Marrin Meyer (eds.), *The Gnostic Bible: Gnostic Texts of Mystical Wisdom from the Ancient and Medieval Worlds* (Boston: Shambala, 2003): 226.

Letty M. Russell and Shannon J. Clarkson (eds.), "Sophia/Wisdom" in *Dictionary of Feminist Theologies* (Santa Ana, CA: Westminster, 1996).

Raphael Patai, *The Hebrew Goddess* (Detroit, MI: Wayne State University Press, 1990).

Suzzanne Schayp, *Sophia: Aspects of the Divine Feminine, Past & Present* (York Beach, ME: Nicolas-Hayes, 1997).

The Wisdom of Solomon, King James Bible, 6:12.

The Old Testament, Book of Proverbs, 28:27 to 30, one of the first references to Sophia as as a feminine entity unto herself.

Some of the research and wisdom for this chapter was contributed by Rev. Victor Fuhrman, M.S.C., R.M., www.victorthevoice.com.

Saint Térèse

Epigraph: Sri Ram quote compiled by Virginia Hanson in *Gifts of the Lotus A Book of Daily Meditations* (Wheaton, IL: Quest, 1974).

"Who Is Saint Térèse?" quote: St. Thérèse of Liseiux and John Beevers (trans.), *The Autobiography of St. Thérèse of Liseiux: The Story of a Soul* (New York: Doubleday, 1957).

"Thought for Today" on completing tasks was drawn from www.relax7.com, courtesy of Brahma Kumaris World Spiritual University.

"St. Theresa" entry in "Catholic Online," www.catholic.org/saints/saint.php ?saint_id=105.

Carol Lee Flinders, *Enduring Grace: Living Portraits of Seven Women's Mysteries* (New York: HarperCollins, 1993).

Alice La Plante and Claire La Plante, *Heaven Help Us: The Worrier's Guide to Patron Saints* (New York: Dell, 1999).

Saint Lucy (Lucina)

Epigraph: Hammarskjöld's words about Eleanor Roosevelt, referring to the famous biblical passage, are engraved on stone at the United Nations Building in New York City.

"Who Is Saint Lucy?" quote: "Santa Lucia" is a famous and traditional Neapolitan song.

Lesley Adkins and Roy A. Adkins, *Dictionary of Roman Religion* (New York: Facts On File, 1996).

Frances Bernstein, *Classical Living: Reconnecting with the Rituals of Ancient Rome*. (New York: HarperCollins, 2000).

"St. Lucy" entry in "Catholic Encyclopedia," www.newadvent.org/cathen/0941a.htm.

Uzume

Epigraph: Widely attributed as a Maori proverb, found at www.quotegarden.com/light.html.

"Who Is Uzume?" quote: Merlin Stone, *Ancient Mirrors of Womanhood: Our Goddess and Heroine Heritage*, Vol. II (Boston: Beacon, 1979).

John Bowker, *The Oxford Dictionary of World Religions* (New York: Oxford University Press, 1997).

Amy Sophia Maranshinksky and Hrana Janto (illus.), *The Goddess Oracle: A Way to Wholeness through the Goddess and Ritual* (Boston: Element, 1997; Stamford, CT: U.S. Games Systems, 2006).

Venus

Epigraph: Widely attributed to Robert Morely, www.ourpla.net/cgi-bin/pikie.cgi?FavoriteQuotes.

"Who Is Venus?" quote: Edith Hamilton, *Mythology: Timeless Tales of Gods and Heroes* (New York: Grand Central Publishing, 1999).

Lesley Adkins and Roy A. Adkins, *Dictionary of Roman Religion* (New York:Facts On File, 1996).

Frances Bernstein, *Classical Living: Reconnecting with the Rituals of Ancient Rome* (New York: HarperCollins, 2000).

Vesta

Epigraph: Adapted from Woolf's famous dictum, "A woman must have money and a room of her own if she is to write fiction." Virginia Woolf, *A Room of One's Own* (New York: Harcourt, 1929; Harvest, 2005).

"Who Is Vesta?" quote: Lesley Adkins and Roy A. Adkins, *Dictionary of Roman Religion* (New York: Facts On File, 1996).

White Buffalo Calf Woman

Epigraph: Courtesy Don Evans, Ojibwa descendant, from his former website and in his writings.

"Who Is White Buffalo Calf Woman?" quote: Arvol Looking Horse, "The Story of White Buffalo Calf Woman," from a speech to the Unrepresented Nations and Peoples Organization, Jan. 1995, the Netherlands. Arvol Looking Horse is Keeper of Original Lakota Pipe. Website, www.kstrom.net/isk/arvol/arv_menu.html.

"White Buffalo Woman Brings the First Pipe," as told by Joseph Chasing Horse and relayed by Arvol Looking Horse on his website, www.kstrom.net/isk/arvol/buffpipe.html.

James R. Walker, *Lakota Belief and Ritual* (Lincoln, NE: University of Nebraska Press, 1980; Bison Books, 1991).

Some of the wisdom and insight into White Buffalo Calf Woman and Native American traditions was gleaned from writings by Don Evans, Ojibwa descendant.

GODDESS RESOURCE GUIDE
A LIBRARY OF CLASSICS FOR MORE INFORMATION AND INSIGHT

Absher, Tom. *Men and the Goddess: Feminine Archetypes in Western Literature.* Rochester, VT: Park Street Press/Inner Traditions,1990. An interesting look at how Westerners view the sacred feminine.

Baring, Anne, and Jules Cashford. *The Myth of the Goddess: Evolution of an Image.* New York: Viking, 1991. A delightfully comprehensive compendium of goddess history.

Graham, Lanier. *Goddesses in Art.* New York: Artabras, 1997. A beautiful collection of female deities as depicted in art.

Jordon, Michael. *Encyclopedia of Gods—Over 2,500 Deities of the World.* New York: Facts on File, 1993. Who's who in all pantheons—half of the deities are goddesses!

Monaghan, Patricia. *The New Book of Goddesses and Heroines.* St. Paul, MN: Llewellyn, 1997. Who's who in the world of the Sacred Feminine.

Muten, Burleigh, ed. *Return of the Great Goddess.* New York: Stewart, Tabori Chang, 1997. Art, inspiration, poems, and ponderings about the Feminine Divine.

Redmond, Layne. *When the Drummers Were Women.* New York: Three Rivers, 1998. A terrific history of goddess worship that traces the practices of ritual, drumming, and gathering in community.

Shlain, Leonard. *The Alphabet vs. the Goddess: The Conflict Between Word and Image.* New York: Viking, 1998. A history of the Goddess approached through a fascinating premise: she was lost to left-brain thinking.

Stone, Merlin. *When God Was a Woman.* New York: Harcourt Brace, 1976. Classic ancient history text.

Interfaith RoundUp of the Divine Feminine

Brown, C. Mackenzie, trans., annotation, commentary. *The Devi Gita: The Song of the Goddess.* Albany: SUNY Press, 1998. Original sacred text of Hindu workshop of the Great Mother.

Gottlieb, Lynn. *She Who Dwells Within: A Feminist Revision of Renewed Judaism.* New York: HarperCollins, 1995. Shekinah and the Sacred Feminine

292

in the Hebrew tradition.

Hawley, John Stratton, and Donna Marie Wolf. *Devi: Goddesses of India.* Berkeley: University of California Press, 1996. In-depth study of Hindu goddesses.

Kinsley, David. *The Goddesses' Mirror: Visions of the Divine from East and West.* Albany: SUNY Press, 1989. Excellent roundup of goddesses of many traditions.

Johnsen, Linda. *The Living Goddess: Reclaiming the Tradition of the Mother of the Universe.* St. Paul, MN: Yes International Publishers, 1999. Brings the daily worship of the Mother to life in a way that Westerners can understand.

Raver, Miki. *Listen to Her: Women of the Hebrew Bible.* San Francisco: Chronicle, 1998. Brings the Goddess alive through stories of the first females.

Young, Serinity, ed. *An Anthology of Sacred Texts By and About Women.* Fort Collins, CO: Crossroad, 1993. Amazing collection of journal entries, musings, sacred writings, speeches, and reports.

Specific Goddesses and Discovering the Goddess Within

Cott, Jonathan. *Isis and Osiris: Exploring the Goddess Myth.* New York: Doubleday, 1994. Extraordinary chronicle of the active worship of Isis today, edited by Jackie Onassis (currently out of print).

Monaghan, Patricia. *The Goddess Path: Myths, Invocations and Rituals.* St. Paul, MN: Llewellyn, 1999. Primer on stepping onto the path; an excellent overview of hundreds of divine females.

de Regula, Traci. *The Mysteries of Isis. Her Worship and Magick.* St. Paul, MN: Llewellyn, 1995. The ultimate book on one of the most famous goddesses.

Stassinopoulos, Agapi. *Conversations with Goddesses: Revealing the Divine Power Within You.* New York: Stewart, Tabori & Chang, 1999. Greek goddesses in everyday life.

Telesco, Patricia. *365 Goddesses: A Daily Guide to the Magic and Inspiration of the Goddess.* New York: HarperOne, 1998. Offers a goddess, her history and mythology, and a ritual for each day of the year.

Waldherr, Chris. *The Book of Goddesses.* Hillsboro, OR: Beyond Words, 1995. Beautiful picture book with brief bios on twenty-six goddesses.

Ritual Work and the Art of Gathering With Others

Baldwin, Christina. *Calling the Circle: The First and Future Culture.* New York: Bantam, 1994. A wonderful how-to book on creating sacred circles and gatherings.

Beck, Renee, and Sydney Barbara Metrick. *The Art of Ritual: A Guide to Creating/Performing Your Own Ceremonies for Growth/Change.* Berkeley: Celestial Arts, 1990. One of the original how-to books on creating rituals for people of all backgrounds.

Biziou, Barbara. *The Joy of Ritual.* New York: Golden Books/St. Martin's Press, 2006. Best ritual book available for people of all faiths, paths, and levels of experience.

Starhawk. *The Spiral Dance: A Rebirth of the Ancient Religion of the Goddess,* 20th anniversary ed. New York: HarperCollins, 1999. A great primer on the religious worship of the Goddess.

Women's Spirituality

Anderson, Sherry Ruth, and Patricia Hopkins. *The Feminine Face of God: The Unfolding of the Sacred in Women.* New York: Bantam, 1991. A compelling look at how women evolve their spiritual lives and needs.

Cabot, Laurie, with Jean Mill. *The Witch in Every Woman: Reawakening the Magical Nature of the Feminine to Heal, Create, Empower.* New York: Delta/ Bantam Doubleday Dell, 1997. Modern insights on ancient earth religions.

Carnes, Robin Deen, and Sally Craig. *Sacred Circles: A Guide to Creating Your Own Women's Spirituality Group.* San Francisco: Harper SanFrancisco, 1998. Best book available to support the spiritual gathering of women in many contexts outside of religion.

Curott, Phyllis. *Book of Shadows: A Modern Woman's Journey into the Wisdom of Witchcraft and the Magic of the Goddess.* New York: Broadway, 1999. Tells of the author's journey as a corporate lawyer and a high priestess. *Witch Crafting: A Spiritual Guide to Making Magic.* New York: Broadway, 2002. A "Goddess 101" book on how to begin learning the Craft with wisdom and creativity.

Special Tools To Help You Learn More

The Goddess Oracle: A Way to Wholeness through the Goddess and Ritual by Amy Sophia Marashinsky, illustrated by Hrana Janto. Boston: Element, 1997; Stamford, CT: U.S. Games Systems, 2006.

This inspiring, informative, and educational divination deck and accompanying book take you on a journey to the Goddess to ask your most pressing questions. The deck contains fifty-two cards representing fifty-two goddesses of all traditions, and offers several spreads you can use to find your answers. Once you've selected the cards, you can then seek deeper insights in the book. For each goddess you'll find a poem, background on her mythology and meaning, and a ritual you can perform to bring healing or wholeness to a particular situation.

Resource for Nondenominational Priestess Training
Crossroads Lyceum/Fellowship of Isis
P.O. Box 19152
Tucson, AZ 85731
e-mail: CRLyceum@gmail.com
website: www.crlyceum.com

The Crossroads Lyceum is a part of the College of Isis, within the Fellowship of Isis (FOI), a multi-religious international organization dedicated to honoring this goddess. Headed by the wise and amazing Connia Silver, the Lyceum offers a wide range of home-study courses in various spiritual topics and also provides priestess training. If you feel it is your path to become a priestess of the Goddess, I highly recommend this route. The teachings are gentle, interesting, comprehensive, and applicable even for those who just want to learn more.

Resource for Goddess Statues and Spiritual Supplies

I highly recommend this shop mom and pop metaphysical and online store. It is run by lovely, caring owners and it offers everything you need to create the perfect Goddess Altar.

Next Millennium Books and Gifts
3141 N 93rd St, Omaha, NE 68134
Phone: (402) 393-1121

The online store is called Magical Omaha and it is filled with spiritual goodies. https://www.magicalomaha.com/

BIBLIOGRAPHY
SOURCES FOR GENERAL INSIGHT AND RESEARCH

Absher, Tom. *Men and the Goddess: Feminine Archetypes in Western Literature.* Rochester, VT: Park Street Press/Inner Traditions, 1990.

Baldwin, Christina. *Calling the Circle: The First and Future Culture.* New York: Bantam, 1998.

Blair, Nancy. *Goddesses for Every Season.* Boston: Element, 1995.

Bowker, John (editor). *The Oxford Dictionary of World Religions.* New York: Oxford University Press, 1997.

Brown, C. Mackenzie, trans., annotation, commentary. *The Devi Gita: The Song of the Goddess.* Albany: SUNY Press, 1998.

Holy Bible. St. James version.

Garland, Linda, and Roger Garland (illus.) and Nigel Suckling. *She: The Book of the Goddess.* Cornwall, UK: Lakeside Gallery, 1998.

Gelberman, Rabbi Joseph H. *Kabbalah As I See It.* Self-published, n.d. Founder of The New Seminary and The New Synagogue in New York City, Gelberman is credited with coining the motto "Never instead of, always in addition to." The New Seminary is dedicated to the training of interfaith ministers.

Graham, Lanier. *Goddesses in Art.* New York: Artabras, 1997.

Hamilton, Edith. *Mythology: Timeless Tales of Gods and Heroes.* New York: Grand Central Publishing, 1999.

Jordon, Michael. *Encyclopedia of Gods—Over 2,500 Deities of the World.* New York: Facts on File, 1993.

Marashinsky, Amy Sophia, and Hrana Janto. *The Goddess Oracle: A Way to Wholeness Through the Goddess and Ritual.* Boston: Element, 1997; Stamford, CT: U.S. Games Systems, 2006.

Monaghan, Patricia. *The New Book of Goddesses and Heroines.* St. Paul, MN: Llewellyn, 1997.

Muten, Burleigh, ed. *Return of the Great Goddess.* New York: Stewart, Tabori & Chang, 1997.

Raver, Miki. *Listen to Her: Women of the Hebrew Bible.* New York: Chronicle, 1998.

Redmond, Layne. *When the Drummers Were Women.* New York: Three Rivers, 1998.

Stone, Merlin. *When God Was a Woman.* New York: Harcourt Brace, 1976.

Young, Serinity, ed. *An Anthology of Sacred Texts By and About Women.* Fort Collins, CO: Crossroad, 1993.

ABOUT THE AUTHOR

Rev. Laurie Sue Brockway has written extensively on women's spirituality, self-esteem, emotional health, relationships, and weddings.

Her deep interest in Goddess studies began when she was a journalist specializing in women's empowerment, and it led her to become an ordained minister focused on interfaith spirituality and women's spirituality. The foundation of her ministry is to celebrate all traditions and to include all aspects of the Divine.

For more than 20 years Rev. Laurie Sue has presided over a multicultural wedding ministry based in New York and is widely recognized as an expert on interfaith, intercultural, and highly personalized nondenominational weddings. She has been called upon by couples around the world for her assistance in complex spiritual and cultural issues, and to help guide families through the interfaith marriage process. She honors relationships between all couples and believes in focusing on the common denominator of love.

Rev. Laurie Sue is author of many books, has written articles for hundreds of publications, and has been editor-in-chief of two national magazines. She also served as a senior editor at *Beliefnet* and *Everyday Health* and as a relationship columnist for *Huffpost*.

She is a graduate of the New Seminary for Interfaith Studies. She received her B.A. in Human Development from S.U.N.Y and studied Marriage and Family Therapy at Mercy College.

Visit her at RevLaurieSue.com.

OTHER BOOKS BY THIS AUTHOR

Lakshmi Magic
Goddess Lessons
Wedding Goddess
Your Interfaith Wedding
Your Hindu-Interfaith Ceremony
Your Perfect Wedding Vows
Your Unique Ceremony
Pet Prayers and Blessings

Lakshmi Magic

We can all use more money, great job opportunities, and goodness in life. This book tells you how to invite material and spiritual wealth on all levels. And it gives you dozens of rituals, prayers, and techniques to draw prosperity and beauty into your life with the help of Goddess Lakshmi. Lakshmi, the Hindu Goddess of Good Fortune, has been bringing good things to life for five thousand years.

In this small but powerful book, the author reveals the spiritual secrets she learned and adapted during many years of study. The writing is fun and easy to follow. You will discover:

- The mythology and meaning of Lakshmi
- How to invite her grace into your life
- Rituals and devotions to attract Lakshmi's attention
- Prayers to ask for her blessings
- Insights into traditional Hindu worship

- Ideas for inviting good fortune into your life
- Peace of mind in times of financial struggle

Lakshmi is famous and beloved for her awesome role of bringing prosperity, opportunity, and success into your life.

Goddess Communications, LLC New York

Made in the USA
Middletown, DE
03 June 2022

66612559R00186